THE TRIBE OF WITCHES

The Religion of the *Dobunni* and *Hwicce*

THE TRIBE OF WITCHES
The Religion of the *Dobunni* and *Hwicce*

Stephen J. Yeates

Oxbow Books

Published in the United Kingdom by
OXBOW BOOKS
81 St Clements, Oxford OX4 1AW

and in the United States by
OXBOW BOOKS
1950 Lawrence Road, Havertown, PA 19083, USA

Text: © Stephen J. Yeates, 2008
Design and layout: © Oxbow Books, 2008

First published 2008
Reprinted 2009, 2014, 2024

Paperback Edition: ISBN 978-1-84217-319-0
Digital Edition: ISBN 978-1-78297-597-7

A CIP record for this book is available from the British Library

All rights reserved. No part of this book may be reproduced or transmitted in any form or by any means, electronic or mechanical including photocopying, recording or by any information storage and retrieval system, without permission from the publisher in writing.

For a complete list of Oxbow titles, please contact:

UNITED KINGDOM
Oxbow Books
Telephone (0)1226 734350
Email: oxbow@oxbowbooks.com
www.oxbowbooks.com

UNITED STATES OF AMERICA
Oxbow Books
Telephone (610) 853-9131, Fax (610) 853-9146
Email: queries@casemateacademic.com
www.casemateacademic.com/oxbow

Oxbow Books is part of the Casemate Group

Front cover: Cleeve Hill (photo Stephen Yeates) and the relief of Mercury and consort, Gloucester (photo courtesy of Gloucester City Museum and Art Gallery).

Back cover: Cooper's Hill (photo Stephen Yeates) and Daglingworth Relief (photo M. B. Cookson, Institute of Archaeology, Oxford).

Frontispiece: The relief of Mars Olludios, from Custom Scrubs near Bisley (photo courtesy of Gloucester City Museum).

For the Muse which inspired this work
and Martin for all his help

Contents

List of Figures		viii
Acknowledgements		xii
1	The *Dobunni,* the *Hwicce* and Religion	1
2	The Deity and the Landscape	9
3	The Sacred Rivers	30
4	The Gods of Tribes and Folk-groups	59
5	Mining and Minerals: Hill-forts and Temples	90
6	The Gods of War	102
7	The Hunter God and the Sacred Grove	107
8	Tree Shrines	117
9	Religion as a Focus for Burial	124
10	The Sacred Horse	132
11	A Goddess for the *Dobunni*	137
12	The Arrival of Christianity: The Locations of Shrines and Minster Churches	147
13	The Never Dying Gods: Natural Deities in a Christian World	157
Bibliography		163
Index		179

List of Figures

1. A map showing the area which has produced Dobunnic Iron-Age coinage, and which is consequently associated with the civitas and tribal area of the *Dobunni* tribe (S. Yeates, based on information provided by de Jersey).
2. A map showing the area of the See of Worcester marked in black, which is equated to the kingdom of the *Hwicce*. The areas shaded in grey can, from historical texts and place-name evidence, be shown to have been annexed from that territory (S. Yeates).
3. The broad topographical divisions of the study area, indicating the main forests (S. Yeates).
4. A map showing the distribution of the corpus of 'Cuda' and *cucullati* sculptures in the Cotswold area. The black circles indicate the locations from where Cuda and *cucullati* sculpture has been recovered and the grey/black circles where *cucullati* sculpture has been found only. The black squares are accepted *Cod names, the grey possible *Cod names. The black circles in grey squares mark temples of a possible Mars deity equated with Jupiter imagery. The black/grey square is the location of Kemble (S. Yeates).
5. A map of the upper Windrush valley showing the place-names and shrines associated with Cuda (S. Yeates).
6. The Daglingworth Cuda and the *Geni Cucullati* (photograph by the late M. B. Cookson, held by the Institute of Archaeology, Oxford).
7. The Cuda relief which was recovered from a well at the Chessels, Lower Slaughter. The relief is similar to that of the Daglingworth and Police Station reliefs but the execution of the sculpture is of a poorer quality. The figure alongside the *cucullati* has been interpreted as a male and is located on the other side to the *cucullati* (photograph used by kind permission of Gloucester City Museum).
8. One of the two seated mother goddesses recovered from the Chessels at Lower Slaughter. The representation is of Cuda, which can be ascertained from the representations on the other sculptures recovered from the same well (photograph used by kind permission of Gloucester City Museum).
9. The plans of the temples at Lamyatt Beacon and Brean Down. Note the division of the ambulatory, to form what both excavators called a vestibulary, the two annexes and the isolated outer building (S. Yeates).
10. A map showing the river shrines which have an associated divine river-name, and the major streams and rivers of the Cotswold region which are tributaries of the Thames (S. Yeates).
11. The church of Saint Mary de Lode, Gloucester (photograph S. Yeates).
12. The cathedral of Saint Mary and Saint Ethelbert, Hereford (photograph S. Yeates)
13. The *parochia* of Gloucester, showing the locations of Roman Gloucester and the minster along with the four Iron-Age hill-forts located in and around the *parochia* (S. Yeates).
14. The hill-fort of Kymesbury on Painswick Beacon (photograph S. Yeates).
15. The hill-fort rampart and shrine which underlie the church of Saint Bartholomew

List of Figures ix

      at Churchdown Hill (photograph S. Yeates).
16 The cathedral of Gloucester (photograph S. Yeates).
17 The *parochia* of Cheltenham, showing the location of the minster and the suspected Roman period settlement along with two recognised Iron-Age hill-forts; one suspected, and Battledown which has been disputed (S. Yeates).
18 The hill-fort of Leckhampton Hill (photograph S. Yeates).
19 The camp at Dowdeswell near the head of the valley of the river Chelt (photograph S. Yeates).
20 The *parochia* of Bishop's Cleeve showing the Roman settlement at Tredington Rise, the minster at Cleeve, and the two recognised camps at Nottingham Hill (Cockbury) and Cleeve Hill, along with a suspected site at Hewletts which was damaged by a landslide, and a possible camp site at Woolaston (S. Yeates).
21 The hill-fort on Cleeve Hill (photograph S. Yeates).
22 The *parochia* of Winchcombe showing the major Roman settlement at Millhampost, and the minster at Winchcombe. There are two confirmed Iron Age hill-forts at Roel and Beckbury, a disputed site at Langley Mount and a probable large prehistoric enclosure under Winchcombe. There is evidence of further prehistoric settlement along with the Roman settlement, along the Hailes Brook and it is this stream which provided the name *Salenses* (S. Yeates).
23 The *parochia* of Withington showing the Roman settlement at Wycomb, the minster at Withington, and where archaeology and antiquaries suggest that there are possible large enclosures (S. Yeates).
24 The church of Withington, Gloucestershire, the location for Finberg's analysis of estate continuity between the Roman and early medieval periods (S. Yeates).
25 The *parochia* of Bibury showing the suspected large Roman settlement of Oldwalls, the mother church of Bibury, the large enclosures of Castle Ditches, Ablington Camp, Winterwell, and the possible site at Hasenbury (S. Yeates).
26 The parish of the mother church of Bourton-on-the-Water, showing the large Roman settlement at Bourton, the three large enclosures around Bourton of Salmonsbury, Knaves Castle, and the defensive site to the south of Bourton. Place-name evidence may indicate that a further enclosure is to be found to the north of Naunton. The location of the Roman period shrine of Cuda is also shown (S. Yeates).
27 The parish of the mother church of Standish, showing the Roman roadside settlement on the Herse Brook at Quedgeley and the defended sites of Haresfield Camp or Ersebury, Harescombe Camp, and the defended promontory at Randwick Wood. There are place-name references to Stanburrow, the Stone Fort at Elmore (S. Yeates).
28 The *parochia* of Westbury-on-Trym showing the Roman small town of Sea Mills, and the large enclosures at Blaize Castle, Coombe Hill, King's Weston Camp, and the possible Bulwark around Sea Mills (S. Yeates).
29 The *parochia* of Bedminster and the parish of Bedminster which show a unified set of settlement features along the Avon. The minster was located at Bedminster and there is circumstantial evidence of a Roman small town at Rosebury. There are three Iron Age hill-forts at Burwalls, Stokeleigh Camp, and Clifton Camp. The

location of a fourth enclosure is not known, but it is evident that Stow place-names turn up in relation to Roman and Iron-Age earth bank enclosures (S. Yeates).

30 The *parochia* of Cheddar, with the Roman small town of Charterhouse, and the minster at Cheddar. The Priddy Circles have the construction features of large Late Bronze-Age or Iron-Age enclosures. One was not finished and it is possible that the circular, and earliest, camp at Charterhouse is also of a prehistoric date (S. Yeates).

31 The *parochia* of Congresbury, with the Roman settlement and minster at Congresbury. There are Iron-Age hill-forts at Congresbury and Cleeve, while the large enclosure recognised as the minster precinct at Congresbury is irregular in shape and may pre-date the minster and the Roman settlement. The place-name evidence and antiquarian accounts indicate that there was a prehistoric enclosure at Bourton (S. Yeates).

32 The *parochiae* of Aymestry and Leintwardine, showing the Roman settlement of the Bury and the churches of Aymestry and Wigmore, along with the hill-forts of Mere Hill, Deerfold, Pyon Hill, and Croft Ambrey. In the parochia of Leintwardine are the Roman settlement and mother church of Leintwardine along with hill-forts at Coxwall, Brandon Hill, and Dervold. There is a further large enclosure along the Deerfold Escarpment at Walford, which has been classed as a Roman camp but is essentially undated (S. Yeates).

33 The *parochia* of the church of Ross on Wye, showing the Roman settlement at Bury Hill, Weston-under-Penyard, and the Iron-Age hill-forts at Chasewood or Cockbury, Camp Field, and Hill of Eaton (S. Yeates).

34 The *parochia* of the church of Warwick, showing what may be a Roman roadside settlement at Sherbourne, and a number of large but essentially undated enclosures at Warwick, Heathcote Hill, Barford Wood, and Grove Park (S. Yeates).

35 The *parochia* of the minster of Eynsham, showing the probable Roman settlement at Cassington and three large enclosures at Eynsham Park, Cassington, and Ambury. The church at Eynsham was established in the enclosure at the centre of a large late Bronze-Age enclosure (S. Yeates).

36 The *parochia* of the church at Wootton, showing the Roman settlement at Samson's Platt, and also some large enclosures of probable late prehistoric date (S. Yeates).

37 The *parochia* of the minster at Charlbury showing the Roman settlement of Wickham and the large prehistoric and undated enclosures indicated at Knollbury, Spelbury, Charlbury, and Wallborough (S. Yeates).

38 The *parochia* of the minster at Shipton-under-Wychwood, which shows the location of a number of large enclosures at Lyneham, Idbury, Fifield, Hill Farm, and also Shipton. The nature of these enclosures has not been determined (S. Yeates)

39 A map showing the mineral locations in the Forest of Dean and the Malvern region. The grey squares indicate major Roman iron production centres while the black squares copper production sites (S. Yeates).

40 A map showing the mineral locations of the Mendip and Kingswood areas. The four divisions of the Mendip Freeminers are marked as Western, Priddy, Harptree, and Chewton (S. Yeates).

41 The hill-fort of Cockbury at Nottingham Hill (S. Yeates).

42 A map showing the distribution of the nemeton. The large black circles represent

List of Figures xi

known late prehistoric linear ditches associated with woodland landscapes and which qualify for the status of nemeton or sacred grove. The large grey circles represent probable locations. The black squares represent the locations of known hunting temples, and the grey squares possible temples. The small black circles represent known sculpture finds associated with the hunter god Cunomaglos. The black and white circle at Gloucester represents the recovery of a plaque showing the hunter god (S. Yeates).

43 The Cotswold hunter-god, from Chedworth, who can be equated with the god Cunomaglos (photograph Martin Henig).
44 The Hobditch bank system which once formed part of the main nemeton of the Forest of Arden (photograph S. Yeates).
45 The Grim's Ditch in the Forest of Wychwood, which forms part of one of the Cotswold nemetons (photograph S. Yeates).
46 The relief of Mars Olludios, from Custom Scrubs near Bisley (Photograph used courtesy of Gloucester City Museum).
47 A map of the Severn valley showing the location of the rich late Iron-Age burials at Crickley and Birdlip, and the other unusual but undated burials at Leckhampton Hill and Nottingham Hill. The grey areas indicate the lines of scarp slopes along the Cotswold Edge and outliers, the Forest of Dean, Malverns, Mendips and Wyre Forest. The enclosed circular valley lies to the northeast of Gloucester and is highlighted in black (S. Yeates).
48 A map showing the distribution of the reliefs showing the mater and Mercury (black circles), which can be interpreted as the mother and father of the Dobunni. The relief from Wellow and Aldsworth (crosses) have also been included because they seem to show the same deities. The Kenchester inscription (black square) has also been inserted. The light grey shading indicates territory which was almost certainly part of the Dobunnic territory (S. Yeates).
49 The relief showing Mercury and the mother from the Leasues site in Cirencester (photograph by the late M. B. Cookson, held by the Institute of Archaeology, Oxford).
50 A plan of the city of Bath showing the temple of Sulis Minerva and that of the mother goddess of the *Dobunni* (S. Yeates).
51 The relief of Mercury and the mother, found in 1857, from Northgate Street, Gloucester. This has the best surviving image of the mother goddess of the *Dobunni*; in it she holds a ladle above a bucket or circular vessel (photograph used by kind permission of Gloucester City Museum).
52 The relief showing the *Matres* from the Leasues site in Cirencester. This shows the consort of Mercury in a triple representation (photograph by the late M. B. Cookson, photograph held by the Institute of Archaeology, Oxford).
53 The mother church of Ross-on-Wye, Herefordshire (photograph S. Yeates).
54 The cathedral church of Worcester (photograph S. Yeates).
55 The Anglo-Saxon priory church of Deerhurst, Gloucestershire (photograph S. Yeates).
56 The minster church of Blockley, Gloucestershire (photograph S. Yeates).
57 The minster church of Dodderhill, Worcestershire (photograph S. Yeates).

Acknowledgements

I would like to thank David Yeates, Martin Henig, David Price, Jean Bagnall-Smith, and Col Saddler for reading through various parts of this work, and David Bland for helping with the aerial photographs. Thank you also to Gloucester City Museum and Art Gallery, Corinium Museum, and the Institute of Archaeology at Oxford for the use of photographs and access to archaeological material.

Chapter 1

The *Dobunni*, the *Hwicce* and Religion

Discussions concerning pre-Christian religion in Western Europe have, for many years, been considered problematic due to a lack of texts, material culture, and the theoretical framework into which place-name studies have been constructed. The first factor to consider is the fragmentary nature of the archaeological, historical, and onomastic evidence; such evidence provides the basis from which narratives about pre-Christian religion are extrapolated. For some time it has been evident that these disciplines, because they often use different evidence or use partial aspects of the same information available, create a variety of views of the past.

The archaeologist uses material culture, the remains of structures and artefacts. This discipline is reliant on an individual of the present day giving an opinion on how such structures or objects would have been used in the past. The interpretation is, to a large extent, determined by the nature of the context in which the site or object was found. Archaeologists create their narratives by fitting the material evidence with theories derived from anthropology, ethnography, and sociology. The historian, on the other hand, uses written texts, which have had the thoughts or observations of an individual from the past recorded. Texts used for this purpose are often written specifically with the aim of preserving information, for example the writing of a chronicle or the granting of a charter. The historian will, from this data, create a narrative of past events. Onomastics is the realm of the philologist who deals with the historical development of names. Names are often built up from components from a mixture of sources. In England this is particularly complicated because its place-names have developed from at least six different languages, and hence, place-names can often be determined as a product of a certain phase of our historical past, thus names are stratified. Together, archaeology, history, and onomastics might be thought able to provide a coherent view of the past; unfortunately, however, they often fail to achieve this. Bringing the evidence provided by these three disciplines together should provide a more cogent view of the past. In assessing all three aspects there is a problem which concerns the weighing of the evidence and the importance one gives to information when there appears to be conflict between these different approaches.

Academically, there are two main approaches to viewing the past; these can be described as a *time-period specific* study or a *di-chronological* study. The former, offers an assessment of a subject at a particular time, and includes works in which certain aspects of a society are categorised over a short time. The studies are, therefore, more interested in discussing the diversity within this period, rather than looking at how the situation was arrived at or what developed from it. Archaeologists and place-name students are adept at these narratives, being concerned with the typology of specific objects or the distribution of a specific name. This approach is two-dimensional. Such approaches have, invariably, produced schemes of classification, which, although useful, do not in themselves produce great revelations, only compartmentalisation and fragmentation. They thus create views of the past which are more prone to be disconnected and incoherent.

The compartmentalisation of history, archaeology, and onomastics into separate disciplines has created problems in understanding. Attempts in archaeology to bridge the classification of the prehistoric or historic periods have led to the construction of a series of monographs on the transition periods, as society moved from one perceived social structure to another. This, it could be argued, is a result of the fixed way in which academic structures, based on disciplinary hierarchy, have come to view history. Di-chronological approaches to the past attempt to adapt to the evolutionary thrust that underlies many academic arguments; it is this approach that is used here through the use of Braudel's (1972) geo-historical approach which he called the *longue durée*. In this approach is an attempt to understand humanity in relationship to their environment; changes are perceived as happening gradually with constant repetition and ever-recurring cycles. This approach gives archaeologists the opportunity to develop a more four-dimensional interpretation of the past, developing a view of the use of space over time.

The development of narratives as a linear story line, although important, fails to encapsulate the complex nature of human activity. In order to understand religion it is necessary to grasp this multifaceted world-view and integrate it into a richer, more cohesive narrative, albeit with many caveats. The linear narrative, the great picture, becomes composed of a series of smaller stories.

The *Hwicce* have an unusual name, one which will be returned to later, but their territory coincided with that of the Iron-Age tribe called the *Dobunni*. These two territories overlap or coincide with each other but it has until now been difficult to directly associate the two groups over time. The association of these two groups will also be considered here. Even though this assessment represents the study of the religion of a British tribe, the implications of this analysis may influence other studies in Western Europe generally.

THE HISTORY AND ARCHAEOLOGY OF THE *DOBUNNI*

When the age of bronze gave way to that of iron in *c.* 800 BC the dwellers of the Severn Valley were still among the nameless peoples of prehistory. It was only much later that the designation *Dobunni* is known to have been used. There are some seven references to this tribe although some of them are considered to be conjectural (RIB(I) 1995, nos. 621, 2250; Rivet and Smith 1979, 339–340). The first surviving account occurred at the beginning of the Roman period in the work of Dio Cassius, but the name is considered to have been misspelt. The second instance is to be found in an inscription recorded on a diploma, dated to AD 105, in Pannonia, central Europe. The third recorded case is in Ptolemy's *Geography*, dated *c.* AD 130–150. The fourth reference relies on interpretation. It is an inscription on a milestone found at Kenchester dated to the reign of the Emperor Numerian, AD 283–284. The four letters on the inscription have been interpreted as R(*es*) P(*ublica*) C(*ivitatis*) D(*obunnorum*). The fifth is on a probable third century inscription on a tombstone from Templeborough, Yorkshire, to *Verecunda* (of the) *cives Dobunna*. The *Ravenna cosmography* of *c.* AD 650–700 provides the sixth and referred to *Cironium* (sic) *Dobunorum*, the *Civitas* of the *Dobunni* – the town that later became Cirencester. The seventh and final case is on a mid sixth-century AD commemorative stone from Tavistock; it has the inscription DOBUNNI [...] FABRI FILI ENABARRI.

Numismatics has provided other insights into our understanding of the *Dobunni*. The first coins minted in Britain were produced in the late Iron Age. These often had distinctive inscriptions and symbols and it has been established that coins with certain names and emblems have been found in discrete clusters (Allen 1944, 1–46; Sellwood 1984, 191–204). These have been associated with historically documented peoples. From this distribution it has become evident that the *Dobunni* territory was focused on Gloucestershire and that it extended in various directions into the neighbouring counties, see Figure 1. In these discussions, however, there is an assumption that the coinage provides evidence for the projection of the tribe into the Iron Age. With no legend referring to the tribe the argument may be considered somewhat circular at present.

There have been a number of studies on the *Dobunni*, which have tried to assess Kingship, the invasion of Britain, and the division of the tribe. These discussions were stimulated by excavations carried out at the Iron-Age centre of Bagendon. The Iron-Age coins contain a series of legends, which are usually considered to be the names of kings. The coins, on stylistic grounds were initially considered to give a royal list as follows: ANTED, EISV, CATTI, COMUX, INAM, CORIO, and BODVOC (Allen 1944, 1–46). Since then the metal content of the coins has been tested and the order reversed (van Arsdell and de Jersey 1994). However, there are some discussions which maintain that the reference to CORIO is in reality derived from the name *Corinium*. The second major debate on the invasion of Britain stems from the work of Dio and the misspelling of the *Dobunni* tribal name. Traditionally the invasion is portrayed as coming through Kent, but the reference to the *Dobunni* and the location of that tribe means that the route was further west, perhaps on the Hampshire or Sussex coast. Various other ideas have been put forward concerning the division of the tribe related to pottery distribution patterns and settlement development patterns, which have been used to suggest that society was in a state of flux.

THE CULTURE, HISTORY AND ARCHAEOLOGY OF THE *HWICCE*

In the early medieval period a group of people called the *Hwicce* are recorded as living in the Severn Valley and Cotswold region. Their name is one of the most unusual of tribal names in Britain recorded at that date, as the word which is of an Old English

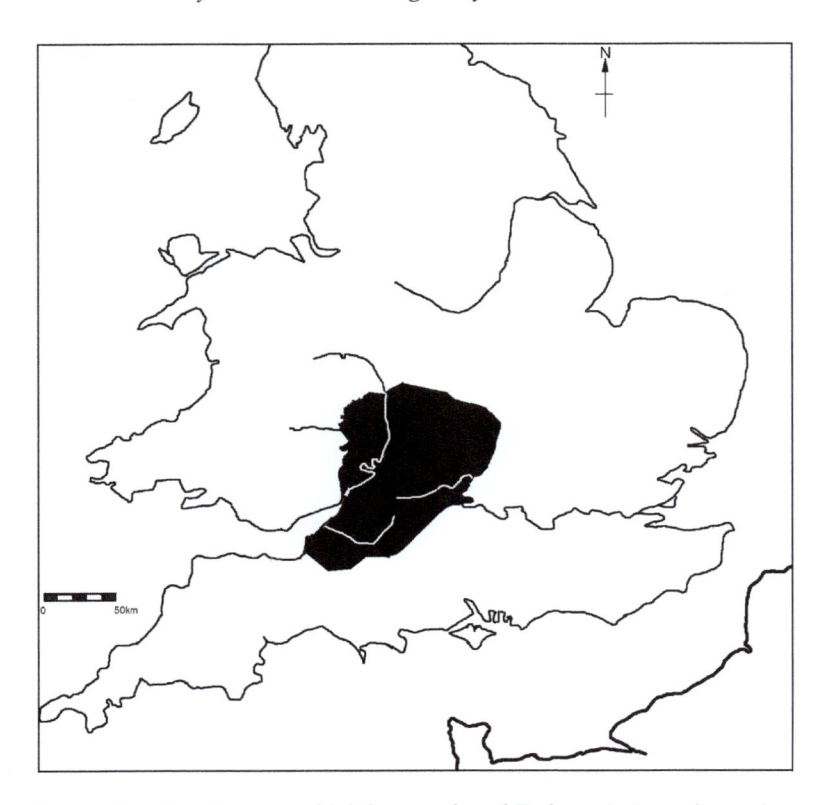

Figure 1: A map showing the area which has produced Dobunnic Iron-Age coinage, and which consequently has been associated with the civitas and tribal area of the Dobunni tribe (S. Yeates, based on information provided by de Jersey).

origin has been interpreted as meaning **Sacred Vessel**. This word is directly associated with the Old English words *wicce*, a female participant of witchcraft, which provides the origins for the modern word *witch*. This means that the tribe was only one of two in Britain which potentially had a name directly associated with pre-Christian religion. It is the aim of this discussion to investigate why this occurred, and it will be shown that this name, which was given out in the migration period, was possibly given by others due to already existing local factors from the development of religion in that region from a far older time.

The *Hwicce* name has survived in a number of written sources, the earliest of which is Bede's *Ecclesiastical History*, where there are four accounts, the first for AD 603 (Colgrave and Mynors 1969, *EH*.II.2). It is also mentioned in numerous charters (Finberg 1972), by Nennius (Morris 1980, *the wonders* nos. 67–68), and in several chronicles, for example the *Worcester Chronicle* (Darlington and McGurk 1995, *Worcester Chron.* 486–487). These texts have been used to assess when the *Hwicce* became integrated into the West Saxon or Mercian Kingdoms. They have also been used to carry out an assessment of ethnic affiliation, Kingship, the establishment of multiple estates, and the development of the Church.

A number of historical facts concerning the *Hwicce* have been questioned; these concern the conflicting evidence about the battle of Dyrham and the meeting at Saint Augustine's Oak. The battle is reputed to have taken place in AD 577, when the rulers of the Severn valley were conquered by Wessex expansionism. However, in AD 603 Bede, by his use of language, implied that the *Hwicce* were Christian and British and adhered to the rules and regulations of the British Church and not the Church based at Canterbury. There are also factors concerning the integration of the *Hwicce* into the Mercian state in AD 628, and the construction of a genealogical list of *reguli* and *subreguli* from charter evidence from *c.* AD 670 to *c.* AD 760 (Finberg 1972, 167–180). These included a series of joint rulers, Eanhere and Eanfrid; Oshere, Osric and Oswald who founded minsters *c.* AD 670; Æthilhard, Æthelric, Æthilweard and Æthilberht; Ælfred and Osred; and the final group Eanberht, Uhtred and Ealdred who reigned till *c.* AD 790. The territory had, therefore, a semi-autonomous status. This degree of independence is also reflected in the founding of a Bishop's See for the region at Worcester, as churches were founded for distinct groups of people, as shall be discussed later in chapter 4. Because of this the See has been used, in historical studies, to establish a basic outline of the tribal territory, see Figure 2.

The charter evidence from the early medieval period can be used both to assess early medieval multiple estates and to interpret the establishment and spread of the Church. Besides considering the relationship between parish and estate boundaries, the earliest assessments of the multiple estates attempted to plot boundaries and relate place-names to their surroundings, for example the work by Grundy (1927, 1–183; 1928, 18–131; 1932, 161–192; 1933; 1936). There has been considerably more work carried out on the early medieval multiple estates in the area; by Finberg (1972) and Hooke (1985) for example, concerning agricultural and woodland practices. A linguistic study of the *Hwicce* has determined that once the *Hwicce* had been absorbed into Mercia, they spoke an Anglian dialect of Old English (Smith 1965a; 1965b).

The relationship which existed between these two peoples, the *Dobunni* and the *Hwicce*, has not been resolved, but has been considered on a number of occasions. Due to the lack of textual sources it was considered that this issue would not be resolved, the problem with this assumption is that the Roman period religious landscape and the survival of pre-Old English folk-names had never been assessed, and the trends which are evident in these traditions had never been identified.

THE SIGNIFICANCE OF BELIEF SYSTEMS

Although there has been much social and economic analysis, the true nature of pre-Christian religion in this area has not been looked at. Much has been written world-wide about the historical development of religion and probably all of it has been criticised. With respect to the pre-Christian religion of the *Dobunni* the subject could be approached on a number of different levels. Sociologists and anthropologists tend to consider that belief systems and ritual activity are associated fundamentally with

Figure 2: A map showing the area of the See of Worcester marked in black, which is equated to the kingdom of the Hwicce. The areas shaded in grey can, from historical texts and place-name evidence, be shown to have been annexed from that territory (S. Yeates).

ideology, society and culture. In contrast, historians attempt to describe the religion of pre-Christian Europe from the unreliable Roman textual and more reliable epigraphic sources.

The sociologists and anthropologists Feuerbach (1957), Marx and Engels (1957), Durkheim (1964), and Geertz (1975) have persistently contextualised the role of religion as a reflection of man and his social world. *The Essence of Christianity* interpreted religion as a child-like condition of humanity, and thought that the divine being was none other than the human being purified. Thus, the relationship between the divine and the human was taken to be illusory, the belief system being but a projection of man's essential nature. In the *Philosophy of Rights*, there was a declaration that man made religion, rather than religion making man. Religion was deemed, therefore, to be the self-consciousness and the self-feeling of man, and that it was state and society which produced religion; thus, religions were in effect general theories reflecting a society's view of reality. In later discussions religion became, therefore, a unified set of beliefs and practices associated with sacred things, and basic religious rites were created around the basic human needs of both individuals and the social group. The final definition of religion quoted here saw religion as a series of symbols acting to establish powerful, pervasive, and long-lasting moods and motivations in men by forming comforting conceptions of a general order. This order then becomes so entrenched that the conceptions develop an aura of factuality and the moods and motivations become realistic.

RELIGION IN THE *DOBUNNIC* TERRITORY

Religion and religious action in the Roman world are not often discussed in a tribal context. On the one hand there are discussions on religion at a national or an empire level, and on the other a series of excavations at sites which are locally specific. There are a number of problems that archaeologists have when assessing beliefs, which was termed the ladder of inference by Hawkes (1954, 155–168). This placed religion and beliefs beyond the reach of direct material interpretation. Due to the insistence that archaeology could not provide a direct answer to any religious questions, interpretation of this sphere of society has often been attempted through the use of Roman ethnographic sources, for example, the works of Caesar, Strabo, Diodorus Siculus, Ammianus Marcellinus, and the text of Posidonius, which is no longer extant but has been reconstructed partially. To the information obtained from Classical writers can be added that derived from Irish traditional sources and from Welsh sources. This information was fed into the interpretation of archaeological data, and since then the interpretation of the classical sources has also been reassessed. There have been discussions on temple designs and on the deposition of votive artefacts within these sites. Further to this there have been discussions on the sculpture of Britain and Gaul, its significance, and its relationship to cult.

Since the 1990s, the study of religion in north-west Europe became influenced by two key surveys of north-east Gaul that had been carried out by Derks (1998) and Roymans (1990, 49–94). The first pursued an environmental determinist approach and the second an anthropological cultural approach. There have also been discussions of the process of integration of the Roman and native traditions.

Locally, the first temples of the region, under discussion here, to be located and recorded by antiquaries were those at Lydney Park and Bath. The initial finds from the Roman temple in Lydney Park came to light in 1723. Between then and 1805 random excavation for artefacts took place and the god *Nodens* was identified. In an early interpretation of the site in 1826 Drummond and D. Lysons suggested that the temple was a shrine associated with healing. The major excavations took place in 1928 (Wheeler and Wheeler 1932), and subsequent excavations in the 1990s.

The finds at Bath were first documented from the late eighteenth century. Much of the early work at Bath was catalogued in the 1800s, when the name of the deity *Sulis* was identified. The plan of the temple and bathing establishment were only ascertained in excavations in the 1960s and 1980s (Cunliffe and Davenport 1985). Other important temple sites in the region have also been examined, most notably at Lamyatt Beacon, Brean Down, Henley Wood, and the Uley shrines (Woodward and Leach 1993), dedicated to Mercury. In the latter, for the first time within the area, a

Roman religious site was proved to have had a late Iron Age predecessor. It has also been suggested that there was a later church, albeit on minimal evidence. Local discussions on the Roman sculpture have developed over time. The most recent is a corpus of sculpture for the Cotswold area (Henig 1993), which is a companion volume to that for Bath and Wessex (Cunliffe and Fulford 1982).

Little information is available concerning 'Anglo-Saxon' pagan beliefs. Traditional approaches have assessed religion using the documented mythological past of the Germanic world, and a number of shrines have been identified from the fifth to sixth centuries AD, and place-names have been related to these gods.

Assessments have been made nationally and locally of Christianity in Roman Britain (Boon 1992, 32–52; Thomas 1981). These indicated that Christian symbols and objects can be found and confirms that Christians did live in Britain during the period under discussion. There has also been an assessment of the survival of the Christian church and parochial system; however, this has been generally questioned because Christianity does not seem strong at an early date. There is some evidence also that pre-Christian wooden temples were maintained.

In the area under consideration, the early medieval charters preserved at Worcester Cathedral represent one of the most important collections of authentic documents from the 'Anglo-Saxon' period to have survived in the country. These have, as a result, become an important source for assessing ecclesiastical development. The main ecclesiastical survey of the area was carried out by Sims-Williams (1990), who deduced that many of the large *parochiae* were constructed through the growth of the monastic culture of the tenth and eleventh centuries AD.

THE ISSUES

There are major issues in the Severn valley area concerning the survival of pagan traditions from the Iron Age and Roman period through the introduction of Christianity and into the early medieval period. The major question, perhaps for all three periods, is whether it is possible to obtain a definition of pre-Christian religion and ascertain the motivations which underlay this? Various associations have been constructed between religion and other areas of knowledge, for example between religion and the environment, between religion and socio-political organisation, and between religion and other social themes. It must be asked whether these associations are valid. If it is possible to identify some of the underlying principles behind religious activity, then it must be asked how they relate to each other. Then there are the archaeologists' debates focused on continuity and discontinuity, and hence the issue of the relationship which existed between the *Dobunni* and *Hwicce*, and whether they were one and the same people.

Chapter 2

The Deity and the Landscape

Studies of Pre-Christian religion in Britain have focused largely on the participants' views of nature and the use of natural loci. This view has been expressed by a number of scholars on the subject including Henig (1984, 17), Aldhouse-Green (Green 1986, 19–22), Webster (1995, 445–464), and Derks (1998, 134–144) and is, to some extent, part of a longer tradition of association; however, this notion has also been criticised, as a sweeping application of geographical determinism, by Drinkwater (2000, 458–459).

The part of Britain loosely associated with the tribal group called the *Dobunni*, the notional *Civitas Dobunnorum* (which included the *colonia* of Gloucester), later to be occupied by the *Hwicce*, comprised the ancient counties of Gloucestershire and Worcestershire, as well as large parts of surrounding counties including east and north Herefordshire, much of south and west Warwickshire, west Oxfordshire, north-west Wiltshire, and a considerable tract of north Somerset. The region has a number of discrete topographical zones, which require some definition and assessment.

These areas in the landscape can be categorised topographically as the following: the Cotswolds, the upper Thames valley, the rag-stone ridge or Braydon Forest, the upper Bristol Avon valley, the Mendips, the Kingswood, the Somerset Levels, the lower-middle Severn valley, the Forest of Dean, the Hereford plain, the central Lugg plain, the Bromyard plateau, the Wyre Forest, the Birmingham Plateau, and the Vale of Evesham or Feldon. We will need to investigate every potential source of information on these areas, drawing on archaeological, historical, and onomastic sources. Each zone will be discussed with respect to its topographical extent, associated historical knowledge of the forest landscape, the etymology of the name, and any factors which might reveal its past religious significance. These large topographical areas were often viewed as having distinct characters; consequently, it has been decided to discuss the topography of the zones as distinct entities rather than presenting a series of discussions on the list of subjects quoted above.

We need to relate the discussion of the development of individual areas to the creation of the forest landscapes of Britain in general. Development of these landscapes has been thought to have occurred primarily during medieval times, but when place-name evidence and Roman-period landscapes are considered, it becomes apparent that far older traditions, stretching back into the mists of time, have been involved. The forest landscape is stratified, yet there are only two forests whose creation is documented in the whole medieval period in Britain; these are the New Forest and

Windsor Forest. Even these, however, were probably carved out of far older and larger topographically defined forests, see Figure 3.

To further this discussion it is necessary to establish whether there is a correlation between the location of certain types of natural features and temple and shrine sites. To do this, one would need to identify known, possible, and probable religious sites' locations, to assess the associated iconography, and to analyse the onomastics and identify any association with the deity's name, and any homonyms.

Describing the locations of such sites and developing criteria that could be used to compare them will be problematic, as the locations of the sites are extremely diverse and some of the sites cover large areas. Having said this, it is possible to recognise certain patterns which give confidence about the location of temples despite evidence

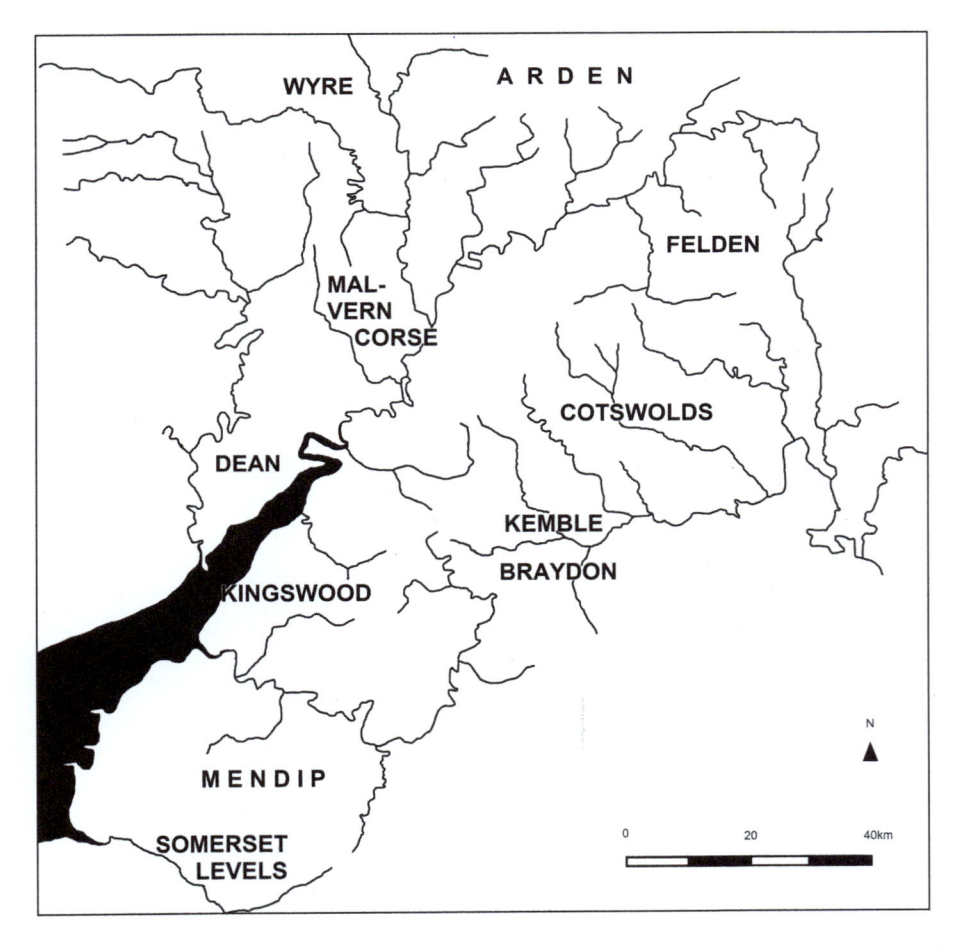

Figure 3: The broad topographical divisions of the study area, indicating the main forests (S. Yeates)

being patchy. Examples include urban and rural sites (both ascertained from the work of Blagg), and peripheral urban sites (located on the edge of a settlement), besides hilltop, hill-slope, spring, river bank and confluence sites, to name but a few. It is true that often the available information is very fragmentary; sometimes there are structures, and votive objects, in other examples there are other artefacts which hint at the location of a shrine but do not necessarily prove its existence even though it is in a potentially important topographic location. Despite these problems a number of shrines have been located across this region. In some of the areas there seem to be significant finds which provide ample evidence of an association between religion and the landscape; in others, the evidence is less well-defined. Despite this it is possible to see patterns emerge which help identify sites in areas where the evidence is scarce.

THE COTSWOLDS

The Cotswold Hills are the largest massif within the study area, forming the eastern upland. There are steep escarpments on its northern and western sides and a gentler dip-slope on its southern and eastern sides. On the northern border of the Cotswolds is the aptly named Edge Hill, and in the south Bath and Bradford-on-Avon.

The earliest records of the name Cotswolds, from the medieval period, are associated with a number of different locations in the range (Smith 1964a, i.2, 199; 1964b, ii.7–8; Yeates 2004, 2–8), for example *Codeswauld*, in 1225, was the name for the pasturelands of Blockley and Chipping Campden; *Newenton(e)-in-Cotswold*, the name used for the village of Naunton, in 1289, and also around Clapley. These names identify an upland area lying between the rivers Stour and Evenlode in the east, and the Coln and Isbourne in the west and south. Further names with similar etymology include: *Cottesdene* or *Cotesdene*, in 1210; *Codestun*, in 977; *Codeswellan*, in 780; and *Codesbyrig*, in *c*. 1055. Historically, therefore, the name Cotswolds has not been perceived as applying to the whole area (Beckinsale 1991, 20–30). The eighteenth century writers Atkyns (1712, 31–32) and Rudder (1779, 392) are considered the first to have used the term Cotswold to describe the whole of the upland area, from Bath to Chipping Campden.

The study of the historical recording of the name Cotswolds has been criticised by other studies carried out on the southern English *wald* and the Midland version *wold* by Everitt (Everitt 1977, 1–19) and Fox (1989, 77–101). These suggested that the word was used at an early stage of the development of Old English for cohesive topographical areas. Gelling and Cole (2000, 257) also agreed that a district, not a specific locality is what would have been described by the name Cotswold. This implies that the name was used at a far earlier date and on a far larger scale than is immediately obvious from the limited textual references.

Another name was used for the Cotswolds, but it is apparent that this developed at a far later date (Yeates 2006, 14). A charter of AD 780 used the name *mons Huuicciorum* and, in AD 964, *monte Wiccisca*. The same first element also occurs in Wychwood in the eastern Cotswolds. The name Wiggold is recorded north of Cirencester, as *Wiggewald* in 1109; as a *wald*, Old English for wooded upland, the name must have been derived from the name of a region, and one should not simply assume that the first element was a personal name, as has been put forward. All of this means that the Cotswolds probably had two distinct names: the Cotswolds and the Wiggold derived from a version of *mons Huuicciorum*, presumably *Hwicce Wold*, being the wooded upland of the *Hwicce* tribe. The latter name probably developed around AD 600–780, as part of a bilingual (British and Old English) tradition. The latter name is clearly of a medieval origin but the former (Cotswold) has a more complex development.

Only one of the Cotswold forests has surviving perambulations or boundaries and that is Wychwood, for the years 1298, 1300, and 1605 (Schumer 2004, no.100). These, together with other place-name evidence, indicate that the Wychwood once extended from the base of the lee slope of the Cotswolds as far north as Bloxham, and to the Gloucestershire border around Langford and Shipton-under-Wychwood.

The origins of the name Cotswold are more complicated than the later alternative name, but it is only with this range of hills that the information survives to create a more cohesive understanding of the origins of how the names of a topographic area developed and how they became associated with a religious belief system. Initially, it was considered that the name was derived from the Welsh *coed*, **a wood** (Rudder 1779, 392), however, in the early twentieth century the assumption was that it derived from **Cod's* or **Codd's wold*; it is this derivation that was accepted by the place-name studies of Worcestershire and Gloucestershire (Smith 1964a, i.2; Mawer and Stenton 1927, 50). No Anglo-Saxon called **Codd* or **Cod* is known, however, as indicated by the asterisks. If **Cod* was not an Old English personal-name it may be that it was a word, whose meaning had been lost, that had developed from an earlier word. The process which is most likely to have taken place is *a*-affection. This would mean that the Old-English **Cod-* was probably derived from the British *Cuda-* (Yeates 2004, 2–8; 2006b, 63–81). That a British prefix and the Old English suffix *'wald'* could be combined is not unheard of; another example is *Andredesweald*.

Place-names with similar derivations as Cotswold place-names have already been discussed by Yeates (2004 2–8). Of names associated with **Cod*, the two most important are *Codeswellan* and *Codesdene*. The place-name *Codeswellan*, **Cod's stream*, recorded in 780, was the name of a sub-manor of the bishop of Worcester's Bredon estate. The name seems to have applied to the river Eye, while the name *Codesdene*, **Cod's valley*, applied to this valley, and must have been located originally near Trafalgar Farm. These names are important because they combine a major land-toponym with a river-name, which seems to be a recurring theme.

The Cotswolds area is the most significant part of the region for the assessment of religious iconography in relation to topographical features. The information available indicates that there were a number of important shrines associated with a mother goddess called *Cuda*. These can be identified from the very south of the region right up to the north. The two most significant shrines are at Daglingworth and the Lower Slaughter Chessels; however, others were surely located at Easton Grey, Cirencester, and Bradford-upon-Avon, (see Figures 4 and 5).

Recovery of material from the shrine at Daglingworth, near Cirencester, has occurred over centuries. In 1690 a Roman slab was recovered; it was inscribed with

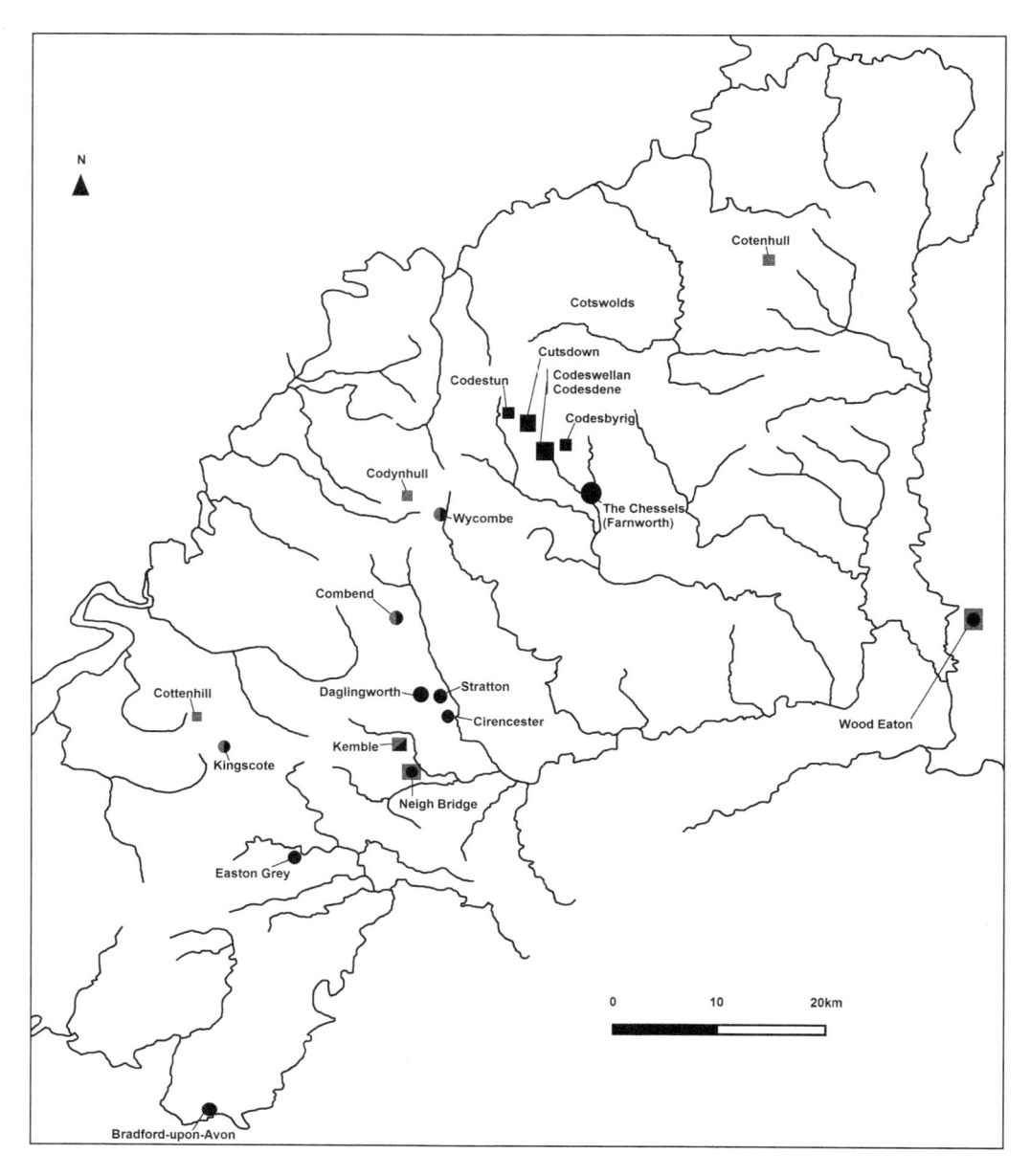

Figure 4: A map showing the distribution of the corpus of 'Cuda' and cucullati *sculptures in the Cotswold area. The black circles indicate the locations from where Cuda and* cucculati *sculpture have been recovered and the grey/black circles where* cucullati *sculpture has been found only. The black squares are accepted *Cod names, the grey possible *Cod names. The black circles in grey squares mark temples dedicated to a possible Mars deity equated with Jupiter imagery. The black/grey square is the location of Kemble (S. Yeates).*

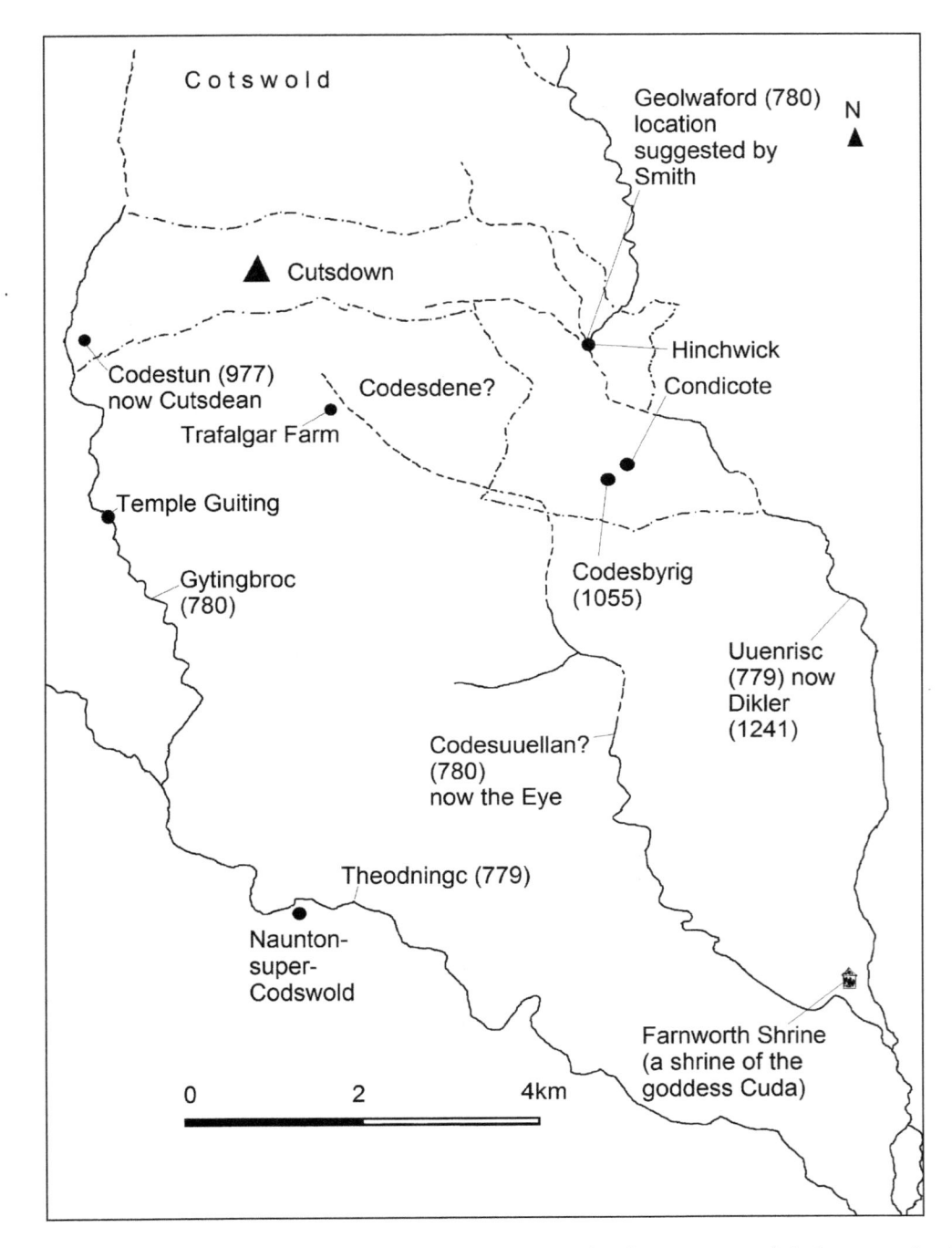

Figure 5: A map of the upper Windrush valley showing the place-names and shrines associated with Cuda (S. Yeates).

MA]TRIB[US ET/GE]NIOL[OCI, which has been translated as *to the mother goddesses and the genius of the place* (RIB(I) 1995). The word *genius* is translated as the **guardian** or **presiding spirit**. A votive relief inscribed CUDAE LOC[..]V[.] was ploughed up in a field in Daglingworth in 1951 (see Figure 6); at the same time, a mosaic pavement was uncovered (Henig 1993, no. 102). It was assumed that both the relief and the mosaic came from the same Romano-British building, perhaps a shrine or temple. The relief portrays a seated mother goddess accompanied by three standing hooded male figures, called by scholars the *genii cucullati*. This name refers to their hooded cloak or *cucullus*. In 2000, survey work was carried out in a field near the site and uncovered Roman pottery, ceramics, and stone building materials.

The full meaning of the inscription on the relief found in 1951 is unknown, but it is believed by Alcock (1966, 45–86; 1986, 113–133), Aldhouse-Green (Green 1986, 90), and Henig (1998, 186–189) that *Cuda* was the name of the goddess depicted on the relief. Although there is no firm evidence of a goddess *Cuda* elsewhere, this idea should not be discounted, and some support can be found on the continent for the use of this name. An inscription from Roman Spain that refers to TRANSCVDANI implies that *Cuda* was the name of a river in Lusitania (CIL 1869, ii.i.no.760); another from Cisalpine Gaul implies that *Cuda* was a feminine cognomen (CIL 1872, v.i.no.2708). The connection between river-names and deities, as illustrated by the river Seine and its goddess *Sequanna* (Aldhouse-Green 1999, 1–9), suggests that the Lusitanian *Cuda* may also have been a deity; this provides support for the divine interpretation of the name on the Daglingworth inscription. It should also be noted that the name *Cuda* is the same name from which *Cod* of Cotswolds was derived (see earlier).

The Daglingworth relief is similar to others from Cirencester, Stratton, and Lower Slaughter Chessels, while a lost relief from Easton Grey also showed a seated divinity with three standing male figures (Henig 1993, nos. 95, 98, 102–103; 1998, 186–189; Cunliffe and Fulford 1982, no. 120). The Cirencester example is particularly well preserved. Yet another relief from an unknown location, but probably one in Gloucestershire, shows a seated goddess accompanied by three cloaked warriors. It may be assumed that, due to the composition of the sculpture, the Easton Grey relief and the unprovenanced one are of the

Figure 6: The Daglingworth Cuda and the Geni Cucullati *(photograph by the late M. B. Cookson, held by the Institute of Archaeology, Oxford).*

same mother goddess. Recent renovation of a house at Bradford-on-Avon has uncovered a broken Roman relief showing a seated mother goddess with at least two standing male figures on the left of the slab. Bradford-on-Avon lies at the very southern end of the Cotswolds and may represent the location of a key shrine. Thus there are at least six known representations of a mother goddess portrayed alongside the *genii cucullati*, all located in the Cotswold Hills

Another sculpture, found at Daglingworth in 1953 shows the lower part of a niche-framed figure wearing a *cucullus* (Henig 1993, no. 100). The *genii cucullati* were presented with a distinctive localised iconography in certain parts of Germany and Britain. In Britain they occur in two main groupings; one in the Cotswolds, the other along Hadrian's Wall. Reliefs depicting them have been found at the Lower Slaughter Chessels, Cirencester, Kingscote Chessels, Chedworth, Bath, and Wycomb (Henig 1993, nos. 95–99, 104–108). In the Cotswold examples, the iconography used is fairly uniform, with either a seated mother goddess with three *genii cucullati*, a seated mother on her own, or the *cucullati* on their own. At Wycomb, the sculpture recovered includes separate representations. It has been suggested that the *cucullati* belonged to the world of dwarfs and goblins, forces for good or evil that had to be propitiated. In Irish mythology, however, the goddess *Danu* was associated with her three sons who were mythical brothers. This would be a more appropriate association and a similar one appears in the Mabinogion where three brothers, called Bwlch, Kyvwlch, and Syvwlch, were associated with sharp swords, dogs, horses, and wives; all of which seem to indicate an underlying association with pestilence of war. The cult of the *cucullati* appears to have been connected, in some way, with the worship of a mother goddess; however, only at Daglingworth, has an inscription with the name of the mother goddess been found.

The shrine at Daglingworth is important because it provides the cult of *Cuda* with an image and a name. However, the full range of sculptural representations of

Figure 7: The Cuda relief, which was recovered from a well, the Chessels, at Lower Slaughter. The relief is similar to the Daglingworth and Police Station reliefs but the execution of the sculpture is of a poorer quality. The figure alongside the cucullati *has been interpreted as a male and is located on the other side to the* cucullati *(photograph used by kind permission of Gloucester City Museum).*

this local cult has been found only at the Lower Slaughter Chessels gravel pit (O'Neil and Toynbee 1958, 49–55), and at the confluence of the Eye, or *Codeswellan*, where eight religious sculptures, believed to have come from a shrine at this site, were recovered from a Roman well. One of the reliefs has images of the *genii cucullati* standing alongside a smaller figure wearing a pleated tunic (Figure 7). Two of the other sculptures are of the remains of two, now headless, seated goddesses; these have been interpreted as representations of Minerva, see Figure 8. Minerva is usually shown standing and holding a spear, but has been also shown in a seated position. The seated goddess, however, fits into the general representation of what is known of the cult of *Cuda*, with the seated mother and the *genii cucullati*. One possibility is that the goddess represented is *Cuda* but that she is shown in the guise of Minerva. Another sculpture from the Chessels at Lower Slaughter is a relief of the *genii cucullati* on their own. It can be claimed that not only is there enough sculpture at the Chessels to assume that it must have come from a shrine, but also that the types of figures in this assemblage indicate that the shrine may have been to the goddess *Cuda*. The sculptures from the Chessels also give an indication of the meaning of the name, as on the gable of the relief with the four figures, there are two unidentified birds facing inwards. One of the seated mothers has an unidentified bird sat on the seat of her chair. They have the general form of a pigeon. This may point to the derivation of the name from the Old Cornish *Cudon*, **a pigeon**, but there are certain philological problems with this *Cuda*, *Cod*, and *Cudon* relationship concerning the long and short u (Yeates 2006b, 63–81).

In and around the Cotswolds it is, therefore, apparent that the topography, the historical forest, onomastics, and Roman period religious sculpture can be used in unison to indicate that there was a mother goddess called *Cuda*, who was revered at a number of shrines in the

Figure 8: One of the two seated mother goddesses recovered from the Chessels at Lower Slaughter. The representation is that of Cuda, which can be ascertained from the representations on the other sculptures recovered from the same well (photograph used by kind permission of Gloucester City Museum).

region. Many of these shrines were located at key places when entering the Cotswolds, at Daglingworth, overlooking the main road north out of Cirencester, and at Bradford at the southern end of the hills. The most significant of these shrines seems to have been located at the confluence of the rivers Eye and Dickler, and it is apparent that in the eighth century AD the Eye was called the *Codeswellan* (Yeates 2004, 2–8). Here, the river seems to be acting as the main focus for, both a river cult, and a cult of the goddess of the land massif. How and why they are interacting in this way is not apparent, but it seems that the shrine did cover a far larger area than the other possible shrines to *Cuda* in the area. As a personification of this landscape this goddess was responsible for its fertility and fecundity, and so one would expect many more, as yet unlocated, shrines to this goddess in the region. Language and sculptural relief has also combined in such a way as to hint at the totem of this deity which was possibly the **pigeon**, or another bird with a similar philological name.

THE FOREST OF KEMBLE

The Thames rises on the Cotswolds' dip-slope and flows out onto an area of gravel deposits and clay which is today called the Cotswold Waterpark. This area is bounded to the north by the edge of the Cotswolds as far as Bladon Heath, and to the south by a broken range of hills from Minety to Wytham Hill.

Historically, this area is known to have had two forests, one at the western end of the valley, which was called the Forest of Kemble, the other at the eastern end of the valley which was recorded in 1170 as the Forest of Stanton or Piriho. References, from AD 688, to the extent of the Forest of Kemble described a territory of 132 *cassati* or 140 *manentes* (Finberg 1972, nos. 4, 4A). The exact significance of the phrase *cassata* is, however, not known. In the second charter the extent of the forest is described as being defined by the Thames and the path of 'the streets', thought to refer to the Roman roads, Fosse Way, and Ermine Street. This would place a number of historic parishes between Kemble, Cirencester, and Latton, in this Forest of Kemble.

The old name of part of this region survives as the place-name Kemble. In the charter of AD 688, the area was described as the wood of *Cemele*. Ekwall (1960, 271) suggested that the name was derived from the war god *Camulos*, recognised amongst Belgic tribes of Gaul, and also in some British place-names. Later interpretations have, however, attempted to move away from this, deriving the name Kemble from the Welsh *cyfyl*, a **border**, **brink** or **edge**, derived from the British **comel-*, meaning **boundary**. Watts (2004, 339) believed that Kemble lay in an area of fluctuating territorial control in the Iron Age or early medieval periods, but this evidence exists only for the upper Thames valley in the late Anglo-Saxon period. During the Iron Age it lay within the *Dobunnic* coin distribution area, while during the early medieval period Malmesbury minster was believed to have been founded through Mercian influence. It is only the Thames Valley, to the east of Kempsford, where this theory holds water, and certainly not in the area where the village now stands. One can assume that the forest once covered a far larger area than is presently the case, or that there is an unrecognised factor involved. The forest of Stanton, which is also in the area, is from looking at place-name evidence, a late derivation and must have been created out of a larger and older forest.

Of the known temple sites in the upper Thames valley, there are two which have similar imagery and could be associated with a single cult. They lie at either end of the valley and are the temples of Woodeaton and Neighbridge. Excavations at Neighbridge, by the Thames, have uncovered an enclosure and produced two pieces of sculptured stone from near a proposed temple site (Henig 1993, nos. 167, 171). One depicts an eagle, the other a shield associated with drapery. This material has been associated with a *Capitolium*, yet the fragment of sculptured shield is also comparable to the circular shields depicted on other reliefs from the *Dobunnic* areas; these are associated not only with Minerva but also with Mars. The location of these finds might be used to argue that the sculpture was part of a statue or relief of a standing Mars figure, with shield and spear, and that the associated image of the eagle is representative of Jupiter. The only god who is known to have been represented in such a way is *Mars Camulos*, who, though equated with Mars, has symbols of an oak and wreath on an altar. These are images of Jupiter, and this particular sculpture was found at Rindern (Espérandieu 1925, no. 6595).

The images found at Woodeaton are comparable with those from Neighbridge. Excavations in 1965–6 re-examined the Iron Age deposits under the temple (Harding 1987, 27–56). The features found included post-holes, associated with middle to late Iron-Age pottery, and a cobbled working surface, which lay between the upper and lower pre-Roman surfaces. During the Roman period a temple, in the Romano-Celtic style, was constructed. The earliest Roman finds from the site include: votive axes, bird images, a prick spur, scabbard chapes, chains of mail, an Aucissa derivative strip bow, and some flint arrow heads; there was also some miniature military equipment including: a sword, a shield, eight crudely made model spears, and a rider brooch. Sculpture from the site includes the lower half of the image of a standing figure, wearing a tunic, who seems to be holding a spear. There is also a plaque which portrays Mars. The bird images have been interpreted as those of eagles, although Bagnall Smith is not convinced. It is possible that here also is a Mars divinity conflated with images of Jupiter, and again *Mars Camulos* may be a possibility, which supports the apparent dedication to Mars, the eagle image, and also the votive weaponry. The temple has been associated with the River Ray, but it is located on a hill that does not overlook this river; rather, it has a view through the gap between Wytham Hill and Bladon Heath, straight up the upper Thames valley.

The upper Thames valley has produced similar information to that found in the Cotswold area, but it is less precise. There are two shrines with similar religious images located in key places on the periphery of the natural feature. The Celtic name of one of the surviving forests has been associated with the name of a Celtic god *Mars Camulos*, yet it lacks certain epigraphic material to demonstrate this association categorically.

THE FOREST OF BRADON AND THE UPPER AVON VALLEY

The rivers from the Forest of Bradon feed into the upper Thames and Bristol Avon rivers. The ridge is formed of Correlian Limestone, and extends from near Minety to Wytham Hill. A perambulation of the forest in AD 956 (Akerman 1857, 257–315) indicated that the boundary of the forest was marked by the rivers Bradon, Woburne, Garesbourne, Idover, Avon, and Ray. It is known that the Forest extended as far east as Lydiard Millicent and Wotton Bassett, and as far west as Hankerton; at all these locations are names which refer to the Perlieu, that is the bounds of the forest. The range of hills which run from near Minety to Wytham contains the ancient Forest of Braydon, which was recorded as *silva Bradon* in AD 688, and *silva Braden* in AD 796. The name is evidently pre-Old English but the etymology is obscure. The forest shared its name with a river, the oldest known name of the Swill being the Braydon Brook, from AD 956.

A possible shrine has been located at Blunsdon Hill, or Groundwell, which seems to have been focused on a spring, while another possible shrine has been identified at Down Farm, near Purton. Here, there is evidence of an isolated square building, where a number of coins have been found. A further shrine site has been located at a hill-top site near Faringdon, but no associated images or epigraphy are known.

The information on the Upper Avon valley is very sparse and there is little to discuss concerning the extent of forests or of the archaeology.

THE MENDIPS, ZOYLAND AND KINGSWOOD

The landscape to the south-east of the Severn consists of the upland zone of the Mendip Hills. They are bounded by scarp slopes to the south and west, facing the Somerset Levels and the Severn Estuary respectively. The eastern boundary is much less distinct as the hills merge gradually with the Wiltshire downland. The Mendip plateau is dissected by a number of river valleys, most notably those of the Yeo, Chew, Cam and Wellow, which form a series of passes through the hills. Beyond the Mendips' northern scarp a ridge runs from near Clevedon towards the Avon Gorge, where it is dissected; beyond this it continues towards Berkeley. To the south-west and west of the Mendips lies a series of levels.

The Royal Forest of Mendip can be identified in a number of place-names and descriptions of mining legislation, as well as a number of thirteenth-century perambulations (Yeates 2006, 12–15). Chewton Mendip obtained the Mendip suffix as early as 1313, in 1277 *Cheddre* was described as within '*the forest of Menedep*', as was *Hidun*, near Charterhouse, in 1235, and Dundry, in 1309, while Beacon Hill is considered to mark the heart of the forest.

The etymology of the name Mendip has not been fully resolved (Watts 2004, 407). The oldest recorded forms of Mendip were *Munedup*, in AD 705–712, *Menedip*, in AD 740–756, and *Menedipp*, in *c.* AD 1150. Ekwall suggested that it was derived from the Welsh word *mynydd*, a **hill** or **mountain**, and the Old-English *hop*, a **valley**; Coates from the Welsh *mönið*, **a hill** or **mountain**, and the Old-English *yppe*, **a lookout place**, **a hunters' platform** or **a chair**.

A number of sacred sites lying within or around the Mendip landscape can be identified, for example those at Brean Down, Henley Wood, Lamyatt Beacon, and Pagans Hill. Other indicators of religious activity have been found at Cadbury Tickenham, and, more problematically, at Cadbury, near Congersbury. Two of the sanctuary sites, Brean Down (ApSimon 1965 195–258) and Lamyatt Beacon (Leech 1986, 259–328), stand out due to the similarity of their general ground plan. Both are variations of a Romano-Celtic temple with a central *cella* and an *ambulatory*. In both, part of the a*mbulatory*, called by the excavators a *vestibule*, was separated from the rest of the complex. Each temple also had two annexes of similar size (between 4.5–5m^2), and a small outlying building. One could argue, tentatively, that both were used for a similar cult purpose. If this was the case, then we can surmise, from their general ground plan, that the other temples were not related to this particular cult. The temples at Brean Down and Lamyatt Beacon lie on key locations at the edge of the Mendip Hills, see Figure 9.

The temple at Lamyatt Beacon has produced more evidence for the nature of its cult. The stone statuary recovered from the site showed a male figure with a tunic and a long cloak with a shield by his left side. Other reliefs found at the site possibly portrayed a Mercury-type figure. The site is, it seems, associated with a male divinity. A hand from a figurine found in *c.* AD 1958–1960 was designed to have held a sceptre. The site has also produced two other objects of interest; one of these has been

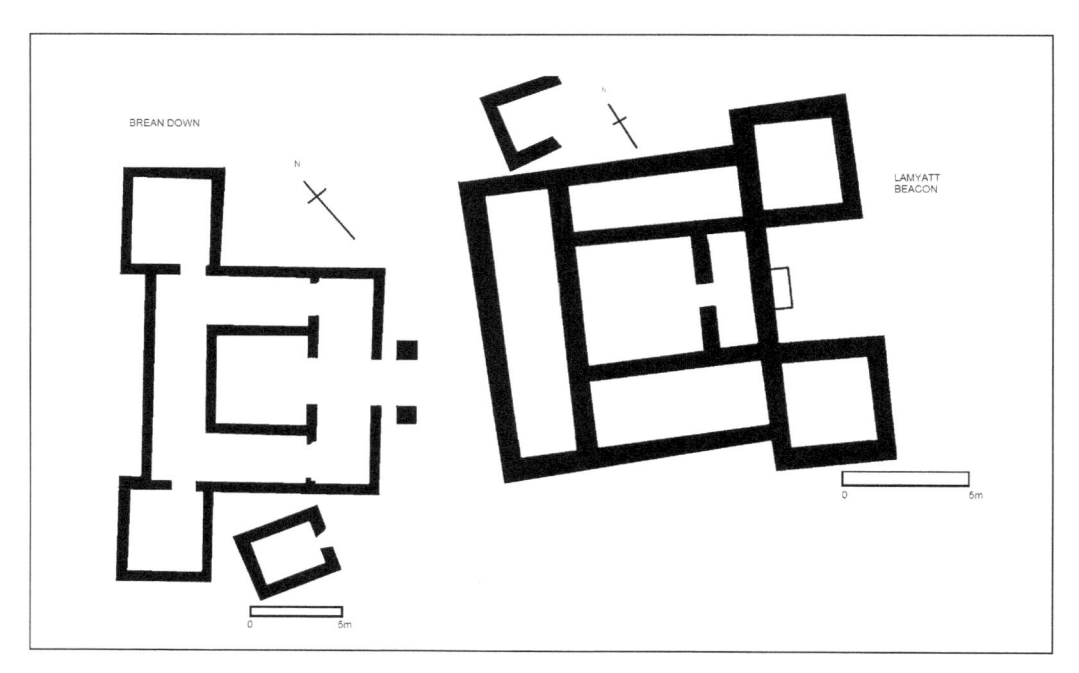

Figure 9: The plans of the temples at Lamyatt Beacon and Brean Down. Note the division of the ambulatory, to form what both excavators called a vestibulary, the two annexes and the isolated outer building (S. Yeates).

interpreted as a sceptre head, the other was the end of a possible votive sceptre. The votive objects found at Brean Down are less informative, although images on coinage may provide some insights. 41% of the coins from Brean Down and 14% of those from Lamyatt Beacon (Besly 1986, 304–316) were of the 'fallen horseman' type. These percentages are above the average.

The shrines in the Mendips, like those in the Forest of Kemble, seem to have been sites of worship for similar deities, based on temple design. The same can not be said for shrines in the Levels or Zoyland, and the forest of Kingswood.

Zoyland may be an older name for the Somerset Levels, as it is derived from the ancient river-name Sowe, which is considered to derive from Indo-European *souo (Watts 2004, 563). The Sowaie was one of the rivers which flowed into Meare Lake and must, therefore, be an old name of the Whitelake. This would mean that there was an area of the levels to the south and north of the Polden Hills which can be associated with this name.

Kingswood has been interpreted as King's Wood; no pre-Old English name of the region has been identified. Place-name evidence and other documentation exist to indicate that this forest extended from Berkeley and Kingswood in the north, to the south of the Avon Gorge.

THE FORESTS OF CORSE AND DEAN

At the heart of the *Dobunnic* territory are the Severn and Avon valleys, which are bounded on the south-east by the Cotswolds, on the north-east by the Birmingham Plateau, and on the west by the Forest of Dean, Malvern Hills, Bromyard Plateau, and Wyre Forest. At the centre of this region there is an old Forest with a pre-Old English name, the Forest of Corse, whose Chase was not confined to the modern parish of Corse, but extended into neighbouring parishes such as Ashleworth. The name was derived from the common Welsh river-name cors, **reed** or **bog** (Smith 1964c, iii.146–147) and was possibly a name for the low-lying land in the lower Leadon Valley and the Vale of Gloucester. There was also a reference to a *Corswelle* in AD 1100–1135, which is the name of a stream in the later parish of Corse.

The upland area, which is now called the Forest of Dean, is primarily a plateau, dissected by streams, which occupies the triangle of land between the rivers Severn and Wye. Topographically, Crew Hill, a spur extending north from the Forest of Dean towards the Woolhope Dome, is also part of that upland area.

In the medieval period, the extent of the Forest of Dean was defined by charters (Grundy 1936a, 65–155). The earliest surviving perambulation, of AD 1227–1228 indicates that the forest was bounded by the Wye to the west and by the Severn to the east. To the north-east it was bounded by the Leadon, and to the North by the Ell and Rudhall Brooks. Only one topographical feature within the Forest of Dean has had a name that can be associated directly with the name Dean; and that is *Dennshill*, recorded in AD 1591, as a name for the Edge Hill ridge; it is the only feature on which both Mitcheldean and Littledean stand.

Many have suggested etymological sources for the name Dean and even though the present etymological associations may fit there are certainly problems in their application. The first attempts derived it from the name Arden. However, Rudge first suggested that it came from the Welsh *dyfn* or the older British word *dubn*, **a valley**, or from the Old-English *denu,* **a valley**. Smith (1964c, iii.209–210), for example, suggested that the name referred to 'the valley of the Cannop Brook'. This topographical suggestion raises, however, a number of problems; the first concerns the location of the earliest recorded name, *Dene,* for Littledean, and the location of the Cannop Brook. There are also problems with some of the older spellings of the name; including *Danica Sylva or Danubia, Dana sylva*, and *Dane(i)um nemus*, which are all names provided by Welsh or Marcher sources such as Giraldus Cambrensis, Orderic Vitalis or Geoffrey of Monmouth. Lewis (Lewis 1845, ii.20) suggested that the name was derived from Danys Coed, **the wood of the fallow deer**. This, presumably, is using the Welsh *danas*, **deer**, which would perhaps more readily support the latter group of names. This suggestion, although generally dismissed, may have further support due to mythological or traditional Welsh associations with the area, implying that *Dene* was an Anglicised form of an earlier name.

Roman sanctuary sites are also known in the Forest of Dean, most notably the temple of *Nodens* at Lydney Park; this god has no known association with the Forest of Dean, although it is possible the name could be a reduced form. It also seems that the temple was a focus of the goddess Fortuna or Abundantia. Another temple, dedicated to an unknown divinity, has been found at High Nash. The claimed site of a temple at Little Dean has now been discredited; as have the carved stone heads from Ruspidge. It has been claimed that Harrow Hill was the location of a pagan shrine, but this has not been verified satisfactorily. Harrow Hill is part of Edge Hill, which is associated with the earliest Dean place-names. Another possible shrine site may be near Linton, where a carved head was recovered. A square or rectangular enclosure, which was removed from Bishop's Wood, may also have been a temple site, due to the discovery of a large coin hoard, which could be votive. Surprisingly the present information on the religious dedications and any association with the landscape can not be resolved.

The Forest of Dean is one of the few upland areas which is associated with a mythical beast in medieval texts. In the tale of *Gereint and Enid* (Jones and Jones 1974, 260) there is a passage which describes how Arthur and his retinue travelled to the Forest of Dean to hunt the white hart which had been sighted there. This mythical tradition fits in with the interpretation of the name by Lewis that this was the forest of the fallow deer. Interestingly, white stags are known in the current fallow deer population. The association of the deer is also interesting in that the area has strong mining traditions; the earliest picks used were probably deer antlers.

THE MALVERNS AND THE HEREFORD PLAINS

The Malvern Hills are a distinctive chain running north to south, situated on the border between Worcestershire and Herefordshire. They are steep-sided, with the Severn Valley on the eastern side and Herefordshire, with an undulating area of smaller random hills, on the western side. To the north-west of the Malverns proper is a ridge which extends intermittently towards the Teme and the Bromyard Plateau. Topographically, these two areas form part of the same upland area.

The historical extent of the Malvern Forest remains unresolved. Malvern was first used as the name of a forest, and then a chase. There are indications that in 1086 Malvern was being used as a forest name; as the manor of Ripple had rights in Malvern and was referred to as lying within the forest (Thorn and Thorn 1982, 2.31). The southern-most of the Malvern Hills is called Chase End Hill, thus implying a boundary.

The landscape feature that is generally called the Bromyard Plateau seems to have lost its old name, unless it was known as the Malvern Forest. The name Malvern is derived from the Welsh words *moel*, **bare**, and *bryn*, **hill** (Ekwall 1960, 312). The name is, therefore, a pre-Old English name of unknown antiquity. It may be that the ancient name for the area was recorded in the Gloucestershire part of the *Domesday Book* of 1086, where the manor of Clifton-upon-Teme is associated with **the Sapina (fir-wood) in King Edward's revenue** (Moore 1982, 1.11 and note). The name Sapey was first recorded in AD 791 as *Sapian* and as *Sapina* in AD 1180. The suggested etymology was Old-English; from *sæpig*, **the sappy one**, and that it was originally a river-name. The context in which the name was used in *The Domesday Book*, however, indicates that the word derived from the Latin *fir-wood*, or **pine tree**.

Little is known about religion in the Bromyard area. One possible religious site is at Upper Sapey Common Camp (Stanford 1959, 19–32). Stanford has claimed that this was a military site but the late dates from the site do not support this. The small nature of the enclosure coupled to the name Sivy Yarn Field, **a pavement**, and the hill-top location, imply a temple rather than a villa, but no votive material has been located.

The lowland area of the Herefordshire plains lies to the west of the Bromyard Plateau and has two clear topographical areas. The first of these is located around Hereford, and the second lies to the north around Leominster. Both of these areas seem to be associated with pre-Old English regional names.

The name *Magana* was recorded in *c*. AD 675 as a district name and has been discussed by Gelling (1978, 102–105), Shepperd (1979, 30–34), and Coplestone-Crow (1989, 13). It is the root of the old district name, recorded as the *Magonsetum* in AD 811, and provides the basis of a number of place-names in the area including Marden. Gelling pointed out that the philological development of the word *magen*, equates it with the Welsh *maen*. The etymology of *maen* is **a stone** and is used in the original sense of **a plain**. Other words related to this are the Irish *magen*, **a place**, and the Welsh *mago-*, **a field**. The name is linked to Magnis, a recorded Romano-British name that came from the British word **magno-*. Many of the place-names associated with *Magana* lie along the south side of a valley whose river is a tributary of the Lugg at Bodenham.

The name Lene was recorded as a regional name as early as AD 958, and again this is recorded in a number of local place-names. The word is derived from the Old Welsh *lion* or *lian* (Coplestone-Crow 1989, 6–9); believed to be derived from the root **lei-*, **to flow**. This indicates that it was the name of a river or stream.

Little is known about the religious activity in this area; few temple sites are known and few sculptures have been uncovered. The remains of a temple at the hill-fort of Sutton Walls were described before it was destroyed by gravel extraction. The gateway of the hill-fort has a major Roman period reconstruction. Little can be said of the religion of the Lene valley and the only significant cultural find is a sculpture of Mercury; its context, however, is unknown. The priory at Leominster was founded in a large enclosure and underneath the priory church geophysical survey work has discovered evidence of a circular building.

THE WYRE FOREST

The Wyre Forest lies to the north of the Teme and to the west of the Severn. Prominent hills include the Clee Hills and Wenlock Edge. Ekwall (1960, 541) was the first to suggest a connection between the names Worcester and Wyre Forest. The earliest known reference to the Wyre Forest is from AD 816. Ekwall decided that *Weogorena leage* meant **the forest of the tribe Weogorena**. Mawer and Stenton (1927, 19–20) suggested that the name was derived from the Gaulish stream-name *Vigora*. Gelling (1969, 26), in an assessment of the name Worcester, accepted Ekwall's argument in principle but argued on the detail. One of her concerns was that there must have been a river *Vigora* in the area of Wyre Forest from which the name of the wider landscape was derived. The association of such a river-name, with an upland area, is a common theme in the vast majority of these regions, and should be considered a strong possibility.

THE FOREST OF ARDEN AND THE FELDON

To the north-east of the Severn and Avon Valleys is the upland area now called the Birmingham Plateau, which was originally the Forest of Arden; to the south-east of this is the Vale of Evesham or the Feldon. The Forest of Arden extends from Spring Hill in the north-west towards Dudley and Oldbury, with a nodal point around the Lickey Hills; it continues with lower rolling hills to the east and south where it would have extended to Evesham and Coventry.

Historically, the Forest of Arden covered much of north and west Warwickshire; it also extended into Worcestershire and Staffordshire. There are no known perambulations of the Forest but there is remaining evidence to indicate the area that it covered (Yeates 2006, 13). Near Lapworth is Arden Hill, for which there are no recognised ancient recordings. There are also a number of villages with the suffix, for example: Hampton-in-Arden, in AD 1200; Henley-in-Arden, in AD 1343; Great Packington, in AD 1405; Weston-in-Arden, in AD 1372; and Tanworth-in-Arden. To the north, the Forest of Arden is known to have included Coleshill, which was described as being in Arden in *c*. AD 1290, and Yardley, which in AD 1221 came under the jurisdiction of Eyre Court in the Law of Arden. In *c*. AD 1540 Leland said that the Forest of Arden lay to the north of the Avon. In the far west of the hills Penkridge was regarded as being in Arden in AD 1791, when this forest was regarded as the largest in all Britain.

In the Worcestershire and Staffordshire part of this upland other names can be recognised, such as: Clent, the Forest of Kinver, the Forest of Feckenham and the Black Country. The Forest of Kinver lies across two topographical areas either side of the river Stour. The Forest of Feckenham covered part of the ridge running south from the Lickey Hills; while the Staffordshire or north part of the forest became known as the Black Country. There may have been an attempt to replace the name Arden in the Snitterfield area, where the name *Griswolds* was recorded as *Grumeswold* in AD 1227, and a reference to the *Wolds* was recorded as *Wald* in AD 1240, the first part probably a derivation from Grim. Due to the use of the name *Wald* it can be surmised that the names must have been applied to a region.

The name Arden has two interpretations; one of which is ancient, the other a corrupted medieval development (Watts 2004, 17). The name of the Forest of Arden is regarded as being of early origin and related to the Ardennes (*Arduenna*) of Caesar. The root of the word is the British **ardu-*, **high** or **steep**. Later, it was decided to reinterpret this and give it the English interpretation **eardærn*, **a dwelling house**. Both are probably valid, the one ancient with an added suffix *–enno-* and the latter **eardærn*, being a later development through more recent folk etymology. A possible Romano-British place-name *Ardua* has been recorded but the reference is garbled and should not be given too much credence. The name Kinver seems more localised; it was first recorded as *Cynibre* in AD 736 and is now considered to be derived from the British word **Cunobriga*, the etymology of which is *cuno*, **dog** and *breiga*, **hill** (Watts 2004, 349). Clent can be explained as an individual hill name developed from the old English **clent*, the **rock** or **hill** (Mawer and Stenton 1927).

There is very little evidence of religious activity in the Arden region, the Coleshill temple being the only major example (Yeates 2006, 20–21). Who or what was deified at this site is, however, unknown. There is a major shrine on the northern edge of the forest at Wall, in Staffordshire, just outside the study area. Further religious sculpture has come from Alcester, while the site of a possible temple has been located, tentatively, in the vicinity of Alcock's Arbour, near a major Roman road crossing the southern part of the Forest of Arden. Near Leek Wootton, a *Roman goddess* was reputedly found, and at Hagley the carving of a rude idol reported; it is not known, however, exactly what these references mean. The name Arden is derived from a similar etymology to that of the Ardennes in France where there is evidence that the goddess of the region was associated with a boar and was conflated with the Roman hunter goddess Diana. The reference to the recovery at Leek Wootton of an image of the goddess makes this the most plausible location for a hypothetical temple to the goddess of the Arden. The area around Leek Wootton and Blacklow is known to have undated enclosures the size of temple enclosures, along with Roman artefact scatters and an early medieval religious complex.

Folk-tradition could be looked at in a sceptical manner, but for the Forest of Arden it may produce the best surviving evidence of a goddess akin to *Arduinna* who was associated with the Roman goddess Diana and a boar. It is in the southern part of the area where the earliest evidence concerning deification of this landscape may be found. In the foundation legend of Evesham Abbey, of *c.* AD 700 (Macray 1863, 8–9, 18) a swine-herder called *Eoves* (the boar) followed a lost sow into the wilderness. Once he had found her he had a vision of three women. This image was associated, subsequently, with the image of the *matres* found so frequently in the land of the *Dobunni*; it has, thus, been used to imply that Evesham Abbey was built on the site of a pre-Christian temple or shrine. Nevertheless, it may be that a mother goddess, associated with a sow and a boar is being recollected, and that she acted as the personification of the Forest of Arden. There is a further legend concerning Swanwell, near Coventry, which seems to have been recorded in the work of Campden as the location where Diana of the Forest slew a great Boar. One wonders if these came into being randomly or whether the traditions have derived from now lost sculptural pieces, like the Roman goddess found at Leek Wootton.

The ancient name of the plain to the south of the Warwick Avon is not readily apparent, but one possibility is that it may be connected to a Celtic word which developed into the form of Wickham, now a village near Evesham. Mawer and Stenton (1927, 273) identified this with the word *Uuiguuennan*. Smith (1964b, ii.6) suggested that it was derived from the Old-Welsh *guic* or *guoun*, **the wooded plain**. There is some circumstantial evidence that the name of the area may have been related to that of the river Sowe.

The identification of temples in the area south of the River Avon is also problematic. A temple probably stood at Harrow Hill (Cox 1979, 31–38), to the north of Badsey, as the Old English place-name referred to the location of a pagan shrine. Quarrying in the area, in 1822, uncovered one of the largest hoards of Iron-Age currency bars in the country, an artefact type which has been shown to have been deposited deliberately behind ramparts or palisades. A river shrine, comparable to that of *Cuda*'s shrine at the Lower Slaughter Chessels, has been identified at Baginton, where the remains of a seated mother goddess was recovered from a well, see chapter 4.

CONCLUSIONS: THE DEIFICATION OF THE WOODLAND

A number of forest areas can be recognised across the territory of the *Dobunni* and *Hwicce*, but it is evident that the names used for these territories came into being at different times and, presumably, by different means. Only two forests are actually recorded as having been created during the high medieval period in the whole of the country. There is also a further group of forests, including Chippenham, Pewsham, and Feckenham, which, due to their name, must have been established during the early medieval period, as their names derived from specific Old English place-names. The name Kinver may also fall into this category even though Kinver itself is of a British origin. It is possible that, during the time of the Norman Conquest, and in the years prior to this, forests were reorganised, and pre-existing topographical regions were broken down. It is also apparent that there are a number of earlier names which, even though they were recorded in the early or high medieval periods, are far older, and share their names with discrete topographical areas.

In the territory of the *Dobunni* are a number of upland and lowland zones which contain pre-Old English place-names. These have already been discussed, and include

Cotswold (*Cuda*), Kemble (*Camulos*), Braydon, Zoyland, Corse, Arden (*Arduinna*), and Wyre (*Vigora*). Others can possibly be inferred from estate names which seem to have applied to far larger topographical areas in the past. The Cotswolds and the Forest of Arden may be the only examples of any of these place-names being recorded and surviving from the Roman period although the *Cudæ* inscription is badly preserved, and the *Ardua* is in a garbled text. That the names are old is recognised by the onomastic evidence, which considers them to be derived from pre-Old English source words and, therefore, must predate AD 600. The next step is to comprehend how these names were used and how the religious activity operated; this will mean that Continental parallels will have to be considered.

Other parts of Britain and adjacent areas of the Continent can provide Roman period parallels that will exemplify the thinking of the peoples of Europe at that time. A number of topographical names containing *silva* as a prefix or a suffix have survived. The usual translation of the word is **woodland**. The Roman historians mentioned a number of them; Caesar, for example, referred to the *Silva Arduenna* and the *Hercynia Silva*, while in Britain; Pliny mentioned the *Silva Calidonia*. Another British example can be found in Kent, the *silvam Verlucium*; this name has been preserved in a wooden writing-tablet from London, which formed part of a grant (Tomlin 1996, 209–205). It seems that these *silva* names were used to designate large topographical areas. They continued to be used in the medieval period; for example, Asser referred to the *Berroc Silva*, the old name of the Berkshire Downs. They often contain pre-Old English names, and in some cases it is apparent that they were the names of recognised divinities. As Old English and even Norman French became more prevalent, replacing the British and Latin languages in oral and written practices, it became apparent that the term *silva*, which means woodland, was replaced by the terms *wold*, which indicated a high wooded area, or forest, set aside for royal hunting.

There is, throughout the region, a disparity between the information available through archaeology, that derived from historical sources, and that obtained through onomastics. For the Cotswolds, it has been postulated, that the old regional name derived from the pre-Old-English *Cuda*. Considering that *silva* was probably a term applied to a topographic area; then the Cotswolds would have been either the *Silva Cuda* or the *Cuda Silva*. Evidence for the existence of the widespread cult of the goddess *Cuda*, and her associated *genii cucullati*, has been discussed. At least five shrines have been located in the Cotswolds; one to the north of Cirencester, one in Cirencester, one at Easton Grey, one at Bradford-on-Avon, and the other at the Lower Slaughter Chessels. The location of the shrines at Easton Grey and Bradford in the South indicates that the name *Cuda* applied to the whole range of hills. The name of the landscape and the name of the goddess are, according to this hypothesis, one and the same, and presumably their origins are intertwined. In the images of *Cuda* as well as in her name it is possible to see that the landscape was deified to a great extent. During the Roman period, the landscape was spiritual and imbued with the divine. Although barely proven in other parts of the *Dobunnic* area, for example the Forest of Kemble, the Mendips, and Forest of Arden, continental parallels could be used to show that the name *silva* was attached to other names which were also those of divinities.

Not all of the regions and names highlighted have been termed *silva*, but some of them certainly were. The interpretation of the religion of Roman Gaul provides many useful ideas for the study of Roman period religion with respect to religious action, iconography and landscape perspective. Derks's (1998) reinterpretation of the two upland landscapes, the Vosges and the Ardennes, associated them with strategically located religious sites where the regional divinities *Vosegus* and *Arduinna* were worshipped. He suggested that shrines were placed on focal mountains, for example at Le Donon in the Vosges, and also at points of key access into the landscape. The access points operated as boundary markers to that landscape. All that lay within the boundaries were the *Vosegus Silva* (the Forest of *Vosegus*) or the *Silva Arduenna* (the Forest of *Arduinna*). The location of shrines on boundaries of the forests is important but this demarcation is not political; the naming and designation of the earliest *silva* names was a means by which the natural world could be divided into zones for human activity, for the assessment of resources, and for cultural integration, thus suggesting practical reasons for the deification of the landscape.

Chapter 3

The Sacred Rivers

In the territory of the *Dobunni* it is apparent that the rivers were deified to a significant degree and this was one of the main concepts which bound together the sanctity of the landscape and the portrayal and cohesion of the community (Yeates 2006, i.57–66; forthcoming 2007b). How this occurred will become more apparent as the next two chapters progress. There are many aspects to the river system which can be assessed; first, with regards to their physical properties and their natural resources; second, through onomastic evidence (the origins of names and the apparent survival of the pre-Old English river names); and third, through the archaeology of spring and river-sites. Each river will be discussed here as a unified whole, so that the name and character can be assessed in a consistent way.

The land associated with the *Dobunni* lies in at least two, and possibly three, major river catchment areas. The majority lies in that of the river Severn, and its major tributaries: the Teme, the Wye, and the Warwick and Bristol Avons. Part of the east of the territory drains into the Thames, and it is from amongst the tributaries of this river where some of the best surviving evidence for the deification of rivers comes. A further part of the territory may extend into the catchment area of the Trent-Humber basin, but this cannot, as yet, be confirmed.

Ritual or religious focus on rivers in prehistory can be identified through the deposition of votive objects in rivers. The evidence for this activity has been assessed for the south and the east of the country and can be seen to date back to at least 1000 BC (Bradley 1990). At this time, major ritual sites were constructed in wetland zones, the primary example being Flag Fen (Pryor 1991), which lies outside the *Dobunnic* tribal area. In the *Dobunnic* region numbers of trackways have been located in the Somerset Levels, one documented on the Severn near Powick, and another, possibly, at Old Weir on the Wye. Votive objects have been recovered from the Thames, around the confluences of the Churn and the Evenlode, which date to the Iron-Age. The locations used along these rivers seem to fall into three general categories: those at the source, those at a spring beside the river and, lastly, those at confluences (Yeates 2006, 39–56). Certain rivers were venerated more than others and the reasons for this varied. This will be explored further later, but must surely have been related to the communities' perception of themselves and others around them.

The river shrines generally had a temple, usually within an enclosure, constructed alongside the spring (either at the source of the river, or on the bank of a river).

Associated with these are a series of wells or votive shafts which were also constructed within enclosures. It seems also that there was a period when the shrines were going out of use, when sculptural material was deposited into the shafts. This will be considered in more detail later. This process may help explain why so little of the sculptural evidence from Britain has been recovered, as so few of these sites have been identified and excavated systematically. Most of those found have been destroyed by gravel extraction.

In considering that rivers were deified in some way it is important to understand the origins of their names. Here, the archaeological information is too fragmentary and only brief glimpses of the past can be identified. Therefore, the assessment of river names from textual sources becomes extremely important. The basic work carried out on the survival of Brittonic river-names was by Ekwall (1928). The Severn Valley and the Cotswolds lie in an area of Britain where there is considerable survival of British river-names; however, it is not always clear that the names are now applied to the correct river, see Figure 10.

It will become apparent that the artefacts and structures of Roman temples, and their association with springs, were important in this respect. It is also evident that, in some circumstances, the name of a spring was associated with the guardian or presiding spirits of that place and that this name was often incorporated into the place-name. What is not totally apparent, however, is whether this association can be projected back into the Iron Age, although there is certainly a desire to. At Bath, for example, medieval romantics claimed that the healing springs had been founded by Bladud in the eighth century BC, an assertion which can not at present be verified. Part of the problem with backward projections is the difficulty in recognising religious activity in the Iron Age.

Many of the rivers mentioned have no evidence, as yet, of deification, but this is probably because the field research has not been carried out. In certain river systems every major stream source has a shrine located at one of its more unusual springs. The evidence for this survives best in the Cotswolds.

THE SEVERN – THE GODDESS SABRINA

The longest river in Britain is the Severn which rises on the slopes of the Welsh mountain Plynlymon. Folk-lore has it that she was one of three sisters born of their mountain father. No evidence of a sanctuary site has yet been produced at its source, but there very likely could be one for such an important river. The river flows through the Welsh county of Montgomeryshire, and then through the English county of Shropshire or Salop. The river passes a number of significant places along the way, the Breiddin Iron-Age hill-fort, the Anglo-Saxon burh of Shrewsbury, the Roman *civitas* capitol of Wroxeter, and the significant industrial site of Iron Gorge. Where the significant religious sites lay await further investigation, but there are undoubtedly a number of them. One would expect one of these shrines to have been located overlooking the river in the vicinity of Wroxeter. It is only when it passes through the Iron Gorge that the river approaches the territory of the *Dobunni* and the later *Hwicce*,

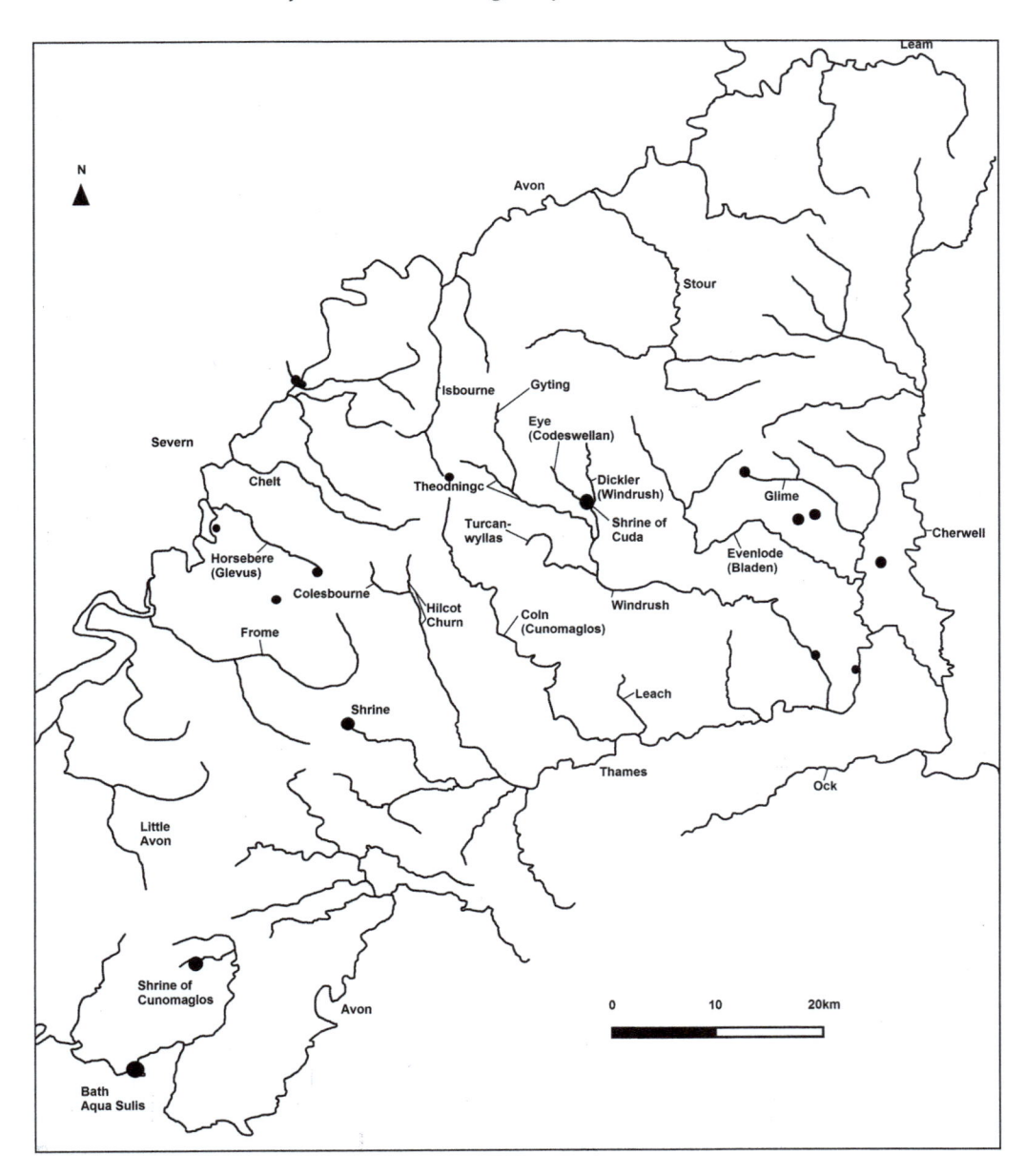

Figure 10: A map showing the river shrines which have an associated divine river-name and the major streams and river-names of the Cotswold region which are tributaries of the Thames (S. Yeates).

but it is not now apparent where the borders of the *Dobunnic* territory were. It is quite likely that the boundary fluctuated. After this point the river flows in a generally southerly direction past the Roman town of Worcester and on through to the Roman *colonia* of Gloucester. From Gloucester the estuary opens out, and its mouth lies between Weston-super-Mare, on the English side, and Penarth, on the Welsh side.

The Severn, whose ancient name was *Sabrina*, a female cogname, was probably an important deity (Ross 1967, 47) of the *Dobunnic* people. The fact that the river had a feminine cogname has led to the suggestion that there must have been a goddess for the river; this has been accepted in the Cambridge Dictionary of English Place-Names (Watts 2004, 537). The name was first recorded by Tacitus (Annals xii.31) and Ptolemy (ii.3.2), and shares a common origin with the French river-names Sèvre and Sèvres. The meaning of this word is, however, unknown. It has been claimed that the name was derived from the Celtic *sab* or *sabar*, **the milk**, or Illyrian *Sab*, meaning **shaft**, but this is all doubtful. The early Welsh form of the name was *Havren* which may be related to the Cornish and Welsh *haf*, **summer**. That such a river would have a seasonal name is probable as, in the winter, much of the land around the river was flooded and dangerous.

The first site with evidence for the ritual deposition of objects, that one comes across as the river flowed into the territory of the *Dobunni* and *Hwicce* is probably in the vicinity of Lincombe and Holt where Bronze-Age objects have been recovered (VCH(Wo1) 1901, 194–195). Worcester, as it was such an important Roman settlement on the Severn, would also be expected to have had a shrine associated with the river. Wells of Roman date have been identified at the Castle, in the Deansway, and in the Butts. None of the deposits found in these are definitely religious, although numerous Roman coins were reported from under the Castle, and a stone column was deposited in the stone well at the Butts. One possible location for a shrine in the vicinity of Worcester could be Beavere Island, but this would need further investigation. At Powick there is evidence of a probable prehistoric site in the form of a series of piles extending into the river from the west bank. A Bronze-Age spear is known to have been recovered from this location (Allies 1852, 52–60). It is probable that there were other religious sites on this river between Worcester and Gloucester, but none has been identified as yet. It is possible that the minster of Deerhurst, which is known to be located on a Roman site, may, due to its location on the banks of the Severn, have been a temple site, but this also remains unproven.

The goddess of the Severn has not been identified but it is probable, if not highly likely, that she shows up in the sculpture recovered from Gloucester. It is believed, from archaeological remains and antiquaries' sources, that there was a temple located on an island in the stream of the Severn under what is now Saint Mary de Lode's church (Yeates 2006, ii.832–833), see Figure 11. Also, religious sculpture, reused in the neighbouring priory of Saint Oswald, shows a seated Fortuna type figure. It is believed to have come from the temple site at Saint Mary's. Further upstream, near a spring, a similarly clad image of a female has been recovered. These sites, an island in the Severn and a mineral spring rising on a gravel terrace above the Severn, are possible locations at which the river could have been venerated. Fortuna was used, through the

Figure 11: The church of Saint Mary de Lode, Gloucester (photograph S. Yeates).

process of *interpretatio* to represent important female deities associated with water; there are examples on the Continent, including the goddess *Nehalennia* (Green 1989, 10–16). The shrines' locations and the image of a female goddess tend to indicate that there was a cult associated with *Sabrina*, goddess of the river Severn; however, no inscriptions to confirm this have been found.

    The Severn estuary starts to broaden after Gloucester and this stretch of the river is one of the most important for its natural resources and natural phenomena. Eleventh-century Anglo-Saxon charters indicate that the river was important for the catching of herring, porpoise, and sturgeon, while later Welsh sources indicate that the salmon had a particular association with the Severn. Church texts indicate that lamprey were a major catch of the river. The most comprehensive list of the produce of the Severn Estuary was written by Smyth (Maclean 1885); it dealt with the fish and sea mammals caught in the manor of Berkeley which had access to the deep water between Slimbridge and Sheperdine, *c.* AD 1605. The catch included: sturgeon, porpoise, thornpoles, jubetas (young whales), *herringe hogge*, seals, swordfish, salmon, trout or *suen*, turbot, lampreys, *lamperne*, shad, twaite, rays, *hound fish*/dogfish, sole, *flooke*, flounder, *sand flooke*, *barne*, cod, *card*, *eele pout*, mackerel, sun-fish, hake, haddock, *roucote*, *sea tad*, plaice, millet/mullet, lynge, *dabbe*/dab, *yearlinge*, *horncake*, lumpfish, red and grey gurnard, cuttlefish, whitinge, *little crabbe*, *conger eele*, *shee fish*/quaver, dory, *huswife*, herring, sprats, pilchards, prawns, shrimps, eels, *fauzon greated*, elvers (young eels), *base*/bass, sea bream, and halibut.

The most important of these fish were probably the migratory fish because they would invariably attract hunter-gatherers, throughout the Mesolithic, and up to the present day. The most important of these was the salmon, and it is evident that it is associated with much of the lower Severn's folk tradition. Other important species included the allis shad, which migrated up the river in April and May, and the twaite shad, which migrated up the river in May and June. Besides this young eels entered the estuary between March and May.

The traditions of the Lower Severn, and the significance of the river are hinted at in the work of Nennius (Morris 1980, 40 no. 68), at the beginning of the ninth century AD. He described the Severn Bore as the fifth wonder of Britain, and referred to it as the Dau Ri Hafren, **the two kings of the Severn**. Geoffrey of Monmouth stated that Avern was born in a cave under the estuary and that she was condemned to swim in the shallows where she drowned (Palmer 1994, 24–27). Local, and undated, traditions suggest that the Broadstone at Stroat marked Sabrina's grave. How these legends and traditions were romanticised and evolved over time is unknown, but it is evident that the Severn may have been thought to end near Beachley, which is now known not to be the case. It is possible that the estuary and the bore may nave been seen as separate entities known under different names.

There is evidence for a shrine on the eroded cliff at Aust, where there is an excellent view across the river. Place-name evidence, in the form of Buryhill, indicates that the site was fortified. The remains of a bronze statuette, of late Iron Age date, found at the site could only have come from a shrine site. During work on the construction of the Severn Bridge Roman deposits were uncovered. Another shrine is believed to overlook the Severn Estuary at Whorlebury. Numerous coins have been recovered from the hill-fort, and also on the island of Steepholm (Green 1993, 241–242). This island contains the remains of two Iron-Age hill-forts. From one, religious sculpture, including, an early Roman head, has been recovered while the other contains the remains of a circular Roman structure. The circular Roman building has been interpreted as a signal station, but on the available evidence may equally have been a Roman shrine. The islands of Steepholm and Flatholm would have provided ideal locations for the deification of the river Severn at its mouth.

THE WYE

The river Wye was considered to be one of the sisters of the river Severn as she was born from the same mountain father. Again no shrine has been located near her source but it is highly likely that there was one, as with the Severn. The Wye flows from the

Welsh county of Montgomeryshire, before passing between the counties of Brecknockshire and Radnorshire. The nature of the river and its veneration are little understood, but it is known that salmon spawned on the gravel beds above Clifford.

The name of the river is considered to have derived from *uogia-*, **a wagon**, or *uegh*, **to carry**, or the Welsh *gwy* or *weg*, **water** (Watts 2004, 706). The interpretation of the name as water may imply that this is not the original name of the river and that aspects of the name have been lost in translation.

There are important gravel beds, which acted as spawning grounds for salmon, between Breinton and Hereford. At the head of this area are the probable remains of a major river shrine complex at New Weir and possibly another at Old Weir (Shoesmith 1980, 135–145). At New Weir there are the remains of a villa complex, an elaborate water cistern or spring head, and a series of columns which once supported platforms out over the river. The site has been claimed as a religious complex, but no temple has been located. However, there is a large double-ditched enclosure adjacent to the site which would have acted as a temenos boundary. At Old Weir there is evidence of wooden posts in the river bed, but no evidence of a bridge. When trying to contextualise this evidence it seems that the site does have many of the characteristics for a river-side shrine, a possible temenos, a spring, a villa complex, and also a platform for walking out over the river. The platform over the river may have been a Roman version of the prehistoric trackways that extended into marshes, lakes, and rivers, as discussed previously. Fish were an important aspect of the river around Breinton, which is indicated by reports of sturgeon, lamprey, and shad in this part of the river. Other fish are recorded at sites lower down the river, around Hoarwithy, Ross, and Ganarew but no potential religious sites are known in these areas.

Below Ross the Wye enters its lower valley, or gorge, at Symond's Yat, but it is not until the river reaches its estuary or confluence that significant references are made to a series of important shrines. Nennius not only provided descriptions of the significance of the Severn Bore but also referred to an ash tree which produced apples, and a cave from where the wind blew constantly. At Chepstow, Roman religious sculpture has been recovered and Roman deposits found, which may have come from a possible Nymphaeum or river shrine. The Roman material has been claimed to have been imported from Caerwent or Lydney, but it is more likely that it originated from a more local site in Chepstow itself. The Roman deity represented seems to be Venus, and not Mithras as claimed (Brewer 1986), an appropriate figure to represent the deity of the Wye.

THE STOUR

There are numerous other tributaries of the Severn. Two of them, the Stour and Smerstow Brook flow from the west part of the Forest of Arden. Stour is an important river-name, which is considered to be pre-Old English by some, but has no known derivation. Other Stours in the region include: the Warwick Stour, the Bradley Brook, and a tributary of the Ampney Brook, both formerly known as Stours. There are references, from 1636, to the weak brine springs at Saltwells Spa, Kingswinford, but no known Roman activity has yet been identified there. One of the tributaries of the Stour also had an open stretch of water called Ismere.

SALWARPE AND WORFE – THE GODDESS VERBEIA

The river Salwarpe rises in the Lickey Hills, in the Forest of Arden, and flows south-west towards Ombersley. It has a number of tributaries including the Salty Brook, and the Elmley Brook. The name Salwarpe (Watts 2004, 525–526) is derived from the Old English *weorpan*, **to throw**, which in turn evolved from the British *verbia*, **to turn** or **twist**. The river-name is, therefore, an adaptation of the common river-name Wharf. In the case of the Yorkshire Wharf it is known that this was derived from the name of the goddess *Verbeia*, which has been determined from an inscription from Ilkley. Due to the early recording of this name it is evident that the river Wharf had a femine cognomen, which applied to the goddess of that river and presumably every Wharf. More recently, it has been suggested that the name was derived not from an adjective but from a noun, the Old Irish *ferb*, **cattle**, a suggestion which seems more likely as it is a recognised pre-Old English word.

On the north side of the river, at Hawford, are the remains of Roman period enclosures of an unknown purpose, which are associated with crop-marks (Yeates 2006, iii.877–878). The enclosure is in a classic location for a Roman period river shrine. To the south of the confluence is Beavere Island, which has produced a Bronze-Age axe and scatters of Roman finds.

There were also other rivers in the region called Wharf, most notably the Wiltshire river which is now called the Ray and flows north from Swindon.

THE PERDISWELL

To the north of Worcester there is potential evidence of a Roman period shrine at Perdiswell (Yeates 2006, iii.1391). There was a large triple-ditched enclosure with evidence of internal features and a substantial building. The area was recorded in antiquity as the source of an Iron-Age torque. This, coupled to the place-name, which is derived from a well, spring or even the stream which flows from the area of the enclosure, indicates that this was probably a substantial shrine site in the hinterland of Worcester.

THE SALTY BROOK – SALINAE

There are many springs in the vicinity of Droitwich and Stoke Priors which rise from an extensive Salt-pan in the Keuper Marl beds. One of the streams which flows into the Salwarpe at Droitwich is called the Salty Brook. Due to the Roman name of Droitwich, *Salinae* (Rivet and Smith 1979, 451), which derives from salt, it is highly probable that this is perhaps an English translation of a river-name *Salinae* or *Salia*. The name of the Roman settlement went through a similar development from *Salinae*, or *Salinae Vicus*, to the early medieval place-name *Saltwich* in AD 717 (Mawer and Stenton 1927, 285).

The salt springs at Droitwich were considered to have been extremely important in the past. Nennius (Morris 1980, 40 no. 67), between AD 796 and 820, described the salt springs of the kingdom of the *Hwicce* as the fourth wonder of Britain. Droitwich was quite a large Roman town due to the presence of its significant mineral springs; it was highly likely that there were not only temples but also a significant spa infrastructure. Two probable shrines at Droitwich have been identified; the first at Bays Meadow, the second at Upwich. Bays Meadow is the location of a villa complex, with two aisles ancillary buildings, and a central square building which has the appearance of a Romano-Celtic temple (Rahtz 1971, 18–19; Wilson 1972, 317) though later reports ignore the evidence for the shrine. It was constructed over earlier Iron-Age salt production sites. The main spring at Droitwich was at Upwich and it is here that the remains of a large cruciform timber building have been located (Frere 1992, 283). The only buildings which provide parallels with this are those identified at Sanxay in Vienne, France and at South Cadbury in Somerset; both of these are considered to be temples. The name of the deity worshiped at Droitwich is not known, but one could consider it safe to hypothesise that there was a goddess called *Salina*.

There are other river-names, possibly derived from *Salina* or *Salia*, which are basically pre-Old English words referring to salt (Ekwall 1928, 188–189; Smith 1964a, ii.15–16). The name of Hailes Brook, Gloucestershire, is probably derived from the river-name *Salia*. There is also a Sawcombe near Winchcombe, a Salt Brook near Stoulton, and a Saltwell near Kingswinford, to name but a few.

THE DOWLES

The river Dowles rises in the centre of the Wyre Forest and flows north then east before it reaches its confluence with the Severn. The name is pre-Old English and considered to be derived from the Welsh, *dulas*, **blackish** (Ekwall 1928, 131). That the river was important in the past is known from its use by salmon as a spawning ground.

GLADDER AND GLEVUM

The Gladder was a tributary of the Severn flowing from the Wyre Forest, while the Horsebere brook rises on the slopes of the Cotswolds and enters the river Severn to the North of Gloucester. The Gladder is an ancient British river name, the later part of which is derived from *dubro-*, **water**, while the former comes from *gloyw* or *gloew*, **bright** (Ekwall 1928, 173; Mawer and Stenton 1927, 11). The name, therefore, means **the bright water**. Along this stream very little is known of the archaeology, but the same first part of the name occurs in the name of the colonia of Gloucester, *Glevum*. This is why Ekwall considered the name of the Roman *colonia* to be derived from a river name. The river to which this applied is now no longer evident in place-names but the most likely candidate for this is the Horsebere Brook.

There are three streams which flow from the coombs behind Gloucester to enter the Severn. These are the Twyver, which contains a Latin or pre-Latin name, and the Horsebere and Hatherley Brooks, both of which have lost their pre-Old English names. There are also a number of mineral springs in the area; a saline spring at Dean Farm, and a chalybeate spring near Green Street. It is also considered that the well which rose in the middle of the *colonia* of Gloucester was saline. Of these springs two of them lie in the valley of the Horsebere Brook. For Longford, near the confluence, there are references to an Old Mere and it is possible that where these streams entered the Severn there was a lake until medieval times. The Horsebere Brook also stands out in other ways in that it seems to be the only stream in the area with a recognised major shrine at its source. Survey work at Great Witcombe Villa has identified the remains of a probable shrine or temple (Holbrook 2003, 179–200), and it is possible that this was the primary structure in the complex and that the villa was secondary to it.

THE DOFERIC

There are a number of common Celtic river names which are derived from *dubro*, **water-stream** or **river**, and the related Welsh word *dwfr*, **water** (Ekwall 1928, 136; Smith 1964b, i.6, 9). These include: the *Doferic* (the former name of the Shrawley Brook), recorded in AD 757–75; the Elmley brook, which was called the *Doverdale* in AD 706; the *Doferburna* (the Knee Brook), recorded in AD 977; and the Doverle, recorded as *doferlan* in AD 940, a tributary of the Little Avon. It is not apparent if this was used as a proper river-name or if it just meant stream and was used with a prefix or suffix which was the actual name of the river. In the case of the Doverle, this was *glan*, **pure**.

THE LAUGHERN AND BARBOURNE

The Anglo-Saxon charters for the area to the west of Worcester identify a large number of river-names, of which the longest is probably the Laughern. This river-name is associated with an animal, which in this case is *llywern*, **fox**. It has been argued that this derives from the Gallic *lovernius*, **fox**, a masculine cognomen (Breeze 1998, 251–252).

A further group of river-names in the Wyre Forest and the Worcester areas take their name from the Old English *beofor*, which must have derived from British **bebro*; both mean **beaver** (Yeates 2006, i.149). The first is the Barbourne Brook, to the north of Worcester, which was recorded in AD 904. The second, on the opposite bank of the river Severn, in the Wyre Forest is *Beferic*, which has a Celtic ending.

TEME

The river Teme rises in the mountains of Radnorshire, before it flows between the English counties of Herefordshire and Shropshire. Little is known about religious activity in this part of the territory. One potential religious site is at Tenbury, which has a mineral spring, associated with a burh or valley-fort place-name, and became the later location of a minster church. A calcareous spring at Southstone Rock was once a large source of deposited tufa. The Teme was also renowned for its salmon spawning grounds.

Many of the tributaries in this area are regarded as having retained their pre-Old English names. They include the Onny, the Clun, the Corve, the Leint, the Kyre, and the Sapey. Little can be said, however, about shrines and religious practices.

LEADON

The river Leadon rises in the hills to the east of Bromyard. It flows south and is one of the main drainage systems for eastern Herefordshire. Its confluence with the Severn is at Gloucester. The valley has a number of mineral springs in the Pauntley, Payford, and Durbridge area to the north-east of Newent. The Leadon has a number of tributaries which include the Glynch and the Wyndbrook, both of which have Celtic or British names. The one means **pure**, the other **white** (Mawer and Stenton 1927, 11; Smith 1964b, i.4–5).

THE CARRANT TO THE DANIEL'S BROOK

There are a number of smaller rivers which flow into the Severn between its confluence with the Warwick Avon and that with the Frome. With some of these there is some evidence of pre-Old English river-names and religious sites. The most northerly of these is the river Carrant, which rises near Dumbleton and is joined by the Washbourne. The Washbourne flows from near Stanley Pontlarge, where there is a Saltpool. There is another salt spring at one of the springs which feed the Carrant to the north. The two streams unite near Beckford, and then flow west; a further salt spring rises near Walton. The name Carrant is believed to be derived from the Celtic *caranto*, **a friend** (Ekwall 1928, 70). This river seems to have been deified in the Roman period, as some evidence has been found of a ritual site at the river's confluence; a stone-lined well with apparent ritual activity (Hannan 1993, 21–75) and is evidently part of a shrine complex.

The Tyrel and the Swilgate, once called the South Tyrel, flow into the Severn at Tewkesbury. However, little evidence has been found to identify the name Tyrel as pre-Old English, or of the existence of past ritual activity along the banks of the streams. It is known, however, that one of the springs at the source of the Hyde Brook is saline. The place-name Harrow Farm indicates the location of a pagan shrine, but the farm lies on a terrace between the Swilgate and Dean Brook, and also a series of wells or springs at Hardwick, which feed into the river Chelt. The Chelt valley also has a number of mineral springs, at: Fieldholme, Lansdown Terrace, and Pitville. It is also not apparent what the ancient name of this river was.

The river Twyver, which rises to the south-east of Gloucester, contains an ancient river name which is derived from, at least, a Latin word for Weaver (Smith 1964b, i.13–14). The river enters the Severn at Gloucester and, one would assume, there would have been a significant site near the confluence. The Daniel's Brook was once called the Herse (Smith 1964a, ii.164, 184), a name which once applied to a large territory around the river. The derivation of the name has not been established fully, but was applied to a hill-fort above the brook's source. One of the villas at Stockend, in the Harescombe valley, has produced evidence of religious sculpture in the form of three uninscribed altars, some columns and other sculptural pieces (G.SMR 7085). The material recovered seems to have been located at a possible spring shrine site on the *Herse*. The Arle, which flows to the south of this, rises from a mineral spring in Standish Park.

THE FROME AND THE LITTLE AVON

The Western Cotswolds are drained by the Frome and the Little Avon. The Frome rises near Brimpsfield, near a location where there is thought to have been a small Roman town on the course of Ermine Street (Yeates 2006, ii.460–461). The name Frome, derived from the British **from* or **fram*, **fair**, **fine** or **brisk** (Ekwall 1928, 55–56). No evidence of a shrine has been found at the source of this river, but some has for shrines on some of its tributaries. The source of the Toadsmore Brook is the springs of Bisley, where there is a seasonal flower dressing ceremony, started in 1863. The minster church, above the spring, has had Roman reliefs recovered from its tower, and is believed to have been the site of a shrine or temple. The village may overlie a hill-fort as there is evidence of scarping, above the springs, and a terrace. The Toadsmore brook has two branches; one at Bisley, the other at Lypiate. These two courses unite further down the valley. An ancient river-name was Biss, which means the forked-river, and one could consider that Bisley and the other related names in the area come from this ancient British river-name. There are other tributaries, such as the Slad and Painswick Brooks, from the north, and the Avening and Horsley Brooks, from the south. Many Roman reliefs have been recovered in the area, but their reported locations have been too imprecise to be of any value. There is evidence of a stone structure on one side of the river Frome, near Whitminster. It has been described as a bridge, but it lies off the line of the main Roman road, and may be the remains of a platform similar to that at New Weir on the Wye.

There are two other rivers with the name Frome in the area; one of these is in east Herefordshire and is a tributary of the Lugg, the other is in East Somerset, and is a tributary of the Mells Stream. At neither has any significant evidence for ritual action been found. In the case of the Hereford Frome, however, there is evidence of mineral springs in the parish of Acton Beauchamp, and also in the area around Saltmarsh.

To the South of the Stroud Frome are the rivers Cam and Little Avon. The former is believed to derive its name from the Celtic *cambo*, **crooked** (Smith 1964b, i.4), while the Little Avon was originally called the *Ballestran* (Grundy 1936, 82–85); this is considered to be from an animal name. Saline springs have been reported at Alkington. The tributaries of the Little Avon include the Doverle. There was possibly a shrine set on a bluff at Ryeham, and there has been some speculation concerning a shrine under

Berkeley minster, which sits on a terrace above the Little Avon. These suggestions do, however, need confirmation.

THE WARWICK AVON

The Warwick Avon rises in Leicestershire, near Bosworth, and drains the eastern arm of the Severn basin. It is fed primarily by the Sowe, the Leam, the Alne, the Arrow, the Stour, the Piddle, the Isbourne, and Bow Brook. Three Avon names occur in the area under investigation; the Warwick Avon, the Bristol Avon and the Little Avon of Berkeley. The name Avon derived from the Celtic *Abona*, **a river** (Ekwall 1928, 21–22), and is believed by some to be of ancient use, as it occurs as the name of a settlement on the Bristol Avon in the Antonine Itinerary. There are doubts as to whether this was a proper name, or simply a corruption, through translation into English. In two Anglo-Saxon charters alternative names have been given to two of these rivers; the Little Avon being called the *Ballestran*, as discussed, while Grundy noticed that the Warwick Avon, possibly erroneously, was called the Alne in one Evesham charter. This implies that the names of the deities of the Warwick and Bristol Avons remain unknown.

There are a number of potential shrine sites associated with the Warwick Avon. Near Tiddington, on the south bank of the Avon, a well was uncovered, in 1938, which contained the remains of two pieces of religious sculpture (Henig 1993, nos. 45, 155). The sculpture included the representation of a male head, which could be identified as the chief deity of the Warwick Avon. There is some evidence of another shrine site at Eckington, in Worcestershire (Allies 1852, 74). When the railway line was constructed the remains of a significant building were identified, as well as three wells. No religious artefacts were identified but the site sits on a gravel terrace overlooking the Avon floodplain. The presence of wells seems significant for Roman-period river shrines. There are also indications at the Mythe, near Tewkesbury, of a possible religious site at the confluence of the Avon and the Severn. Aerial photographs show the remains of a square enclosure of unknown use, which is associated with a scatter of Roman material. A number of Roman artefacts have also been recovered from the river Severn at Tewkesbury, near its confluence with the Warwick Avon.

THE SOWE

The river Sowe rises in the Forest of Arden near the village of Astley, from where it travels south-east before turning south-west towards its confluence with the Warwick Avon near Stoneleigh. The river-name was derived from the Gallic *savus* or *sava* which evolved into the root *seu*, and has been given the etymology **to flow** or **to be liquid** (Ekwall 1928, 70; Watts 2004, 563). There is evidence of a major shrine in the area, perched on the edge of a gravel terrace overlooking the Sowe at Baginton. Gravel extraction has uncovered the remains of numerous wells, without any real evidence of standing structures. The site seems to parallel other river sanctuaries in the area, and it seems that one of the wells produced the remains of a piece of Roman religious sculpture. This sculpture is significant because it is of a seated mother goddess (Henig 1993, no. 122). The only parallel for this is that found at the Lower Slaughter Chessels, where the mother goddess *Cuda* was associated, not only with the river, but also with the larger topographical feature, the Cotswolds. It is, therefore, possible that the Sowe did not rise in the Arden Forest, as it does not share its name with the Sowe, but was the original name of the Smite or Withy Brook, which rises in the Leicestershire Uplands. The alternative to this is that the Sowe once gave its name to the lowland region of the Feldon and the Vale of Evesham.

THE LEAM

The Leam rises on the edge of the Northamptonshire uplands. There is one significant mineral spring along its course, which is the Original Spring or Abbot's Well at Leamington Spa. The name Leam is derived from a Celtic word for the **elm** (Ekwall 1928, 243–245).

THE ARROW, THE ALNE, THE PIDDLE AND THE HYMEL (BOW)

The river Arrow is one of a number of rivers which flows from the Forest of Arden into the Avon, along with the Piddle, and the Hymel. The river rises in a coomb on the east side of the Lickey Hills near Alvechurch. In this area there is the place-name Arrowtop Field, which refers to a pagan shrine, but little is known about the site and it may not even relate to this river system. The etymology of the river-name is believed to come from the Celtic *arva*, **swift** (Ekwall 1928, 16–17). There are indications of a saline spring in the lower valley as in 1730 the church of Salford Priors had tithes of salt.

The Alne, the Arrow's tributary, rises in a valley to the east; it has a name with a much discussed etymology, which could be from the Welsh *alaun*, **very white** (Ekwall 1928, 8–9), or even the Gaulish *alausa*, the **alose,** a type of shad (Rivet and Smith 1979, 243–244). Roman votive material has been recovered from near Aston Cantlow, and there is evidence of the mother church of Kinwarton being located on a site with earlier activity, which may point to it being a temple; this information has, however, not been properly contextualised. Roman religious iconography of Jupiter has been recovered from Alcester but, again, this has not been explained properly.

The Bow Brook, which was originally recorded as the Hymel (a name which refers to a plant, possibly the woodbine) rises in the valley between Hanbury and Feckenham (Mawer and Stenton 1927, 135). One of its tributaries is the Sawbrook, while there is a chalybeate spring near Churchill.

Other rivers in this area include: the Piddle Brook, which has mineral springs at Throckmorton and Abberton, and the Ennick and Inkford Brooks from the Welsh *ennick*, **hen** or **old** (Ekwall 1928, 148). The name Ennik is probably derived from the British divine name Senuna, later Senna.

THE WELLESBOURNE AND THE STOUR

The tributaries of the Warwick Avon, which flow from the Cotswolds, include: the Wellesbourne (now the Dene), the Stour, the Noleham, the Badesey, and the Isbourne. The Wellesbourne rises from the Burton Dassett hills, probably from the holy well near Burton Dassett church. The church lies in a large rectangular enclosure, which is essentially undated, but Roman finds have come from the area (Yeates 2006, ii.476–477). The nature of the enclosure and its location, next to a holy well, may indicate that this was the location of a spring shrine. This possibility is strengthened by the fact that the church at Burton Dassett was undoubtedly a minster. The Littleham Brook, which joins the Avon further down stream from the Wellesbourne has, near its confluence, a rectangular enclosure with a central circular building; this seems to have the design of a religious enclosure.

The Stour rises near Tadmarston Hill, and flows west before turning north; it has a number of tributaries, the most notable of which is the Knee Brook. There are a number of mineral springs at Ilmington and Blockley. Further west along the Cotswold scarp, the Noleham Brook rises, and flows towards Welford. At Welford Pasture, near the confluence, are the remains of a rectangular enclosure with a circular building inside, a design common to religious sites. The site has been associated with Roman material. The Badsey Brook is the tributary which flows from near Broadway to the Avon.

THE ISBOURNE, THE SALIA, AND THE SPONWÆLLE

The river Isbourne rises on a north-east facing coomb of Cleeve Hill and flows to the north, where it is joined by the Langley Brook from the west and the Beesmore Brook from the south. Near Winchcombe, are two mineral springs, one a strong salt spring, the other a chalybeate spring. Place-name evidence suggests that there is a saline spring near Sawcombe, which means that *Salbury*, recorded in AD 1482, would have to be located at the disputed hill-fort on Langley Hill. The Isbourne flows north from Winchcombe, where it is joined by the Hailes Brook, before heading towards its confluence with the river Avon. Bronze-Age and Roman metalwork has been recovered from the Isbourne near Sedgeberrow, while at Hampton village, near the confluence, there is a further salt spring.

There is evidence for a shrine at the source of the Beesmore Brook, which, in early medieval charters, is called the *Sponwælle*. The remains of the sculpture of an eagle has been recovered from the site (Henig 1993, no. 168), thus indicating a shrine, associated with Jupiter and his cult bird.

THE BRISTOL AVON

Two sources are claimed for the Bristol Avon; one, the Tetbury arm, the other the Sherston arm; both of which come together at Malmesbury. Religious sculpture and a temple site has been claimed in the area around Grickstone and Badminton on the Sherston arm, but none of this has been verified satisfactorily (Yeates 2006, iii.1172–

1173). At Hyam Farm, to the south-west of Malmesbury, is a concentration of cropmarks on a south facing terrace above the river bank, from which votive material, indicating the site of a shrine above the Avon has been recovered (Yeates 2006, iii.1025). A spring to the north of Malmesbury, at Quobwell, which feeds a tributary of the Bristol Avon has also produced the sort of Roman material that would be expected to come from a spring shrine.

Mineral springs have been located along the course of the Avon at Christian Malford Meadow, Chippenham, Melksham, and Holt. Further mineral springs can be found on the tributaries flowing from Wotton Bassett in the east. In *c.* AD 1670, Aubrey referred to a petrifying spring in the parish which is at Whitehill, and a chalybeate well near Hunt's Mill. Further west there is a mineral spring in Kington Saint Michael Park. In the vicinity of Melksham, the river Avon has produced evidence for a major votive Bronze-Age deposit, with some of the artefacts being deliberately mutilated (Fowler and Miles 1971, 20; 1972, 25; Robinson 2001, 151).

There is a further spring near the banks of the Avon at Horseland which seems to have been the location of a shrine to that river (Collinson 1791, 111). The spring rises from the floor in the middle of a square building which seems to have had a later hypocaust floor built over it. The finds associated with the building included two altars and a coin hoard, thus suggesting a shrine. Despite this, the site has been catalogued as a villa. Springs rising in domestic buildings are not common, and from the description given the site probably originated as a shrine, temple, or *nymphaeum*, similar in design to Coventina's Well, Northumberland. The second floor may relate to later conversion of the site for secular use.

The lower part of the Avon valley is renowned for its mineral springs, especially its thermal springs. Those around Bath will be returned to later and discussed separately. There are five thermal springs in the Avon Valley region, three of which are located at Bath, with a fourth at Hotwells, Clifton, Bristol. This is a high volume hot spring issuing from an aperture in the carboniferous limestone at the foot of Saint Vincent's Rock. This fissure now lies approximately 8m below the high water mark and 3m below the low water mark. *William Worecestre* discussed the source and gave the measurements of Ghyston Cliff, on which the chapel of Saint Vincent stood, in 1480. Rudder discussed this spring, referring to it as being generally above the level of the River Avon and only being affected by high tides. There are reports of complete oaks being dredged from this part of the river Avon, and it is possible that they may have formed the basis for prehistoric or even Roman platforms around the spring. The spring is associated with a mythical giant, and also seems to have been venerated in the medieval period. The last of the sites is at Freshford, on Staples Hill, where there is a hot spring like that at Bath. No further information is available on this site and it needs further investigation.

The last site to consider is the confluence of the Avon and the Severn. A Bronze-Age sword was recovered during the construction of the docks; this indicates a possible veneration site at the meeting of these waters (Brett 1996, 115–120).

THE WEAVER (BY) AND THE *CUNOMAGLOS* (BROADWATER)

The Broadwater and the By Brook rise in the valleys to the north of Bath, from where they flow east and join near Castle Combe. There is an enclosure, on one of the spurs above one of the coombs near the head of the By Brook, which has the appearance of a religious enclosure.

Meanwhile, a major shrine, dedicated to the god *Cunomaglos*, has been excavated at Nettleton Scrubs (Wedlake 1982). The site lies next to the Broadwater Brook and the remains of a wooden structure, which extended out over the stream, have been found. This has been associated with bathing, but may have been for deposition into the river. *Cunomaglos* has a number of attributes and, in a later chapter; he will be discussed as the central figure of a widespread cult amongst the *Dobunni*. Here, we can suggest that he may have been the god of the Broadwater Brook, as the name *Cynfael* (derived from *Cunomaglos*) is recorded in the Mabinogion as the name of a river associated with a hunter-god who kills a stag (Jones and Jones 1974, 69).

There may have been another sanctuary at Box, where a mineral spring is known to be located. The important villa at Box, which lies under the church, has, in the past, been considered to be part of a sanctuary site, as a votive eye was recovered during excavations (Robinson 2001, 150, 161). This has not yet been confirmed.

THE FROME, THE MELLS STREAM, THE CAM, AND THE WELLOW

These rivers drain a large section of the eastern Mendips and flow into the Avon to the south-east of Bath. Three of the rivers still retain derivations of Celtic or British names. One of them, the Wellow, not previously discussed, was derived from the Welsh *gwelw*, **pale** or **pale blue** (Ekwall 1928, 446–447). In these valleys saline springs rise from the Radstock and Farrington rock series. Religious sculpture and other artefacts have been recovered from the area but can not be related to any of these water shrines as yet.

AQUIS SULIS AND THE MINERAL SPRINGS AROUND BATH

Around Bath, or Aqua Sulis, there are numerous mineral springs the most important of which are the hot springs in the centre of Bath. The springs are formed by water seeping into deep fissures in the Keuper marl bedrock, which becomes heated and is then forced upwards and out at the junction of the Keuper marl and the impervious Rhaetic shale beds. Further mineral springs have been identified at Swainswick, Lyncombe Spa, Saint Winifred's Well, Lansdown Hill, Limekiln Spa, Carnwell, Batheaston, and Bathford Spa or Saint Anthony's Well. When veneration of these sites commenced is not known. There are claims that Bladud found the springs at Bath in the eighth century BC, a claim which can not be verified. The Salt spring on Swainswick hill rises from below the hill-fort on Solsbury Hill, a name which has been corrupted but was recorded as *Saltbury* in AD 1480, meaning the salt-fort (Yeates 2006, ii.338).

The hot springs at Bath have a name related to the Welsh *haul* or the Breton *heol*, both of which refer to **the sun** (Rivet and Smith 1979, 255–256); the early recording of the name *Sulis* suggests that it was derived from a noun and not an adjective.

The surviving texts indicate that Bath was a significant religious site in both the Roman and the medieval periods. Solinus, in the *Collectanae rerum memorabilium* (or the Curiosities of the World), referred to the hot springs in Britain, which were furnished for the use of man, and over which Minerva presided. There was a "perpetual fire which never turned to ash, but the flame dies and turns to rocky balls". Nennius (Morris 1980, 40 no. 67), AD 796 to 820, referred to the hot springs in the kingdom of the *Hwicce* as the third wonder of Britain, thus indicating their continued veneration into the ninth century AD.

The temple complex and its surviving Roman material offer one of the best examples of how other more fragmentary remains should be considered (Cunliffe and Davenport 1985). The date at which objects were deposited in the spring is not known, and even though *Dobunnic* coins have been recovered these may have been deposited in the early Roman period following continued circulation. From the late Iron Age or early Roman period, there is evidence of an enclosure with a causeway being built between the three springs. This contained four standing posts. The temple complex was built over a long period, mainly from the late first century into the second century AD. The main spring became located in the south-east corner of a religious enclosed space; a wall was built around the spring and this had a building constructed over it. The temple was a tetrastyle construction, facing east, in which a cult statue of the goddess *Sulis Minerva* was housed. In front of the temple were an altar and a quadrangular monument, all on the same alignment. The finds from the temple complex are numerous, and include altars, reliefs, curse tablets, coins and jewellery and other trinkets; much of this was deposited in the spring. The altars recovered from this site, and in other parts of Bath, are among the most important finds because they inform us of the name of the goddess *Sulis*, who presided over the springs, the temple, the baths, and the town. This goddess was associated with the Roman goddess Minerva. Haverfield stated that the position of *Sulis* as the presiding deity of the site requires us to assume the existence of a temple dedicated to *Sulis*, even if we had lacked the evidence. In many respects the temple of *Sulis* indicates how other topographical rivers and springs sites should be viewed.

The temple was only one component of the religious complex; the other was the bathing establishment, which is probably the largest complex of its type recognised in Britain. This, like the temple, seems to have developed over centuries, and filled in the whole of the area between the three springs. It was fed by the hot springs and is what the Romans would have known as a *Kurorte*, or spa. By extrapolating what has been found at other Roman river or spring sanctuaries it is possible to show that significant elements were missing from the complex; including a series of wells, in enclosures, which would have been used for votive purposes. That such a site existed may be postulated with the consideration that the town wall marked the division between the sacred world and the profane. These may lie under another area of Bath, along the line of the stream flowing from the springs, or perhaps at the confluence of the *Sulis* with the Avon.

THE CHEW, THE BOYD, THE BRISTOL FROME, AND THE TRYM

Before the Bristol Avon reaches the Severn it is joined by a number of streams and rivers. The major ones are the Chew, flowing from the Mendips, and the Boyd and Frome, flowing from the Cotswolds and Kingswood. All of these are considered to have retained their Celtic names; the most interesting of which is Chew, associated with the Welsh *cyw*, **a young chicken** or **bird** (Ekwall 1928, 77). There are a number of unusual springs in the area, including one at Beach, Bitton, called Grand Mere, and holy wells at Pucklechurch, at Saint Jacob's well, near Bristol, and at Stapleton; a well which acts like a boiling cauldron.

Little, if anything, has been recovered on the veneration of these rivers, but antiquaries have claimed that there was a Roman camp at Dodington, a village which is located at the source of the Frome (RCHME 1976, 43). The Chew rises near Chewton Mendip, where a Roman site is known to be located under the village (VCH(So1) 1906, 360); the church is regarded as a minster church. The river Trym, for which the ancient name is lost, has had prehistoric metalwork found in it near its confluence with the Avon.

THE LUGG, THE ARROW, THE LODON, THE FROME, AND THE HUMBER

The largest tributary of the Wye is the Lugg, which rises in the Welsh mountains of Radnorshire. In the same mountains rises the Arrow, and these two rivers unite in the vicinity of Leominster. Both have Celtic names, the first from the Welsh **Lugge*, meaning **brilliant light** (Watts 2004, 386), the one associated with the god Lugus (Ekwall 1928, 239; Mawer and Stenton 1938, 3), while the Arrow is believed to derive its name from the Celtic word *ariant,* **silver** (Ekwall 1928, 13). The only mineral spring in either of these valleys is believed to be at Stockley Cross, Staunton-on-Arrow. Further down its course the Lugg is joined by the Humber, whose name is derived from the common Celtic word *sumbr,* **good** or **well** (Ekwall 1928, 202–205). The only suspected Roman temple site in the area was detected by geophysical survey work under the priory church at Leominster; it is of a circular shape (Barker and Ranity 2003). The location of the site is on a terrace above an area of marshland, where the Lugg is now braided but would once have been fed, not only by the Lugg, but also by the Onny (now the Pinsley Brook), the Whyle, and the Ridgemoore Brook. This was, therefore, a major, or nodal, confluence. The last tributary of the Lugg is the Herefordshire Frome, which is fed by the Lodon. Possible Roman-period religious sculpture has also been found near the confluence of these two rivers (Henig 1993, no. 160).

THE EIGN

The river in Herefordshire which seems to have the most evidence recovered for its veneration is the Eign. It rises near Shucks Bank on the Burton Hills near Yarsop. At Mansell Lacy it reaches the plain, from where it makes its way through the northern suburbs of Hereford, and enters the Wye in an area known as the Widemarsh. The river is believed to have retained its Celtic name which is derived from the Welsh *iagin*, **the cold stream** (Ekwall 1928, 145).

The centre of the city of Hereford was located on a gravel terrace in the middle of the Widemarsh. On this terrace a holy spring, called Saint Ethelbert's Well, rose from the gravel near what was later the location of Hereford Castle. There is enough evidence now to indicate that the cathedral of Hereford was founded over the site of a Roman temple (Yeates 2006, iii.891–892), see Figure 12. Excavations of the Mappa Mundi building identified the remains of a Roman enclosure ditch. The remains of three altars have also been recovered, while antiquarians digging in the cathedral cloister area found the remains of an earlier building which has always been interpreted as a church, but may be the remains of another type of building.

THE THAMES

The Thames rises near the village of Kemble, from where it heads into the Forest of Kemble, and borders the Forest of Braydon as it heads towards Lechlade, around Wytham Hill, and then Oxford. The major tributaries that flow from the Cotswolds

Figure 12: The cathedral of Saint Mary and Saint Ethelbert, Hereford (photograph S. Yeates).

include: the Churn, the Coln, the Leach, the Windrush, the Evenlode, the Glyme, and the Cherwell. The rivers draining into the Thames from the south include: the Swill Brook, and the rivers Key, and Ray.

The Thames once rose from a spring higher up the valley. In Hailey Wood are the remains of a large enclosure with banks and ditches, and cropmarks of ancillary buildings. The artefacts from the site indicate that this was a Roman site, and the lead curse tablets that this was a temple complex. The site is so located that it was undoubtedly the shrine which marked the source of the Thames (Moore 2001, 83–93, 83–93).

The name Thames was initially believed to have been derived from the British *tamaza*, **dark water** (Ekwall 1928, 402–405). It used to be considered that this word came from the Sanskrit *tamasa*, however, this interpretation is now considered to be incorrect and an alternative suggestion that **ta*, in river names means **to flow** (Rivet and Smith 1979, 466). This interpretation may also be relevant for the name of the Tame, and also the Teme, which was derived from the extended British word **Tametio*.

Like the Severn, the Thames must have been a major source of fish; however, due to the industrialisation of the area around London it is more difficult to assess this. The fish discussed include: sturgeon, in Oxfordshire, miller's thumb, ruffe, perch, stickleback, barbell, gudgeon, roach, dace, chub, minnow, tench, bream, bleak, and loach. The migratory fish had problems on the river due to industrialisation but there are accounts of salmon being re-introduced in 1815.

The shrine at the source of the river has been discussed, but few other religious sites associated with the Thames have been identified. The remains of a *genius* with a headdress and veil were dredged from the Thames at Bablock Hythe (Henig 1993, no. 35). It had no inscription so it is not apparent what the *genius* represents. In the same general area Bronze-Age and Iron-Age artefacts were recovered from the river at Stanton Harcourt.

Only well outside the study area can another possible shrine to the Thames be identified (Yeates 2006, i.56–57). Under Southwark Cathedral, on numerous occasions, Roman material has been recovered. From AD 1820–1910 a whole series of mosaics and foundations have been uncovered: under the church, in the cemetery, and also at the grammar school. Excavations in 1977, at the west end of the choir, identified the remains of a first century AD timber structure with a possible clay floor, and a second-century AD pit and hearth along with burnt and unburnt walls. These were sealed by a dump of clay through which a circular pit, 2.5m wide, was cut into the gravel. This was clay lined and proved to be the top of a wood-lined well. From the well a series of sculptures of deities, and two funerary monuments, were recovered. One of the sculptures was that of a hunter god wearing a Phrygian cap and a tunic, and carrying a bow; he was accompanied by a hound and a deer. There was also a well-sculpted local *genius* in fine-grained sandstone. The head and the right arm are missing, but the left hand survives and holds a cornucopia; the lower part of the body is covered in folds of drapery. The remains of hair or a veil can be identified around the neck. There was also an altar with the stump of a damaged sculpture. The remains of a marble statuette showing a leg accompanied by a dolphin have also been recovered. These are believed to be of a male, perhaps Neptune or Oceanus, and to be dated to the first or second century AD. The last of the sculptures is the head of a river god. Further investigation in 1991–8 indicated that the river was braided at this location, and that there were a number of wells on the island. Due to the sculpture found at this site, it has been interpreted as the possible location of a temple complex, the meeting-place of a religious guild, a residence, or a private shrine. The fact that there are so many wells with sculpture deposited in one or more of them has parallels with other known river shrines; for example, that at the Chessels, Lower Slaughter. The fact that the *genius* from the site was damaged in the way that it was is a problem, but enough of its neck and headdress survive to indicate that this is the same *genius* as that portrayed at Bablock Hythe, further up the Thames.

THE CHURN

The river Churn, on modern OS maps, is marked as rising at Severn Springs, but in the Anglo-Saxon charters of the area, that stream was known as the Colesbourne and it was the Hilcot Brook which was referred to by the name of Churn (Yeates 2006b, 63–81). The river head is fed by some nine springs which flow from a bank on the east side of Wistley Hill. These streams would have come together in the vicinity of Pegglesworth Home Farm; however, today there is a fishpond collecting the water and channelling it so as to make the ground where the house and stables are usable. From here the river flows south towards North Cerney, and there is evidence of a Roman religious complex between Baunton and North Cerney on the bluff on the east side of the river. The river flows past Cirencester before it reaches its confluence with the Thames. Here, Iron Age and Roman artefacts have been dredged from the river, thus implying some earlier activity.

It is possible that images of the Churn *genius* have been recovered from Cirencester (Yeates 2006, i.64). The Churn was represented by the image of a *genius loci* with a mural crown, while votive material has been recovered in the vicinity of the confluence with the Thames (Yeates 2006, ii.649–650).

The ancient name of the river was Corin and as yet no satisfactory solution has been produced for the word's etymology. It has been suggested that it is from **cern*, **a horn**, or *ceri*, **a medlartree** (Rivet and Smith 1979, 321–322).

THE COLESBOURNE

The river Colesbourne, presumably, takes its name from *cole*, a Celtic word for hazel (Yeates 2006b, 63–81), a common name as it was used for the river Rea at Birmingham (formerly the Cole), the Cole at Coleshill, and the Colwall in Herefordshire. In the case of the Colesbourne the river-name was used as a personal-name implying that the deity may have been preserved in folk memory.

THE COLN

The river Coln rises in a valley called Cawcombe, to the west of Sevenhampton; then runs east before turning south. On its way it passes the powerful spring at Syreford Mill and below Withington the river flows in a generally south-easterly direction towards its confluence with the river Thames, near Claydon Pike. The name of the Coln has been thought to be undecipherable; the early forms being *Cunuglae* or *Cunuglan* of AD 721–743. It is probable that the first part of the name is the Celtic *cuno*, **dog** (Yeates 2006, i.26, 49–50), and more recently it has been determined that it may also be derived from *Cunomaglos* (Yeates 2006b, 63–81).

The religious site at Wycomb was uncovered in the 1800s (Lawrence 1863, 302–307; 1863, 627). The site had a two phase temple, the last of which was of a Romano-Celtic design, and produced an image of Mars. The main temple is possibly one of three found on the site, one of which may be circular in design. The place-name Wycomb has developed from wic-ham which is derived from the Latin *vicus*, **town**. The survival of this name may mean that the town had a specific status, but there has always been some ambiguity concerning its development and location. There should be no problems in understanding why this religious complex was built in this location, as there is a cliff at Syreford Mill which has several springs pouring straight out of the face of the rock. The volume of water from the spring is powerful even in the summer and for this reason an important medieval mill was constructed there. The medieval channels, ponds, and fish ponds may have destroyed a number of important earlier features at the site, but the proximity of the major temple to one of the most powerful and interesting springs in the Cotswolds should not be ignored. It is possible that, due to the nature of the spring, this was venerated as the source of the Coln.

There is a further shrine, which is likely to have been built for the veneration of the Coln, near Chedworth Roman villa (Saint Clair Baddeley 1930, 255–264). On a terrace above the river are the remains of a tetrastyle temple, with an accompanying Roman settlement of unknown use. At the villa there is also evidence of the veneration of the spring, with a small *nymphaeum*. The only distinctive sculptures to have come from the villa-temple complex are three native warrior figures with schematic images (Henig 1993, nos. 126–128). The first shows the outline of a male figure simply outlined on a miniature altar. The deity has large ears, sunken facial depressions, quincunx settings, and stick arms. A second, smaller, altar also seems to have quincunx settings, thus associating it with the Chedworth warrior god. The third shows a standing male figure with a quincunx of sunken dots; he is believed to hold a circular shield in his left hand, and perhaps an axe and a spear in his right hand. Part of an inscription survives on the relief as [.]EN[.] M, which is normally interpreted as [L]EN[o] M(arti). There is also a circular shrine located in the woods above the villa, it may have been part of the complex for the veneration of the spring, although there are alternative possibilities. The use of Mars at Wycombe and Chedworth may indicate that the local river god was conflated with Mars. As the name of the river was probably the *Cunomaglos* then a hypothetical *Mars Cunomaglos* may be inferred.

The remains of a further shrine site, of two phases, has been located at Claydon

Pike, which lies on a hill near the confluence of the rivers Coln and Thames. This had a circular shrine and a long ancillary building (Miles and Palmer 1982).

THE WINDRUSH

The river-names of the Upper Windrush valley have been considerably confused, not through the introduction of English, but rather by the cartographers of the early post medieval period (Yeates 2006b, 63–81). The Windrush has a number of tributaries, and according to the Anglo-Saxon charters, the river of that name started in the valley above Hinchwick. This is now called the Dickler, but it is apparent that the Windrush, which translates into English as **white rush**, and the Dickler, which means **thick read beds**, are British and English names for the same river. The river was renowned for its trout, eel, crayfish, and greyling.

No known shrine has yet been identified at the source of this river, or at its major natural feature Windrush Mere, which lay between the villages of Bourton-on-the-Water and Windrush. There is evidence of a large riverside stone structure at Asthall, described as a bridge but found only on the one side of the river (Pike 1990, 58). The only clearly recognisable shrine to this river is probably at Gill Mill, where a major Roman period settlement lay on an island in the river. In the low area by the river, spreads of occupation debris were uncovered around two wells in 1990; this has all the indications of a river-side shrine. Amongst the finds were numerous coins and a relief of a *genius* (Henig 1993, no. 36; Bagnall-Smith 1995, 201; Frere 1991, 258; Pike 1991, 95–96).

One of the tributaries of the Windrush rises from a saline spring on the west side of Iccombe Hill. The spring is located outside the site of an Iron-Age enclosure, which has very little evidence of occupation.

THE *CODESWELLAN*, THE *GYTING*, THE *THEODNINGC*, AND THE *TURCH*

There are three rivers which join the Windrush from the West; these are today called the Eye, the Upper Windrush, and the Sherbourne. It is apparent, from Anglo-Saxon charters, that, in the early medieval period, they all had other names. The Eye was previously called the *Codeswellan*, possibly meaning **pigeon** river (Yeates 2004, 2–8; 2006b, 63–81; 2007a, 55–69), and is associated with the deity of the Cotswold Hills, who was discussed earlier. No shrine has yet been recognised at the river's source, but there surely must have been one. A shrine has, however, been located at the confluence of the Eye (nee *Codeswellan*) and the Dickler (nee Windrush). This shrine, at the Lower Slaughter Chessels, is evidently a river shrine with its enclosures surrounding votive wells. Although a shrine or temple was not recognised in the excavations, the complex was renowned for the sculptures associated with *Cuda* and her cult.

The Windrush is now considered to rise from the great spring near Cutsdean, which was actually the source of the Guiting Brook (Yeates 2006b, 63–81). The name of the brook is generally considered to be of an Old English origin. No shrines have yet been located along its course, although one would expect such a powerful spring to have such a site. This stream flows into a river which was, in the early medieval period, called the *Theodningc*, also at present considered to be an English derived name. This river rises near Pinnock and flows into the Windrush to the south of Bourton-on-the-Water. Like the *Codeswellan*, there is evidence of a Roman site at the confluence, which also had wells constructed in small enclosures (RCHME 1976, 21). One can only consider that this was a similar shrine to the Lower Slaughter Chessels site.

The Sherbourne Brook rises near Salperton. It was once called the river Turch; a name derived from the Welsh *Turce*, **a boar** (Ekwall 1928, 420–421). Like the *Codeswellan* and *Theodningc* the only evidence for a potential shrine to this river is at the confluence. On the Edge of the gravel terrace, some way from the Windrush now but possibly once on the edge of Windrush Mere, are the remains of an extensive Roman period site, about which little is known (RCHME 1976). Its location is, however, comparable to the other sites further up the Windrush valley.

THE BLADEN

The river Evenlode, which was previously called the Bladen, may have originally come from a number of spring locations in the Evenlode, Little Compton, and Little Rollright areas. It is only after the confluence at Kingham that we know the river was definitely called the Bladen. There are a number of mineral springs in this valley, located at Churchill Mill, Shipton-under-Wychwood, and Bould. The name of the river is derived from the British word *blatona* or *bladona*, its meaning is unknown. One possibility, however, is that it may be associated with the Welsh *blaidd*, **wolf**, although this has its philological problems (Yeates 2006, i.49; 2006b, 63–81).

A possible temple site has been identified above a combe near Little Rollright (Yeates 2006, iii.903), while a Bronze-Age axe was recovered from the stream at Batsford. The remains of another spring shrine has been identified above one of the river's tributaries to the east of Charlbury. There are the remains of a triple-ditched enclosure at Lee's Rest, from which a sculptured head of Mercury has been recovered (Bagnall-Smith 1995, 177–203); the enclosure sits above the site of a spring. Further prehistoric objects have been dredged from the Thames near its confluence with the Bladen.

THE GLYME

The river Glyme is the major tributary of the Bladen, and rises in the hills to the south-east of Chipping Norton. From here the river flows south-east towards Wootton, where it is joined by the Dornford. It then proceeds south towards the Bladen. The river-name has an etymology which is derived from the British *glimo*, **bright** (Gelling 1953, i.7). Two sites on its course have been identified as locations of religious sites.

The first is at Glyme Farm where a considerable quantity of Roman material lies in the plough soil around the spring (Henig 1993, no. 46). One of the finds from the area is that of a bearded deity, which has been interpreted as Jupiter. It is possible that Jupiter was associated with the deity of the Glyme; both names are associated with brightness, Jupiter being father of the day, and Glyme, meaning **bright**. Another possible religious site associated with the Glyme is Fair Rosamund's Well, near Blenheim Lake (Copeland 2002, 118–119). By this spring there is a small enclosure which, it has been claimed, is the remains of a Romano-Celtic temple.

Evidence of ritual activity has also been identified at one of the tributaries which rises near Ditchley (Yeates 2006, i.53). At Barrow Place there is an enclosure located above a spring, called Devil's Pool, which is claimed as the location of a temple. The Rowel or Begbrook, which on Anglo-Saxon charters may have been called the Humber, rises near Campsfield and enters the Thames to the south of Yarnton. Archaeological observations in the Campsfield area have identified the remains of a Roman settlement which had at least two stone lined wells and some rich artefacts (Marshall 1873, 1–3). The name Campsfield refers to an enclosure. This could indicate that this was the location of a Roman period shrine at the source of the Rowel Brook.

THE CHERWELL

The eastern boundary of the *Dobunni* territory is often speculatively fixed along the river Cherwell, which rises near Cherwell Farm to the north of Charwelton, Northamptonshire. It does not rise in the Cotswolds but in the Northamptonshire uplands. From here the river flows south towards Croperdy, and from there on down to Oxford. In the Cherwell Valley, at Clifton (near Deddington), at Deddington, and at Sutton Bog, there are mineral springs. It has been suggested that the name Cherwell contains a British prefix associated with the suffix well. There are a number of tributaries, most of which join from the west. These include: the Highfurlong Brook, the Sor, the North Aston Brook, and from the east, the Farthinghoe Brook. At one of the sources of the Clayhome Brook, a tributary of the Highfurlong Brook, a lake called the Cranmere once existed. In the valley of the North Aston tributary there was a mineral spring called Saint Stephen's Well.

Little is known about religious activity along the Cherwell, however, there are some points of interest, especially concerning the location of two minster churches, which, when considering the wider landscape and the repetitive use of confluence sites, could be considered to be located on earlier temple sites. The first of these is the church and village of Croperdy which lies at the confluence of the Cherwell and Highfurlong Brook. The name of the village contains the earliest known name of the Brook, which is considered to have been derived from a plant-name. The remains of a Roman altar was claimed to have been built into the wall of a pub at Banbury (Beesley 1853, 18), but this can no longer be confirmed as the building has now been destroyed. Near Shipton-upon-Cherwell the remains of a bronze cauldron has been recovered from the river (Leeds 1930, 1–36). The second minster is Christchurch at Oxford, which sits on the gravel terrace overlooking the confluence of the Cherwell with the Thames.

The locations of Croperdy and Oxford look decidedly suspicious, when one considers what is known of the Roman period religious landscape. In both cases the minster would have required a monastic vallum and a temenos boundary, either a wall or ditch.

THE SWILL, THE KEY AND THE RAY

There are three notable rivers which flow from the eastern side of the Braydon Forest to feed the Thames. All now have new names, but charters do record what their old names were: the Swill was the Braydon, the Key was the *Lortingas*, and the Ray was the Wharf or *Verbia* (Gover, Mawer and Stenton 1939, 8–10). Two saline springs have been identified in this part of the Braydon Forest; at Braydon Manor Farm and Minety Common. The only known potential religious complex is at Groundwell, where a major villa complex has been identified, and an object with the name Isis recorded. The presence of a temple or shrine in the complex is indicated by the place-name as this refers to a well which rises from deep within the earth.

THE OCK AND THE KENNET

Two rivers which lie outside the probable tribal area of the *Dobunni*, have useful evidence of shrines; these are the rivers Ock and Kennet. Some more investigation as to their nature may still be needed, however. The Ock rises, according to Anglo-Saxon charters near the village of Uffington; this is not, however, where modern maps place it. The river's name derives from the Celtic **esáco-*, **salmon** (Gelling 1973, i.14–15). On the lower course of the river there is a major shrine complex with two temples in a large enclosure. A Romano-Celtic temple and a circular shrine were built over earlier Iron-Age deposits (Bradford and Goodchild 1939, 1–70). Outside the temple enclosure there is evidence of buildings looking out onto a cobbled area and, beyond this, a large linear building. There is also a large circular monument which was possibly a theatre, but may also have acted like a seasonal well, with the rise and fall of the water table. Between this area and the river, votive artefacts have been recovered from a further small shrine. If this site was like other river shrines then there should be an extensive area of enclosed wells into which votive material was deposited. Further along the terrace there is a salt spring, around which Roman material has also been recovered. The shrine was once considered as a boundary location, but it is more probable that the river name salmon was more important and that the river was possibly a major spawning ground of that fish.

The river Kennet has two possible sources, the main source being near Silbury Hill by Avebury. This is the accepted source. To the north there is a stream called the Winterbourne which had a seasonal nature and was prone to dry up. Excavations at the base of Silbury Hill, in 1911, identified a series of wells, which were considered to have been ritual shafts associated with a shrine (Robinson 2001, 162; Corney 2001, 26–29). There is further evidence for a large structure in this area, but the significance of this building is unknown. It seems to have been on the periphery of a large Roman settlement over Waden Hill, whose name is derived from *wēo(h)-dun*, **hill with a heathen shrine** (Gover, Mawer and Stenton 1939, 295). There seems, therefore, to have been a major shrine, associated with the source of the Kennet, which exhibits key components associated with typical river shrines in the Cotswolds.

THE AXE, THE BRUE, AND ITS TRIBUTARIES

The major rivers of the north Somerset levels include the Brue, the Whitelake, the Sheppey, and the Axe. The Axe rises from the underground cave system at Wookey Hole, and flows across the levels, and around the north side of Wedmore, to its confluence with the Severn near Brean Down. The river has the common Celtic river name *isca*, **a fish** (Rivet and Smith 1979), but the type of fish referred to is not known. At the entrance to Wookey Hole there is evidence of a Roman enclosure, the nature of which is unknown.

The river Brue rises in the Forest of Selwood near South Brewham, from where it heads west towards Glastonbury; before continuing to the sea. The river's name is believed to be derived from the Welsh *bryw*, **brisk** or **vigorous** (Ekwall 1928, 152–156), but this is a sluggish stream meandering over the levels. There are mineral springs in the Glastonbury area at Chalice Well and on Tor Hill. At South Brewham, in the upper Brue Valley, votive material has been recovered, but the location of the shrine and its significance to the river Brue is not known.

Near Glastonbury there was once a large lake or mere, which is known to have been exploited greatly in the medieval period and was the source of the abbey of Glastonbury's fish wealth. The pre-Old English name of the lake is not known, but *Glas* or *Glast* is attested elsewhere in the region as a lake name, and it is possible that Glastonbury takes its name from this lake. *William Worcestre* stated, in AD 1490, that the meres near Glastonbury were full of fish; he listed trout, coles (miller's thumbs), loaches, flukes, pickerel, minnows, prides (like lampreys), crawfish and *dewdows*. He stated that if the meres were fished out in one year they became replenished the next. Later, the manor of Meare was known to produce pike, tenches, roaches, eels, and other diverse kinds of fish, as well as water birds, including swans and herons. In this area numerous prehistoric wooden tracks were built and possible ritual deposits, including Bronze Age axes, spears and swords are known from Meare Heath (Saint George Gray 1929, 105–106).

The lake at Glastonbury was fed by two other rivers, described as the Croscombe Water and the Sowaie. The Sowaie must be an older name for the Whitelake, and here we may have a late recording of its Celtic name. The Croscombe is the Sheppey, which, in the earliest surviving Anglo-Saxon charters, was called the Doulting or *Duluting* (in AD 705). The river-name Doulting is recognised as being pre-Old English in origin, initially interpreted as Welsh *du*, **black**, and *-lud*, **swift**, or *-loth*, **dirt**, it has subsequently been re-evaluated as being associated with Welsh *dylad*, **flood** (Coates and Breeze 2000, 90–92). The word, in the form Delat, is known as the name of a famous and beautiful woman who was a concubine of king Bleddyn of Powys. The name is, therefore, a recognised female cognomen, which one would expect with river-names. There is a holy well at the source of this river, dedicated to Saint Aldhelm, and one would expect the source to have had a sanctuary. The site is known to be the location of a minster church, and the village retains the name of the river, Doulting.

One of the tributaries to the Sheppey rises from Saint Andrew's Well, near the eastern end of Wells Cathedral. Roman material has been found at Wells and it was the location of a major early medieval church (Rodwell 2001). The nature of the site is unknown.

DISCUSSION

The territory of the *Dobunni* has numerous springs and rivers, and used to have some lakes. Springs, especially mineral ones, were considered to be important sites for veneration. The confluences and certain banks of rivers were also associated with temple or shrine sites. In some cases it is not evident why a particular river-bank would have been chosen, but it is possible that it was associated with natural resources and the spawning grounds of migratory fish, which would have been a huge focus for human activity from the Mesolithic onwards.

Sulis and *Cuda* can be recognised as presiding spirits and it is evident that the names of topographical features were often shared with towns and also, more importantly, with deities. Other river names such as: the Lugg (*Lugus*), the Itchen (*Icauna*), the Wharf (*Verbia*), and the Hennuc (Senuna or Senna) are known to have such associations even if they have not been categorically proven with inscriptions. The names are Celtic or British in origin, and it is evident that votive deposition in rivers became important in the late Bronze Age and persisted into the Iron Age and Roman periods. Shrine locations along rivers seem to have followed a systematic pattern: enclosures located above the springs at the source; enclosures associated with springs along the course of the river; and enclosures at the confluence. Associated with these enclosures are a series of enclosed wells associated with votive deposition, and the placing of sculptured votive material upon the closure of the shrine.

Chapter 4

The Gods of Tribes and Folk-Groups

There has been some discussion concerning the relationship which existed between communities and their gods. These interpretations have been derived mainly from surviving sculpture and inscriptions, and also some anthropological and ethnographic theory. There are indications that deities were established to preside over provinces and their peoples; for example, at Altrip there is a dedication to the *Geni(o) G(ermaniae) S(uperioris)* and a *Genio Loci* (Espérandieu 1922, no. 5993). At Winchester, a dedication was found to the *Matres* of certain Roman provinces, including both Britain and Gaul (RIB(I) 1995, no. 88). It is also evident that these deities represented the origins of certain national symbols, such as Britannia, and Germania. As these provinces did not exist before the Roman period it is difficult to project these figures back into the past, although it could be claimed that the idea of the British, the Gauls, and the Germans existed in a pre-Roman context. The second level of group deification which can be recognised occurred both on the continent and in Britain. From the town of Naix, in Gaul, a sculptured altar, with *Epona* on one side, and a *genius* with a dedication to the *Genio Leuc(orum)*, the presiding spirit of the *Leuci* tribe, on the other (Espérandieu 1915, no. 4650). In Britain dedications have been found to the tribal goddess *Brigantia*, the goddess of the *Brigantes* (RIB(I) 1995, nos. 630, 2091, 1053). From the direct examples, it is evident that Roymans (1990, 49–94) is correct in recognising an association between deity and tribe. This tradition would, presumably, have related to smaller groupings including *pagi* and maybe even smaller units. Dedications at Saalburg, Feldberg, Zugmantel, and Mayence to the *Genius Centurie*, have also been found (Espérandieu 1918, no. 5762; Mattern 2001, no. 8–14, 18–19, 36, 38). This is normally seen as a dedication to an army century, but it, perhaps, only represents the spirit of a part of the Roman people.

For the territory of the *Dobunni* and the *Hwicce* it is apparent that certain folk-names were recorded in charters and in place-names, for example *Weogorena* (Gelling 1969, 26), and *Salenses* (Smith 1964a, ii.15–16). These two examples, however, are both of British origin and are recording part of a stratified linguistic landscape; informing us about the folk-groups which resided in the area prior to the migration period, despite the names being recorded in texts from the eighth to the eleventh centuries AD. To understand how these names could have survived through the migration period, it is evident that there had to have been stable communal development into the fifth and sixth centuries AD. We need to, therefore, divide the landscape into discrete units in which a whole series of key archaeological sites would have been constructed. It is only through such an approach that we can hope to understand how communities developed and how they retained their pre-Old English folk-names.

PEOPLE OF THE RIVERS

A number of folk-names from the area, besides *Woegorena* and *Salenses*, have survived and a very recognisable underlying development pattern can be defined (Yeates 2006, 57–66; forthcoming 2007b). The names are all derived from river-names, *Woegorena* being from the Celtic river-name *Vigora*, an unrecognised stream, presumably to the west of Worcester. *Salenses* is derived from the river name *Salia*, which is the old name of Hailes Brook. Further folk-names can be identified throughout the area; including those containing the suffixes *-sæte, -ingas,* and *–hæme*; all of which indicate **dwellers or community**. These names have been discussed in the past by Mawer and Stenton (1927, 104) for Worcestershire but were not fully understood. Many of the names contain a river-name prefix, along with the **dwellers** suffix, while some other names contain the full name of a village, for example *Wudetunnincga*, in AD 983 (Gover, Mawer and Stenton 1939, 272). These **dwelling** names are probably stratified. The names with only the river-name plus **dwellers** must date from before the development of the present settlement pattern, while those which contain a full village name, and are not necessarily associated with a river-name, must have developed from the time when the present settlement was constructed.

Further examples from Gloucestershire include the *Glevensis* and the *Esingas*. The folk-name *Glevensis,* according to Föester, developed into the early Welsh tribal name *Glywysinga* (Yeates 2006, i.64, 95). The *Esingas*, were considered to be the people of *Esa* (Smith 1964b, i.9); but it is apparent that, as the name later became Isbourne, the name came to refer to **the people that dwelt on the *Esa* river**. Other examples can be found in Worcestershire, including the *Badesaeta*, **the dwellers on the *Badewella*** (Mawer and Stenton 1927); and in Somerset, including the *Lockingas*, and the *Glastingas*. It was considered that the place-name *Lokkinges*, of 1249, derived from **Locc's people**, but it is apparent that this was a river-name (Watts 2004, 378). The name could not have come from the Locking Rind, a drainage channel on the levels, but instead must have come from the Lox Yeo, a river-name derived from the British name **Losca*, presumed to mean **the winding one**. The name Locking probably derived from the word *Loscaingas*, the etymology of which would be **the dwellers on the river Losca**. The name *Glastingaea* (from AD 704) means **the island of the *Glastingas* people** and derived from the Celtic *glast-*, or Gallic *glastum,* **woad** (Watts 2004, 251–252; Ekwall 1960, 198). It probably referred to **the dwellers on the *Glass* Meare**. In Wiltshire there are charters which refer to the *Crodesaeta*, **the dwellers on the Crudwell** (Gover, Mawer and Stenton 1939, 56), and in Oxfordshire were found the *Hensingas*, **the dwellers on the river *Hen*** (Gelling 1954), and the *Glimehæme*, **the dwellers on the river Glyme** (Gelling 1954). The *Arrowsaeta* of Warwickshire represent **the dwellers on the river Arrow** (Gover, Mawer and Stenton 1936), while for the last county in the area, Herefordshire, there is a reference to the *Lionehæme*, who were **the dwellers on the *Lione*** (Coplestone-Crow 1989), probably the original name of the Curl stream. That this type of name turns up right across the region is significant and, in the vast majority of these cases, the name is invariably that of a recognisable pre-Old English river name followed by a prefix of **dweller**.

THE ARCHAEOLOGICAL FRAMEWORK: LATER PREHISTORY TO THE FOUNDATION OF THE MINSTERS

To understand the development of these communities and the survival of their names it is essential to assess the zoning of the landscape and the types of monuments which were constructed (Yeates 2006, i.57–66; forthcoming 2007b). A brief overview of this development will be given before a series of communities are discussed. It is apparent that, in the late Bronze-Age, large unenclosed settlements, often with a smaller enclosure acting as a central focus, developed. This type of settlement probably continued into the early Iron-Age but the evidence for this is more limited. Examples for both middle and late Iron-Age extensive semi-nucleated settlements are known. It is not always apparent where some territories' settlements were located, but the fact that they are evident in other territories, albeit in a fragmentary nature, means that they probably developed in most territories.

The monument of the Iron-Age which is most well known is the hill-fort. Much work has been carried out on these sites and there has been much debate on their development and use (Yeates 2006, i.62–63). They were initially interpreted as fortified towns, but it is apparent they varied widely in their design. Some have much evidence of occupation while others have none. The chronology of these sites has also been discussed; were the sites contemporary or built at different times? A typological series has been proposed but it is apparent, from other research, that dating the use of and even the construction of such sites is problematic. The sites seem to have been constructed and used by communities over centuries, and acted as places where people returned, seasonally, for specific events. Even in those sites which have the remains of dwellings it is evident that they were not places of permanent occupation. These sites' use for gatherings at specific times is also indicated by a number of medieval place-names. Many of these hill-forts are located on or called Maiden Hill, Maiden Bury, Knave Hill or Knave Bury; names which indicate a site where young adults gathered to take part in specific rites. Another group of place-names associated with hill-forts includes Spell Bury, Spell Wall, and Maugersbury. These names refer to a place used for communal gatherings; in the latter case **the fort where people speak**. Some fortified sites were named after rivers; for example, *Codesbyrig*, or *Eresbury*. Previous discussions have suggested that sites on rivers were deified, but the exact nature of the relationship between the forts and the rivers is not obvious. These accounts seem to suggest that hill-forts were used for a central ceremonial function (possibly seasonal and variable); and were built or rebuilt over centuries, with the bank being a symbolic boundary.

There is evidence from the region that single hill-forts were not important in their own right but, rather, operated as part of a group. For Somerset and Gloucestershire especially, it is apparent that hill-forts occurred in groups of three usually with a fourth which operated as an outlier (Yeates 2006, i.57–66; forthcoming 2007b). Such sites occur near Mells, at Priddy Circles, in the Avon Gorge, in the Trym valley, at Condicote, and at Standish, to name but a few.

During the Roman period nucleated settlements, with new technologies and new concepts of planning, developed (Yeates 2006, 59–62). Most of these new settlements, Cirencester being the major exception, had an intramural area and an extramural area. This design followed, to a large extent, the design of the settlements of later prehistory. It has been assumed that ritual activity took place in some of the central enclosures of these settlements, but is not proven categorically. In the region under study something like 80% of the Anglo-Saxon *parochia* have a recognised or partially recognised Roman nucleated settlement in their territory. The names of a large number of such settlements, from across Roman Britain and Gaul, took their names from rivers.

Whatever the status of the Roman settlement; *colonia, civitas, vicus,* or *castellum* there was always a ritual focus for the central area, normally related to a deity associated with the identity of the local folk-group or community (Yeates 2006, i.57–66; forthcoming 2007b). There has been much archaeological investigation in both Gloucester and Cirencester, and in both a central forum and basilica can be identified. Basilicas were large aisled buildings from which *Civitas* and *Colonia* were run. It was common for these structures to contain an *aedes* or shrine, dedicated to the divinity. Even before the arrival of the Romans, the deities and *genii* of folk-communities and tribes were probably worshiped in Gaul and Britain as will be seen as certain deities are discussed later. The worship of city *tyches* (female presiding spirits) can be recognised in Gaul, for example at Paris and Lyon (Espérandieu 1910, no. 1744). The view that only city *tyches* could preside over cities is, however, incorrect as at Hyères, originally *Olbia* (in Gaul), a dedication was found to the *Genio Viciniae Castellanae Olbiensium* (Espérandieu 1925, no. 6688), while in Britain the presiding spirit of Colchester must have been *Camulos*, and that of York, the *Genius Eboraci* (RIB(I) 1995, no. 657). Masculine (gods and *genii*) and feminine (goddesses and *tyche*) deities were, very much, interchangeable. It also seems to have been the case that only certain *genii* were portrayed wearing mural crowns. In Saalburg, Feldberg, Zugmantel, and Mayence they occur on *Genius Centurie*; and at Altrip on the *Genius Germaniae Superioris*. In other cases the *genius* with the crown occurs alongside a goddess as an apparent consort; for example, alongside Minerva, as at *Carnutum*, or Fortuna, as at Changé.

There is increasing evidence that some of these settlements continued in use into the sub-Roman period and that, even though they may have been less densely populated, they may have, in some areas, covered a far larger area (Yeates 2006, i.59–62). In the case of some of the larger towns, however, there may have been a decrease in size. In the early medieval period minsters were established; much work has been done on these monuments. The underlying hypothesis is that central churches were established over a territory; served by a team of priests with control or influence over lesser churches established in its territory. There have been a number of discussions on the territories of these churches, and a suggestion that they developed from Roman period estates (Finberg 1955), or from churches established in the Roman period (Bassett 1989, 225–256). In view, however, of the Wootton Wawen charter it would be better to consider that minster churches were founded for groups of peoples or communities (Yeates forthcoming 2007b). That there was an association between tribe and minster, at least on some occasions, is evident in the textual sources; a landscape study of these sources could help establish the territorial units of the folk-groups, which could be referred to as land-units.

The minster hypothesis has developed from a number of documentary sources, of which the earliest is the Anglo-Saxon legislation of the seventh to eleventh centuries. One of these was the *Law code of Ine* (AD 668–684), which declared that church-scot (tithes) should be paid to the Church at Martinmass (Whitelock 1979, 399, 406, 444). This, and other rights; for example, soul-scot (burial dues), were detailed in the later laws of II, III, IV Edgar and V Æthelred. Later textual sources of the eleventh to fifteenth centuries are also important as they indicate the relationship between mother churches and their daughter chapels (Fosbrooke 1821, 116). Amongst these are manuscripts discussing the payment systems that had developed between various churches; for example, regarding pensions, portions, and rents. The pensions and portions, the argument claimed, were either a one-off payment or, more likely, an annual payment to the mother church to compensate it for the loss of revenue in tithe and soul-scot (burial dues) which had come about through the daughter churches' independence. The longevity of such practices and the ability of the church organisation to reform itself was studied by Sims-Williams (1990) using the West Country examples, and was developed further by Hadley (2000), with respect to the Trent Valley. These discussions were important critiques of early medieval church organisation and how it was portrayed in later texts. The work of Sims-Williams and Hadley demonstrated that church estates were not constant. What we should, perhaps, consider is that the minster or major church presided over a territory which, despite shifting boundaries, had a stable and cohesive core. Sims-Williams considered the area of the West Midlands, which is under consideration here. Blair (2005, 306–307) stated that for minster studies this was the core study area; thus, implying that any discussion of the theories expounded here, have a great relevance for the rest of the country.

IDENTIFYING LONGSTANDING COMMUNITIES

The survival of folk-names based on rivers has been discussed, and a brief outline given of how an underlying framework, which would enable pre-Old English names to survive, could operate. The information available varies greatly amongst the different territories.

The Glevensis

The name *Glevensis* was given to the people who dwelt in and around the *colonia* of Gloucester, see Figure 13. The word is considered to have developed into the early medieval *Glywysinga*, a folk-name associated with Glamorgan. An alternative view is that the name *Glywysinga* derived from a historical figure called *Glywys*. The *Glevensis* have one of the better understood folk-territories (Yeates 2006, ii.845–849). The earliest evidence is to be found along the Horsebere brook where, under much sediment, the

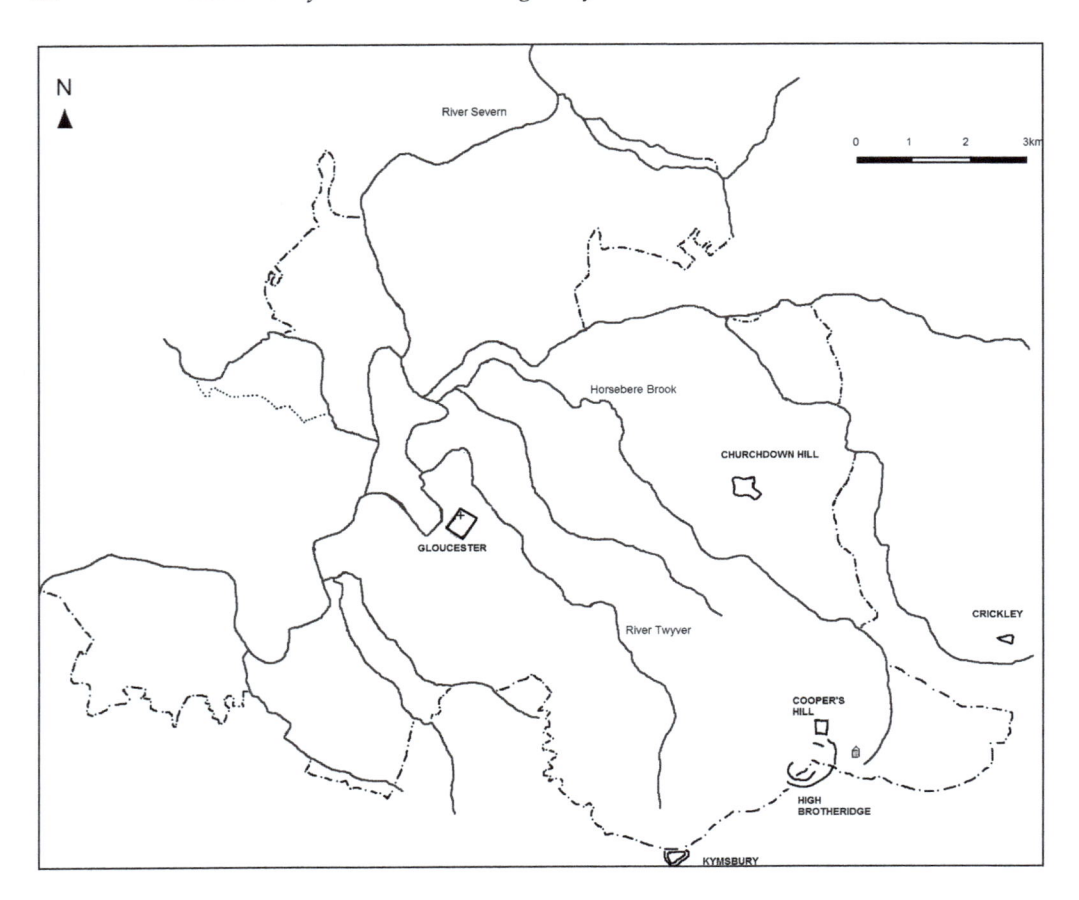

Figure 13: The parochia *of Gloucester, showing the locations of Roman Gloucester and the minster along with the four Iron-Age hill-forts located in and around the* parochia *(S. Yeates).*

remains of part of a late Bronze-Age settlement, between Brockworth and Hucclecote, were identified. The settlement seems to have been associated with earlier middle Bronze-Age burials. Slightly later material, dating to the early Iron Age, was found in the excavations at Hucclecote Roman villa, to the west. Sporadic finds in the Barnwood and Hucclecote area have shown that middle Iron-Age settlement was focused in this area. The full extent of these settlements is unknown and the evidence now lies underneath the eastern suburbs of Gloucester. Place-name evidence indicates that there was a defended enclosure in the Hucclecote area, near the Horsebere Brook and to the west of the Hucclecote Roman villa. Around this valley and also in that of the Twyver there are some four Iron-Age hill-forts or large enclosures. There are three hill-forts located along the Cotswold scarp. The first of these is at Crickley Hill, a site which has seen much excavation (Dixon 1994). The second is the enigmatic site at Cooper's Hill and High Brotheridge (RCHME 1976, 21–22, 40–41), where there is a claimed fort on the promontory and a partial enclosure on the south end of the hill, both probably part of the same complex. On Painswick Beacon is the multivallate hill-fort called *Kymesbury*, see Figure 14. The last hill-fort is on Churchdown, an outlier from the Cotswold scarp, where there is evidence for a platform on the north-east corner of the hill (Hurst 1977, 5–10). It is believed that this was the site of an earlier shrine (Waters 1999, 9–12, 18, 20), see Figure 15. In the medieval period the site must have been called the *Spelwall*, which means **the vallum were people come to talk or discuss**. There are also the remains of a large late Iron-Age settlement at Longford, which was disrupted by the establishment of the Roman fortresses and *colonia* in the first century AD. Gloucester had an enclosed space in which the main civic buildings were located, and an external or extramural settlement. A relief has been recovered from the Bon Marché site which showed three figures. The central figure is a female in a long pleated dress. She has been described as having a coiffure but it is possible that she is wearing a type of mural crown. If so then she could be a representation of the city *tyche*. The *colonia* and Roman city of Gloucester now lie at the confluence of the Twyver and Severn; it is, however, evident that the focus of prehistoric settlement, which seems to have migrated downstream from near Brockworth to near its confluence, was along the Horsebere Brook. It is this brook which has evidence of a shrine, near Great Witcombe Roman Villa, at its source. The Horsebere Brook could have, presumably, given its name to Gloucester and the people who dwelt along its

Figure 14: The hill-fort of Kymesbury on Painswick Beacon (photograph S. Yeates).

Figure 15: The hill-fort rampart and shrine which underlie the church of Saint Bartholomew at Churchdown Hill (photograph S. Yeates).

bank. During the early medieval period a minster was founded in the colonia (Finberg 1972, no. 1), see Figure 16; it had an extensive territory which was focused in the Horsebere and Twyver valleys.

Cheltenham

The archaeology of the folk-groups to the north-east of Gloucester, around Cleeve Hill, shows a number of factors which indicate that there were a number of groups residing in the valleys around it, see Figure 17. As Cheltenham has become built up much of the settlement pattern has been destroyed (Yeates 2006, ii.522–531). There are reports of enclosures and place-name evidence that suggest that settlement existed in the Chelt valley. On the hills to the south of Cheltenham are the remains of three Iron-Age hill-forts; one on Leckhampton, see Figure 18, one probably on Whistley, and another at Dowdeswell, see Figure 19, above the source of the Chelt. The site of a

Figure 16: The cathedral of Gloucester (photograph S. Yeates).

fourth enclosure has not been determined. There is scarping around the hilltop of Battledown, but this has been interpreted as natural as no Iron-Age artefacts have been recovered from the site. Roman material is recovered constantly from certain parts of central Cheltenham, which indicates that, in the west part of the town, there was once a Roman nucleated settlement. A minster was founded at Cheltenham, the parish of which covered the upper parts of the Chelt and Hatherley Brook valley. Settlement in the area seems to have been focused along the Chelt, but it is not known what the old name of this river was.

Bishop's Cleeve the Timbingas (?)

To the north of the Cheltenham territory lay a land-unit which was focused on Bishop's Cleeve (Yeates 2006, ii.590–598), see Figure 21. Early settlement in the area has not been established but there is known to have been a major middle Iron-Age settlement, with a large enclosure, under the centre of the present village of Bishop's Cleeve. On the hills to the east of Cleeve are the remains of a number of hill-forts; most notably on Nottingham Hill, or Cockbury, and on Cleeve Hill, see Figure 21. A camp was claimed at the Hewlett's on a spur towards the south end of the hill. This has been doubted but, as this area of the hill suffered a major landslip in the eighteenth century, it is probable that any remains would no longer be recognisable on the ground. Aerial photographs show the possible remains of a ditch, which may be all that survives of

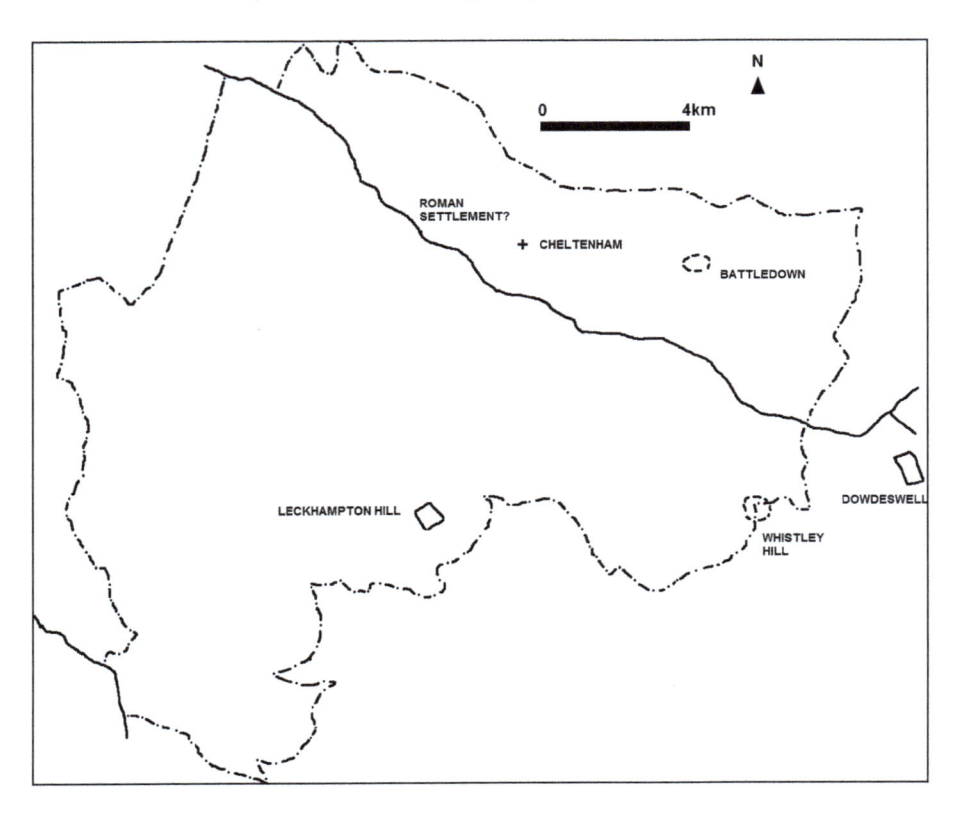

Figure 17: The parochia *of Cheltenham showing the location of the minster and the suspected Roman period settlement along with two recognised Iron-Age hill-forts; one suspected and Battledown which has been disputed (S. Yeates).*

the site. A further camp was described at Woolaston, from which Iron-Age pottery has been recovered. The location of the camp is not known but it probably lay on the summit of a knoll where a whole series of Wall field names, which would once have referred to a vallum, can be found. A nucleated Roman settlement was located at Tredington Rise in the parish, but the layout and even the full extent of the settlement are not known. A minster church was established at Bishop's Cleeve in the large central enclosure of the middle Iron-Age settlement. The parish covered much of the valleys of the tributaries of the Swilgate. The name *Timbingctun* is associated with the village of Bishop's Cleeve, and it is possible that this derives from a river name.

The Salenses

To the north-east of Cleeve Hill lies the territory of the *Salenses* and the same process of development can be recognised here (Yeates 2006, iii.1309–1322), see Figure 22. There is evidence of prehistoric settlement, of an unknown nature, along the course of the Hailes Brook. This includes the small prehistoric camp called Hailes Camp, which

Figure 18: The hill-fort of Leckhampton Hill (photograph S. Yeates).

Figure 19: The camp at Dowdeswell near the head of the valley of the river Chelt (photograph S. Yeates).

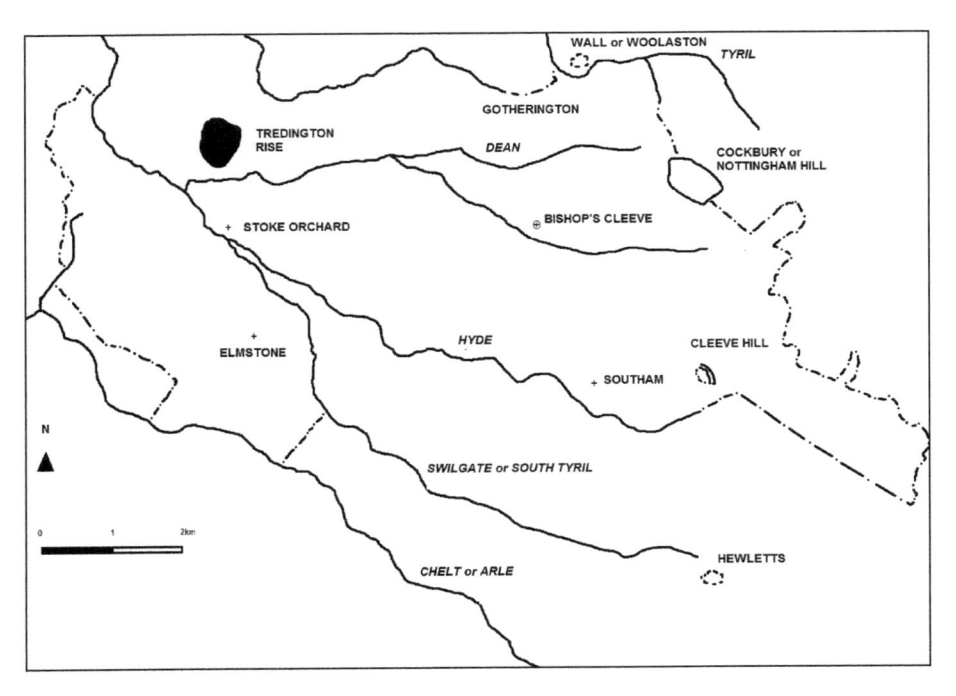

Figure 20: The parochia *of Bishop's Cleeve showing the Roman settlement at Tredington Rise, the minster at Cleeve and the two recognised camps at Nottingham Hill (Cockbury) and Cleeve Hill, along with a suspected site at Hewletts which was damaged by a landslide, and a possible camp site at Woolaston (S. Yeates).*

is believed to have been altered in the medieval period. This enclosure has the size of other lowland enclosures which operated as possible centres of semi-nucleated prehistoric settlements. There are also a number of larger enclosures which can be recognised in the area, including the hill-fort at Roel Gate, near the headwaters of the Beesmore Brook. The hill-fort at Beckbury sits on a pointed spur above the Hailes Brook and it is probably this promontory which gives the camp its present name. There is a large, and severely quarried, enclosure on Langley Mount, which was probably called *Salbury* in AD 1480. It has been doubted that this was a hill-fort, but from our present understanding of such sites, the reasons used to dismiss it seem invalid. Many camps are now known to have no occupation debris, to have dumped ramparts, and to have internal quarry pits. There is evidence of an earlier undated ditch in Winchcombe which underlay the bank of the Saxon burh, and within Winchcombe a ritual shaft was found with prehistoric deposits in it. This may indicate that there was a further large defended enclosure of a late prehistoric date under Winchcombe. The Roman settlement, which covered an area of 34ha, was located at Millhampost, along the line of the Hailes Brook, while the minster at Winchcombe was established in what seems to have been a large prehistoric enclosure. The major prehistoric lowland settlement lay along the course of the Hailes Brook, which is considered to have been the *Salia* river. This river gave its name to the dwellers on the *Salia*, hence the *Salenses*.

Withington Gloucestershire

To the south of Winchcombe was the Anglo-Saxon *parochia* of Withington (Yeates 2006, iii.1322–1337); the location for Finburg's important Gloucestershire study, see Figure 23. Prehistoric material from this area is more circumstantial, but, nevertheless, there are claims of key sites. Prestbury Hill was claimed to be the location of a camp while Anglo-Saxon charters place a dyke in the vicinity. A further camp has been claimed at Arle Grove, where the remains of a curving linear boundary has been identified but not investigated. Puckham, where aerial photographs show a linear ditch which may be one side of an enclosure, has also been described as the location of a dyke on Anglo-Saxon charters. Near Kilkenny is evidence of a partially destroyed prehistoric enclosure with a large ditch. There is also evidence of a possible prehistoric settlement at Square Ditch Farm, where a palisaded enclosure shows up as one of the features. To the west of this lay the major Roman-period settlement at Wycomb, which derives its name from *vicus*, **a town**. Settlement in this area started in the late Iron Age and continued into the sub-Roman period. Later, a minster was established at Withington, above a spring, see Figure 24. The remains of earlier buildings have been found in the churchyard and in the rectory garden, but these are essentially undated.

Figure 21: The hill-fort on Cleeve Hill (photograph S. Yeates).

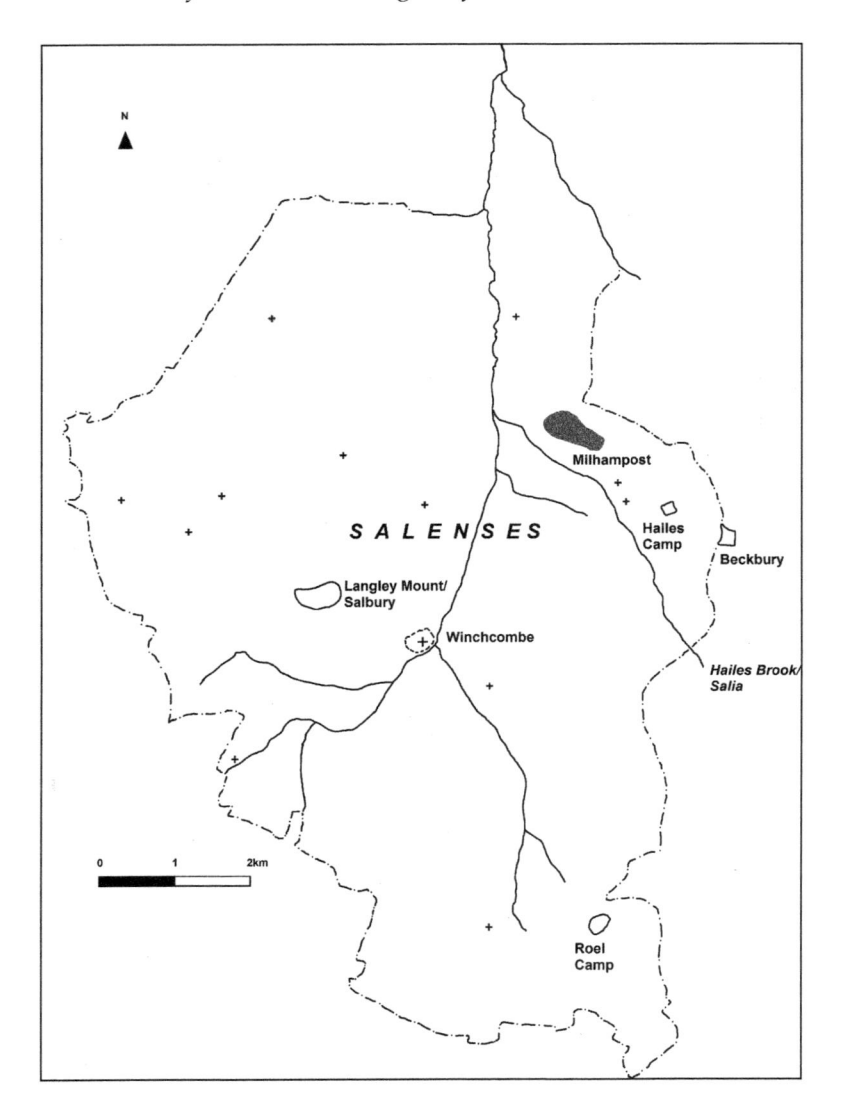

Figure 22: The parochia *of Winchcombe showing the major Roman settlement at Millhampost and the minster at Winchcombe. There are two confirmed Iron Age hill-forts at Roel and Beckbury, a disputed site at Langley Mount, and a probable large prehistoric enclosure under Winchcombe. There is evidence of further prehistoric settlement, along with the Roman settlement, along the Hailes Brook the stream which provided the name of the* Salenses *(S. Yeates).*

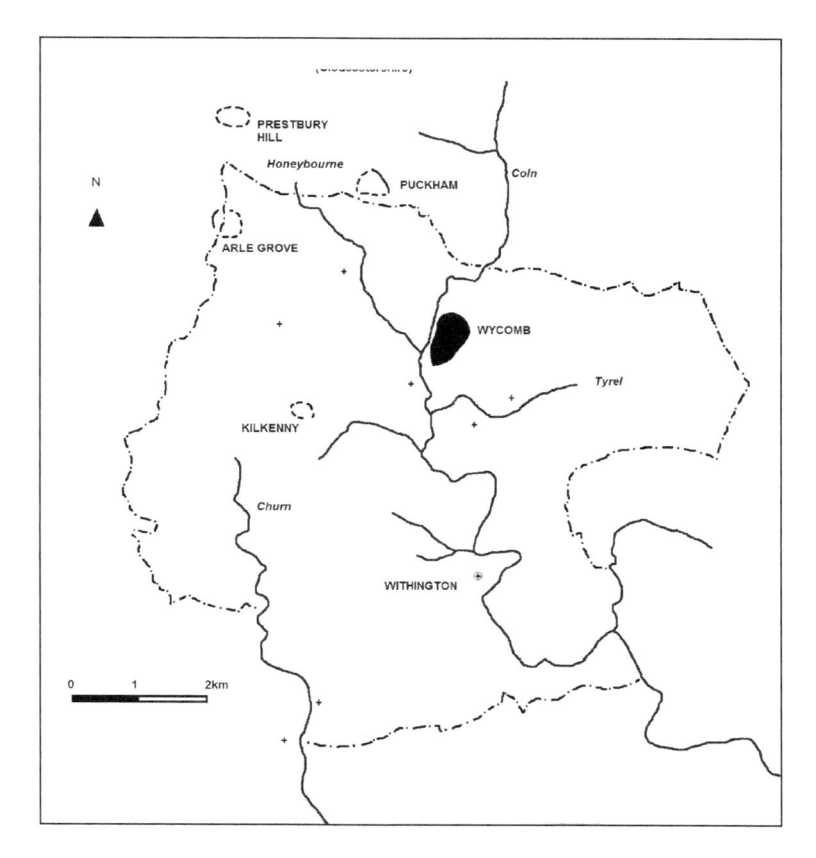

Figure 23: The parochia *of Withington showing the Roman settlement at Wycomb, the minster at Withington, and where archaeology and antiquaries suggest that there are possible large enclosures (S. Yeates).*

Bibury

A similar pattern can be found at Bibury, further down the Coln valley (Yeates 2006, ii.392–397), see Figure 25. There is no evidence for prehistoric settlement apart from three large camps; one of which is located near Winterswell, and shows up as a circular cropmark. This lies at the head of a dry valley, which heads down towards the Coln. On the scarp edge, on the south side of the river, evidence of two fortified sites has been identified, at Ablington Camp and Castle Ditches (or Winson). To the east of these, and also on the scarp slope, the name Hasenbury, which indicates a fortified site, is recorded, but has not yet been located archaeologically. Near Oldwalls, on the line of an ancient Saltway, there is evidence of Roman debris scatters covering an area of 16ha. The minster was established at Bibury; a name which indicates an enclosure the nature of which is unknown. The church has surviving Anglo-Saxon material. A similar arrangement of large enclosures, Roman settlement and major church is found around Bourton-on-the-Water, see Figure 26.

Figure 24: The church of Withington, Gloucestershire, the location for Finberg's analysis of estate continuity between the Roman and early medieval periods (photograph S. Yeates).

Cirencester

Cirencester lies in the lower Churn valley and needs some consideration even if its earlier settlement pattern has not been understood fully (Yeates 2006, ii.557–590). Cirencester is often associated with Bagendon which has been thought to have preceded Cirencester as the main population centre for the tribal-area, but this seems to be incorrect and Cirencester's territory probably lay to the south towards South Cerney. There is a large rectangular enclosure on a hilltop at South Cerney Airfield, perhaps called Lidbury. Place-name evidence indicates that there was a defended enclosure near Barton in what is now Cirencester Park. If there is such a site, which has been destroyed by post-medieval landscaping, then it is in a key location adjacent to Roman Corinium. Where other sites in this area would be located is not known. The Romans established military bases at Cirencester in the first century AD, around which a settlement developed, and over which the later *civitas* town was constructed. To the east of the forum a number of sculptural remains have been recovered. Some of these have been claimed to represent the deity of the city (Rudder 1779, 343–349; Fosbrooke 1807, 479–482; Henig 1993, no. 47). A sculptured head, described as wearing a spiky or turreted crown, no longer survives, but possibly was similar to an image found on an altar recovered from Sheep Street (Henig 1993, no. 33). This altar shows a *genius* with the same spiked priestly head-dress or mural crown, tightly bunched curls, a bare

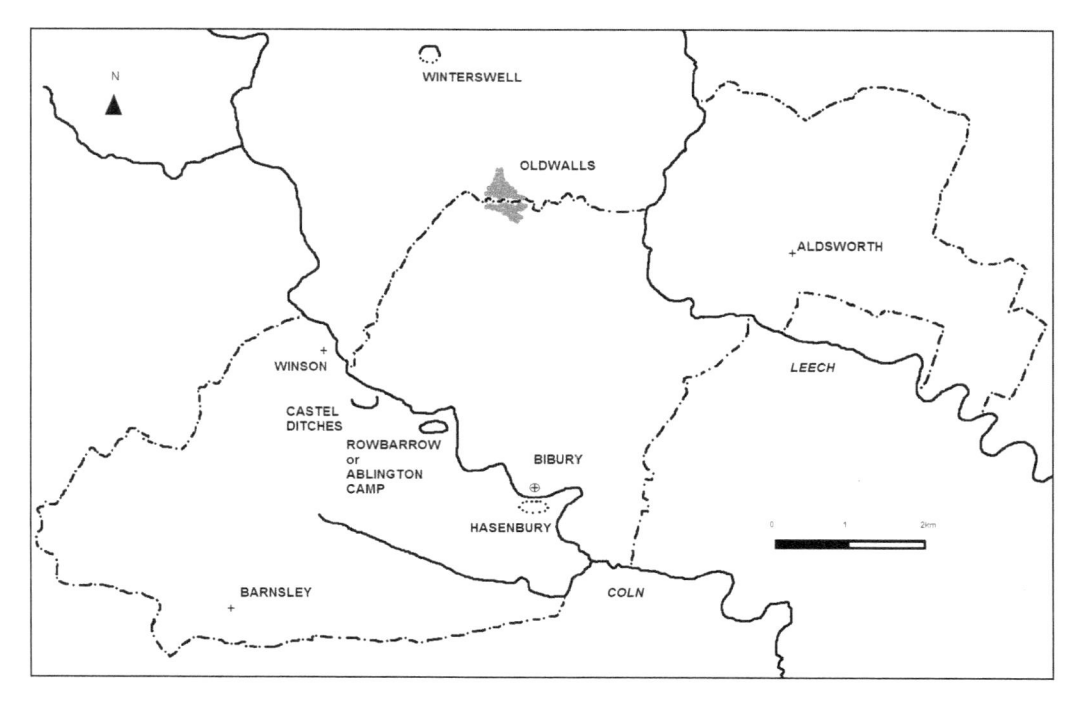

Figure 25: The parochia *of Bibury showing the suspected large Roman settlement of Oldwalls, the mother church of Bibury and the large enclosures of Castle Ditches, Ablington Camp, Winterwell, and the possible site at Hasenbury (S. Yeates).*

torso, and a mantle, or loin cloth, which is draped over an altar by his side. The altar has the inscription G(enio).S(ancto).HVI[V]S.LOC[I], which refers to the *sacred genius of this place*. The spiky or turreted mural crown sets this divinity apart from other *genii*, and may indicate that he was the deity of the town. A minster was established in Cirencester, and although its territory extended partially up the Churn valley most of it's territory was predominantly to the south of the town.

Blockley

Blockley *parochia* was the subject of a further case study by Finberg and, as with Cirencester, the later archaeological features are better preserved (Yeates 2006, ii.409–417). At Dorn, there are the remains of a Roman small town, with intramural and extramural settlement, from which, in *c.* AD 1875, the remains of two altars, showing a *genius* wearing a mural crown (Henig 1993, no. 38, 39), were recovered. A minster was established at Blockley, which is known to have had a large territory in the valleys of the Knee Brook and the Cam.

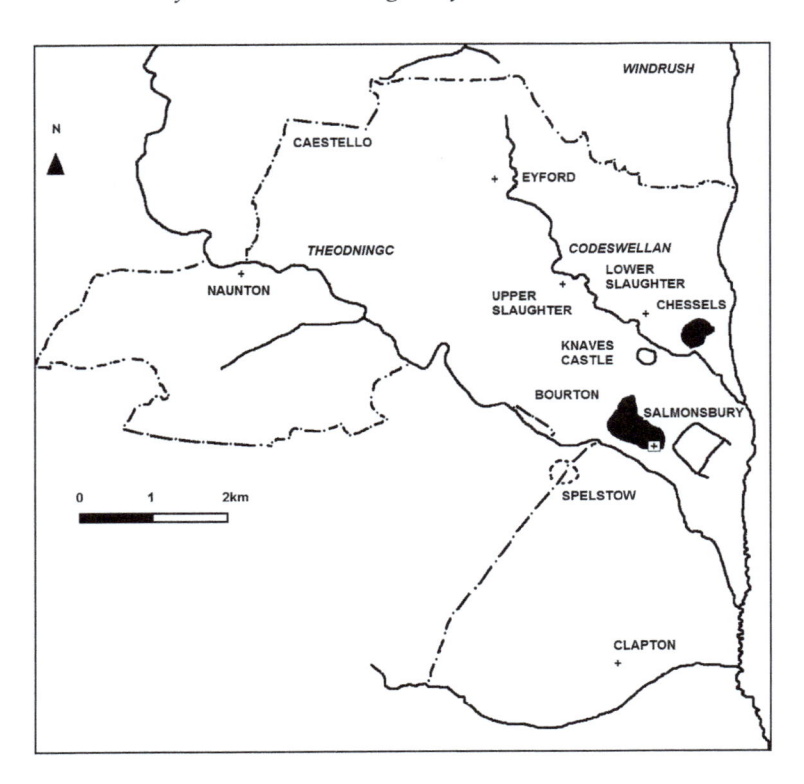

Figure 26: The parish of the mother church of Bourton-on-the-Water, showing the large Roman settlement at Bourton, the three large enclosures around Bourton: Salmonsbury, Knaves Castle, and the defensive site to the south of Bourton. Place-name evidence may indicate that a further enclosure is to be found to the north of Naunton. The location of the Roman period shrine of Cuda is also shown (S. Yeates).

Standish

To the south of Gloucester the same pattern occurs with the *parochia* of Standish (Yeates 2006, iii.1176–1184), see Figure 27. On the Cotswold scarp are three large enclosures or defended promontories. The first is on Haresfield Beacon, where there is a camp once called *Ersebury*. On the highest point of the same hill is a large undated enclosure called Harescombe Camp. In Randwick Wood is a bank which cuts off the promontory of Maiden Hill. At Elmore, place-name evidence, in the form of Stanburrow, describes the location of a stone fort, which has not been located. At Quedgeley, on the Daniel's Brook, there is evidence of a large Roman roadside settlement, which is probably the *wicham* settlement recorded in the medieval period. The name of the brook was originally *Herse*, which has provided the place-names of Harescombe and Haresfield, and the hill-fort *Ersebury*. The mother church was established at Standish, with the territory shifting slightly to the south, presumably due to the influence of Gloucester and its minster.

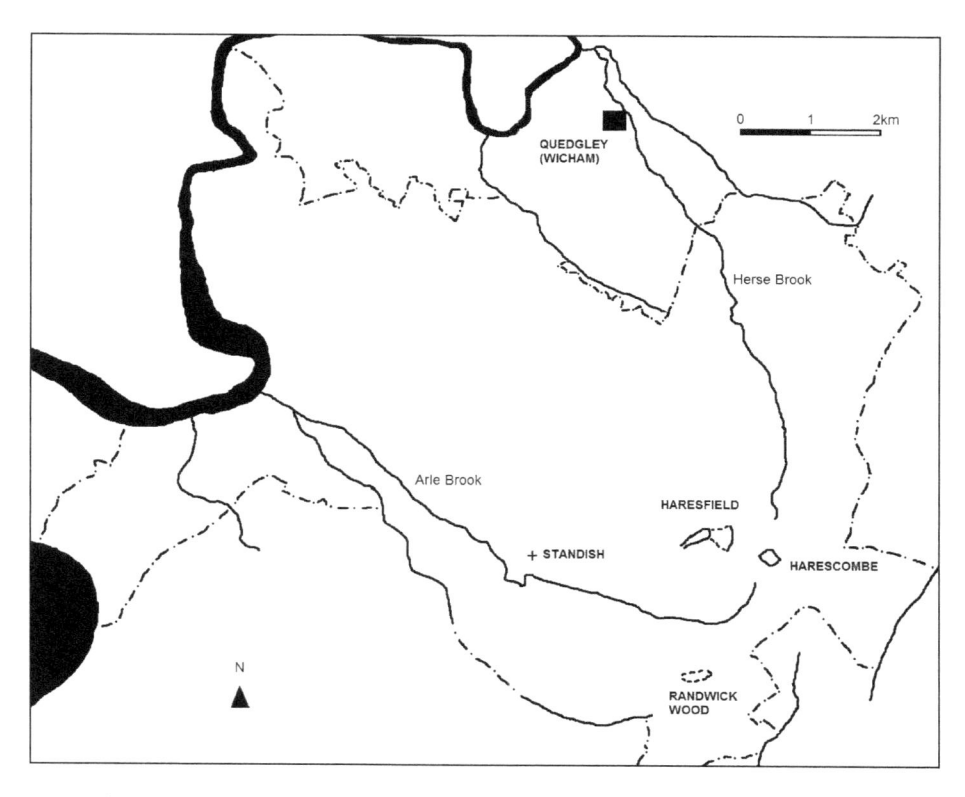

Figure 27: The parish of the mother church of Standish, showing the Roman roadside settlement on the Herse Brook at Quedgeley and the defended sites of Haresfield Camp or Ersebury, Harescombe Camp, and the defended promontory at Randwick Wood. There are place-name references to Stanburrow, the Stone Fort at Elmore (S. Yeates).

Westbury-on-Trym

Even in the far south of Gloucestershire this pattern is still evident; for example, in the Trym valley (Yeates 2006, iii.1294–1309), see Figure 28, there is evidence of three large Iron-Age enclosures, which existed around the confluence of the Henbury and the Westbury Trym: Blaize Castle, Coombe Hill, and King's Weston. There was a fourth large enclosure at Sea Mills, which is described in an Anglo-Saxon charter as "running around the Roman town and its cemeteries". The bank is undated but is considered as the location of an Iron Age Bulwark. The Roman town was established at Sea Mills and the later minster at Westbury-on-Trym. A similar arrangement can be found around Bedminster and Bristol, see Figure 29.

Bath

Further examples of this settlement pattern have been found in north Somerset at Bath (Yeates 2006, ii.324–357). On a hill to the north of Bath is evidence of a large Iron-Age enclosure called Solsbury. On another hill, to the south, is a confirmed Iron-Age hill-fort at Bathhampton. Antiquaries described a further fortification at Berwick, and also a camp at Combe Down, which would have existed between the two other sites. These sites have not as yet been confirmed. The site at Combe Down may have produced an unusual and un-contextualised Roman inscription. The major Roman settlement was established at Bath, and there is evidence of early settlement and descriptions of a camp in the Bathwick area to the south of the river. The main settlement was established around the hot springs, where there was a pentagonal enclosure around an intramural area; extramural settlement was established at Walcot, to the north. The temple of *Sulis Minerva* has already been discussed with respect to the sanctity of the springs, but this deity was multifaceted in that she also presided over the town, and presumably the people. She thus personified Roman Bath. The minster, which seems to have had a double foundation, was established within the walls of the Roman town.

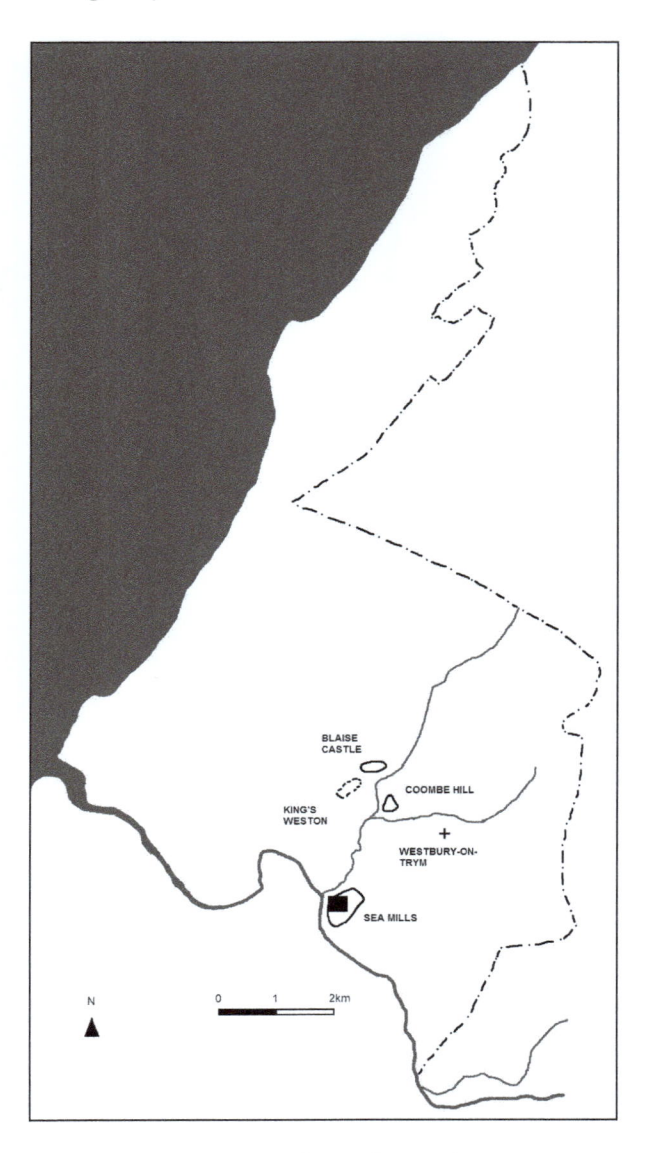

Figure 28: The parochia *of Westbury-on-Trym showing the Roman small town of Sea Mills, and the large enclosures at Blaize Castle, Coombe Hill, King's Weston Camp, and the possible Bulwark around Sea Mills (S. Yeates).*

Cheddar

The land-unit around Cheddar also has many of these features (Yeates 2006, ii.513–522), but here the Iron Age, or later prehistoric, activity is more concentrated, see Figure 30. On the Mendips, to the east of Charterhouse, are the

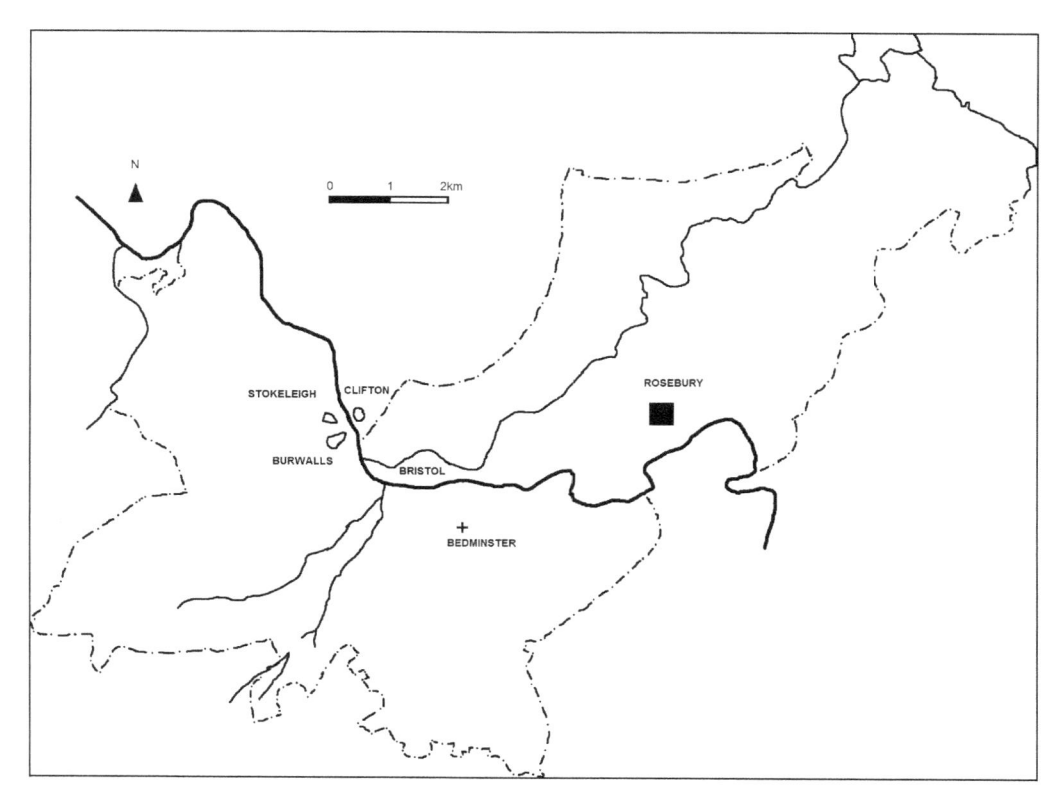

Figure 29: The parochia *of Bedminster and the parish of Bedminster which show a unified set of settlement features along the Avon. The minster was located at Bedminster; there is circumstantial evidence for a Roman small town at Rosebury. There are three Iron Age hill-forts at Burwalls, Stokeleigh Camp, and Clifton Camp. The location of a fourth enclosure is not known, but it is evident that Stow place-names turn up in relation to Roman and Iron-Age earth bank enclosures (S. Yeates).*

Priddy Circles; a group of large enclosures, which contain three completed circular enclosures and one incomplete one. Excavations carried out on the site were inconclusive, and so they have been interpreted as Bronze Age ritual features. The nature of the external bank and the timberlaced rampart have more in common with what is known about Iron-Age hill-forts, and here there are three built in a compact row. The fourth, unfinished, circle may have been replaced by the camp at Charterhouse, which has been described as a fortlet. The earliest enclosure has none of these characteristics and its oval shape and irregular ditch, along with third century BC finds, imply that the antiquaries, who considered this to be a prehistoric camp, were probably correct. The Roman town grew up next to this enclosure, and a smaller enclosure, of Roman date, was established over the earlier enclosure. The minster for this area was established at Cheddar over a Roman site.

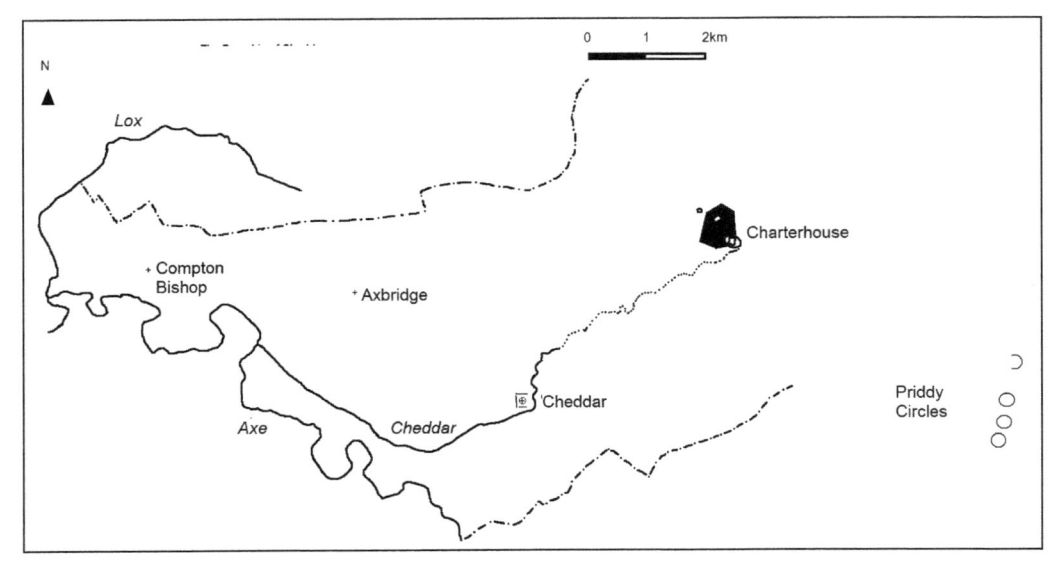

Figure 30: The parochia *of Cheddar, with the Roman small town of Charterhouse, and the minster at Cheddar. The Priddy Circles have the construction features of large Late Bronze-Age or Iron-Age enclosures. One was not finished and it is possible that the circular and earliest camp at Charterhouse is also of a prehistoric date (S. Yeates).*

Congresbury

A similar pattern can be identified on the western end of the Mendips; around Congresbury (Yeates 2006, ii.630–641), see Figure 31. There are three large enclosures in a line facing the levels: the hill-fort at Cadbury, the enclosure on Cleeve Hill, and there is also evidence of a sub-rectangular enclosure at Congresbury, which has given the settlement its name. Antiquaries' accounts describe a camp at Wick Saint Lawrence, which again, although not identified, seems to be supported by the place-name Bourton. There is evidence of a Roman settlement extending under Congresbury, which may also be associated with the large enclosure. The minster church was established in the enclosure at Congresbury; surviving charters indicate that the parish of Yatton was probably subservient to Congresbury church.

Herefordshire

In Herefordshire a similar pattern can be identified at Ross, at Aymestry and at Leintwardine, see Figures 32 and 33. The territory of Ross lies in the valleys of the Coughton and Rudhall Brooks (Yeates 2006, iii.1137–1149). There is evidence of a Bronze-Age settlement, perhaps extensive, near the head of the Coughton Brook. The site is near Wall Hill, a name which may indicate that there was an enclosure associated with this settlement. Three large enclosures or Iron-Age hill-forts have also been identified in the area. The major site is at Chase Wood Camp, which was also called Cockbury. On an Antiquaries' Map, and from aerial photographs, a camp has

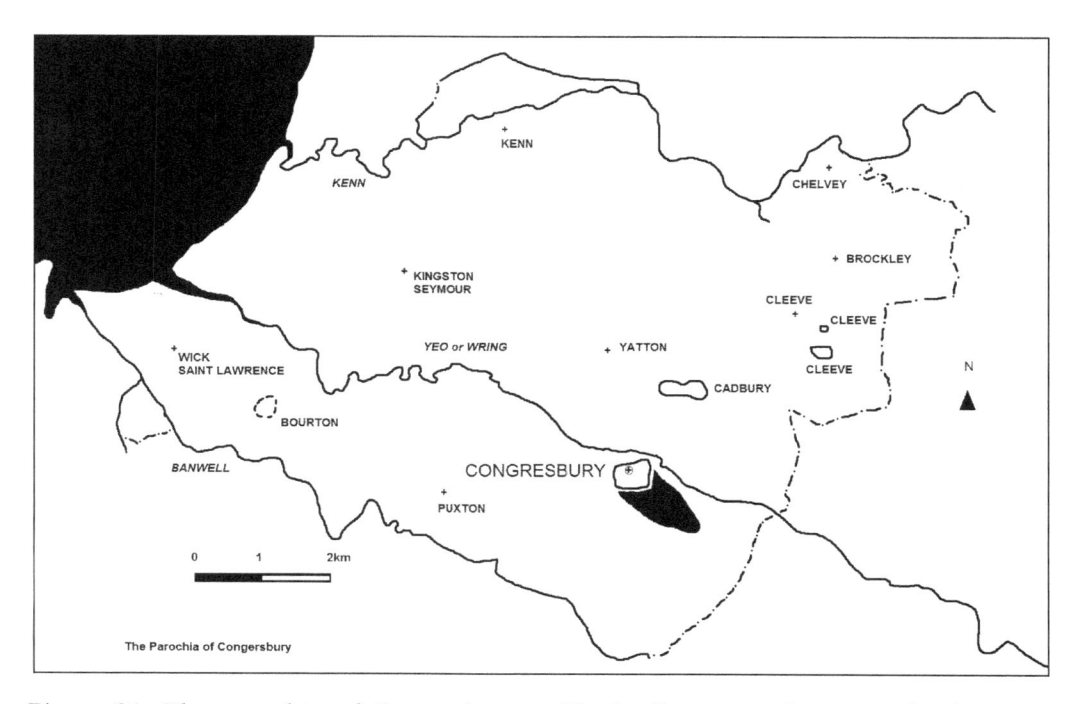

Figure 31: The parochia *of Congresbury, with the Roman settlement and minster at Congresbury. There are Iron-Age hill-forts at Congresbury and Cleeve, while the large enclosure recognised as the minster precinct at Congresbury is irregular in shape and may pre-date the minster and the Roman settlement. The place-name evidence and antiquarian accounts indicate that there was a prehistoric enclosure at Bourton (S. Yeates).*

been located at the Hill of Eaton, while further aerial photographs show a camp covering two fields at Camp Field. The location of the fourth site has not been determined. A major late Iron-Age settlement developed into the Roman settlement at Weston-under-Penyard, covering 50ha. This site had a central enclosure at Bury Hill. This was flattened in AD 1785 when the remains of much Roman religious material was recovered, including what seems to have been the head of a bronze cult statue with rams' horns (Fosbrooke 1821, 36; Jack 1922, Addition 1–44; RCHME 1932, 209). In the early medieval period a mother church was established at Ross, and it is possible that the name Eccleswall indicates that the church at Ross was an early foundation, as the name may refer to the well on the boundary of the Welsh Church's territory.

At Aymestry, in the north of Herefordshire, there is evidence for another set of monuments which show the underlying basis of this structure (Yeates 2006, ii.289–294). Three hill-forts have been identified on the north side of the river Lugg, at Croft Ambrey, at Pyon Hill, and at Deerfold Hill. The fourth camp is at Mere Hill on the south side of the Lugg. Antiquaries' maps mark the site of a deserted Roman settlement on the line of a Roman road at the Bury near Wigmore. The minster church was founded in 704 by a nun at Aymestry.

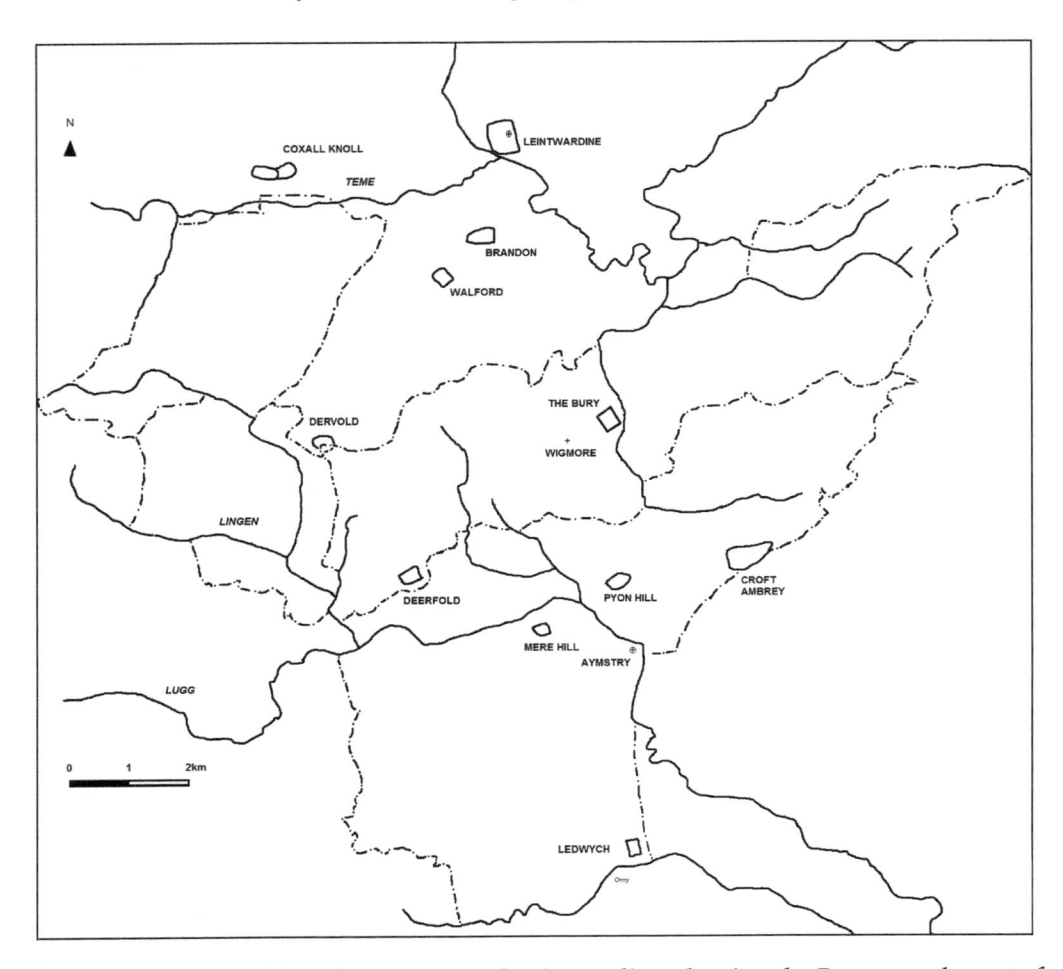

Figure 32: The parochiae *of Aymestry and Leintwardine, showing the Roman settlement of the Bury and the churches of Aymestry and Wigmore, along with the hill-forts of Mere Hill, Deerfold, Pyon Hill, and Croft Ambrey. In the parochia of Leintwardine are the Roman settlement and mother church of Leintwardine along with hill-forts at Coxwall, Brandon Hill, and Dervold. There is a further large enclosure along the Deerfold Escarpment at Walford, this has been classed as a Roman camp but is essentially undated (S. Yeates).*

A similar pattern is found around Leintwardine (Yeates 2006, iii.988–995). Three recognised Iron-Age hill-forts are located in the valley to the south-west of Leintwardine; at Brandon Camp, at Coxall Hill, and on Dervold Hill. Brandon Camp and Dervold Camp lie to the south of the river and between them is a further large enclosure at Walton, which can be seen on aerial photographs. It lies on a spur and has been interpreted as a Roman military camp, but for which no firm date has been given. The major Roman settlement was established at Leintwardine, where a religious

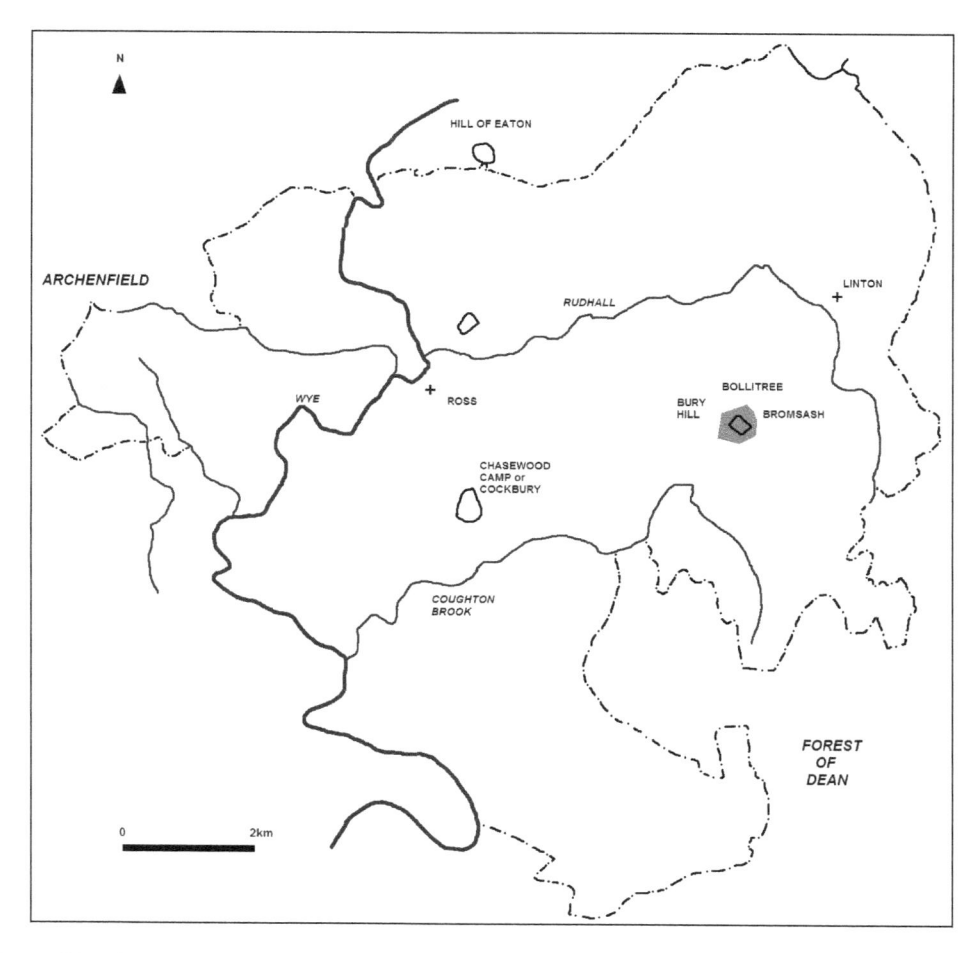

Figure 33: The parochia *of the church of Ross on Wye, showing the Roman settlement at Bury Hill, Weston-under-Penyard, and the Iron-Age hill-forts at Chasewood or Cockbury, Camp Field, and Hill of Eaton (S. Yeates).*

inscription has been recovered which indicates the presence of a Roman religious site. The minster church was also established in the Roman period enclosure.

Oxfordshire

In Worcestershire, Warwickshire, and Wiltshire there is also evidence of similarly constructed landscapes with configurations of hill-forts, Roman nucleated settlements, and minster churches, for example at Warwick, see Figure 34. Three Oxfordshire territories will be discussed: Eynsham, Wootton, and Charlbury, see Figures 35, 36, and 37. Due to gravel extraction in and around Eynsham (Yeates 2006, ii.737–751), this has to be one of the areas in the country for which archaeological knowledge is most complete. A late Bronze-Age settlement of some size, associated with a large enclosure, has been identified under Eynsham. This was superseded by a late Bronze-Age site, on a gravel Island, to the east of Eynsham. Middle Iron-Age settlement has been identified in the Yarnton area. Three large enclosures being identified in the area: at Cassington, at Eynsham Park, and on the Limb Brook, at Ambury. A fourth has not yet been located. There are indications, from the size of the cemetery excavated at

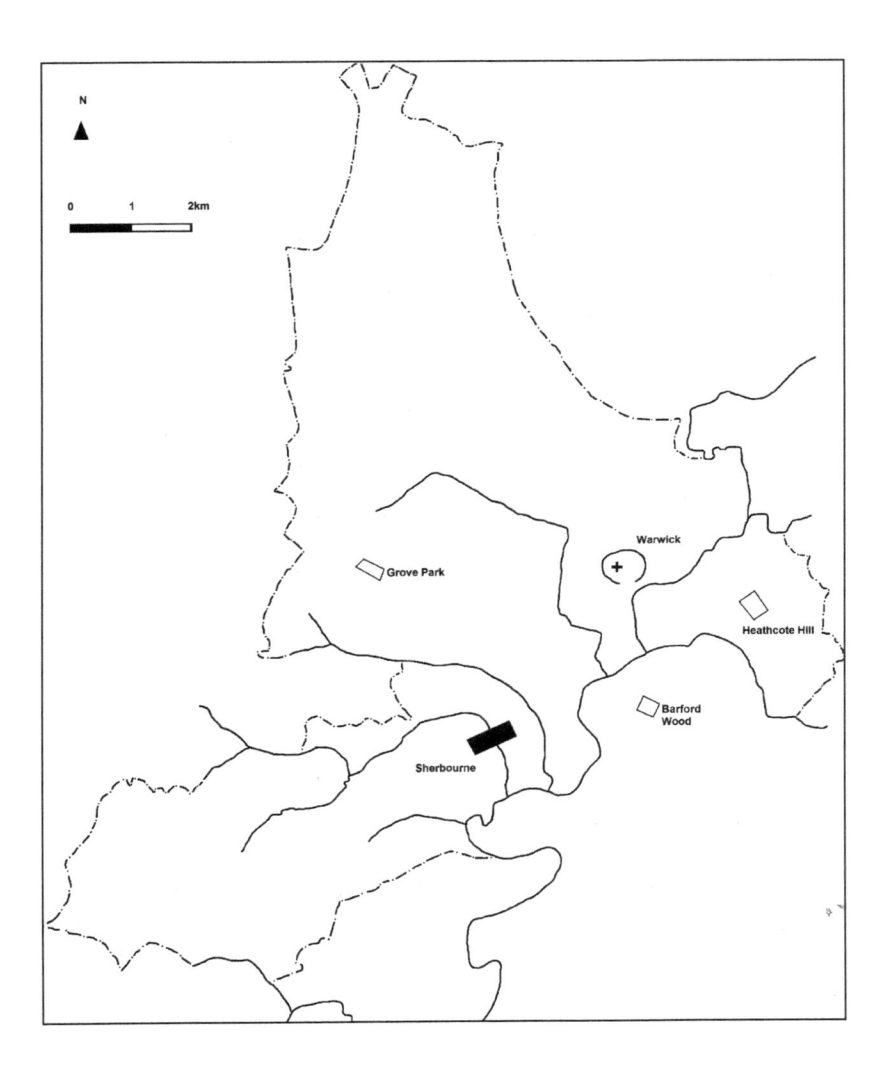

Figure 34: The parochia *of the church of Warwick, showing what may be a Roman roadside settlement at Sherbourne, and a number of large, but essentially undated, enclosures at Warwick, Heathcote Hill, Barford Wood, and Grove Park (S. Yeates).*

Cassington that this may have been the location of a nucleated Roman settlement, built outside Cassington Big Ring. There is also evidence of Roman settlement inside the enclosure. The sub-Roman settlement was larger than the Roman settlement but seems to have been less dense, extending from Cassington to New Wintles. The minster was founded in the late Bronze-Age enclosure at Eynsham. No folk-name has yet been identified.

The *parochia* of Charlbury lies to the north-west up the Evenlode valley; and it also had the same basic design (Yeates 2006, ii.501–512). A hill-fort is known at Knollbury, and there is a description of a large camp being destroyed at Spelbury. The place-name Charlbury and the plan of the village indicate that there was also a large enclosure underneath the village, while for Wallborough there are antiquaries' claims of a camp and indications, from the place-name that one once existed. The Roman settlement was located at Wilcote, on the line of Akeman Street, and was known as a *wicham* settlement, deriving its name from *vicus*. The minster was established at Charlbury.

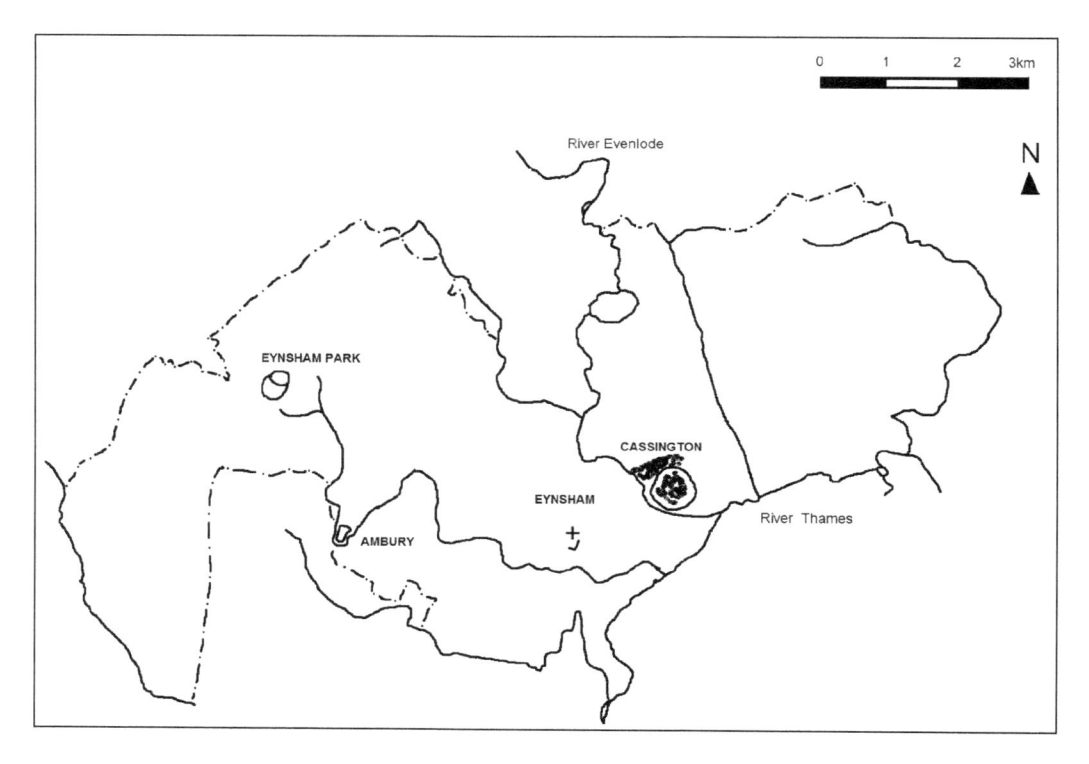

Figure 35: The parochia *of the minster of Eynsham, showing the probable Roman settlement at Cassington and three large enclosures at Eynsham Park, Cassington, and Ambury. The church at Eynsham was established in the enclosure at the centre of a large late Bronze-Age enclosure (S. Yeates).*

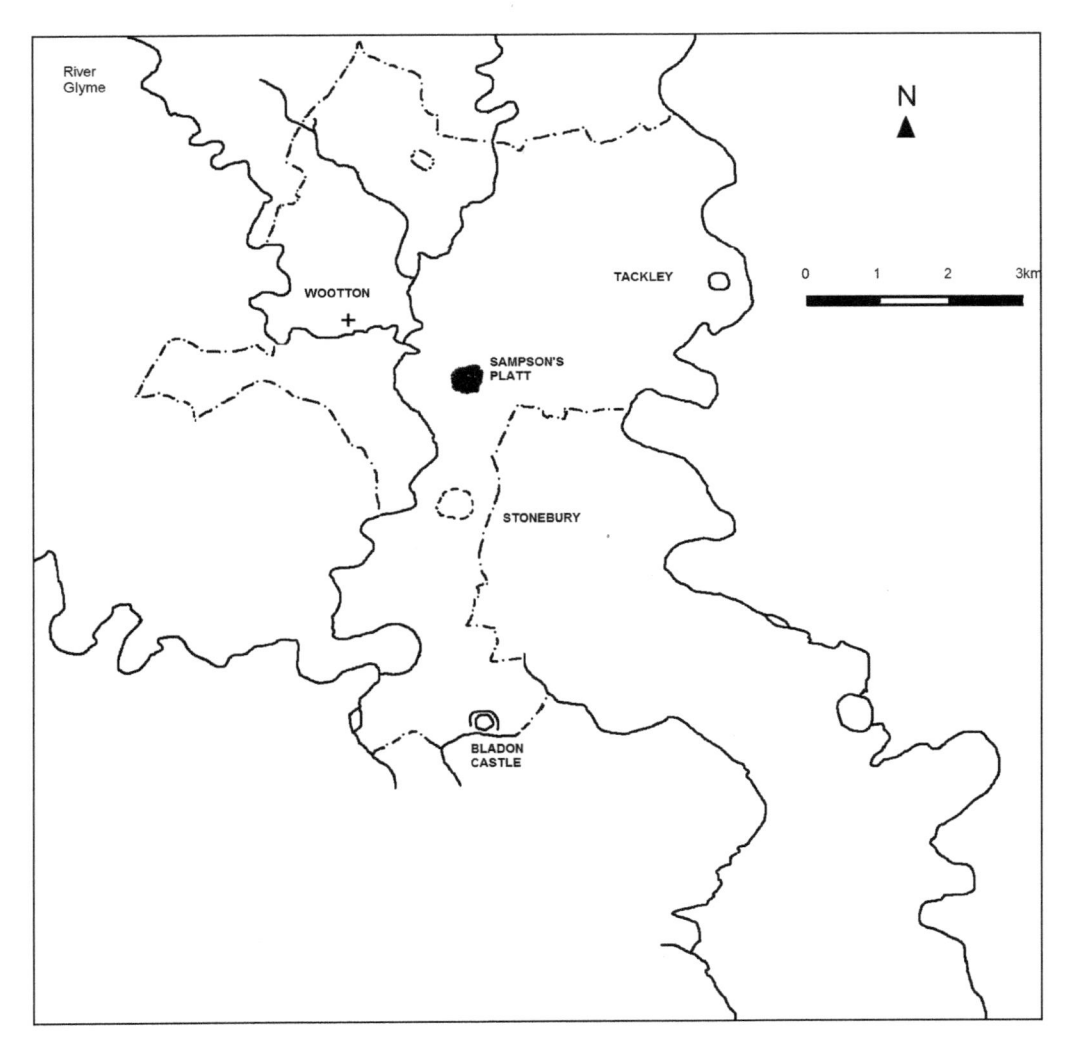

86   *The Tribe of Witches: The Religion of the* Dobunni *and* Hwicce

Figure 36: The parochia *of the church at Wootton, showing the Roman settlement at Samson's Platt, and also some large enclosures of probable late prehistoric date (S. Yeates).*

    The lower Glyme valley and the adjacent part of the Cherwell also contain the territory of Wootton (Yeates 2006, iii.1360–1369), for which the folk-name may have survived. A number of camps, or large enclosures, have been reported in the area, in a number of sources. The remains of an Iron-Age camp have been located at Bladon Heath, while for the Hensington and Woodstock areas there are antiquaries' descriptions of a camp, called Stonbury, which has now been levelled. For Tackley, aerial photographs show the remains of a large enclosure, which is believed to be a hill-fort.

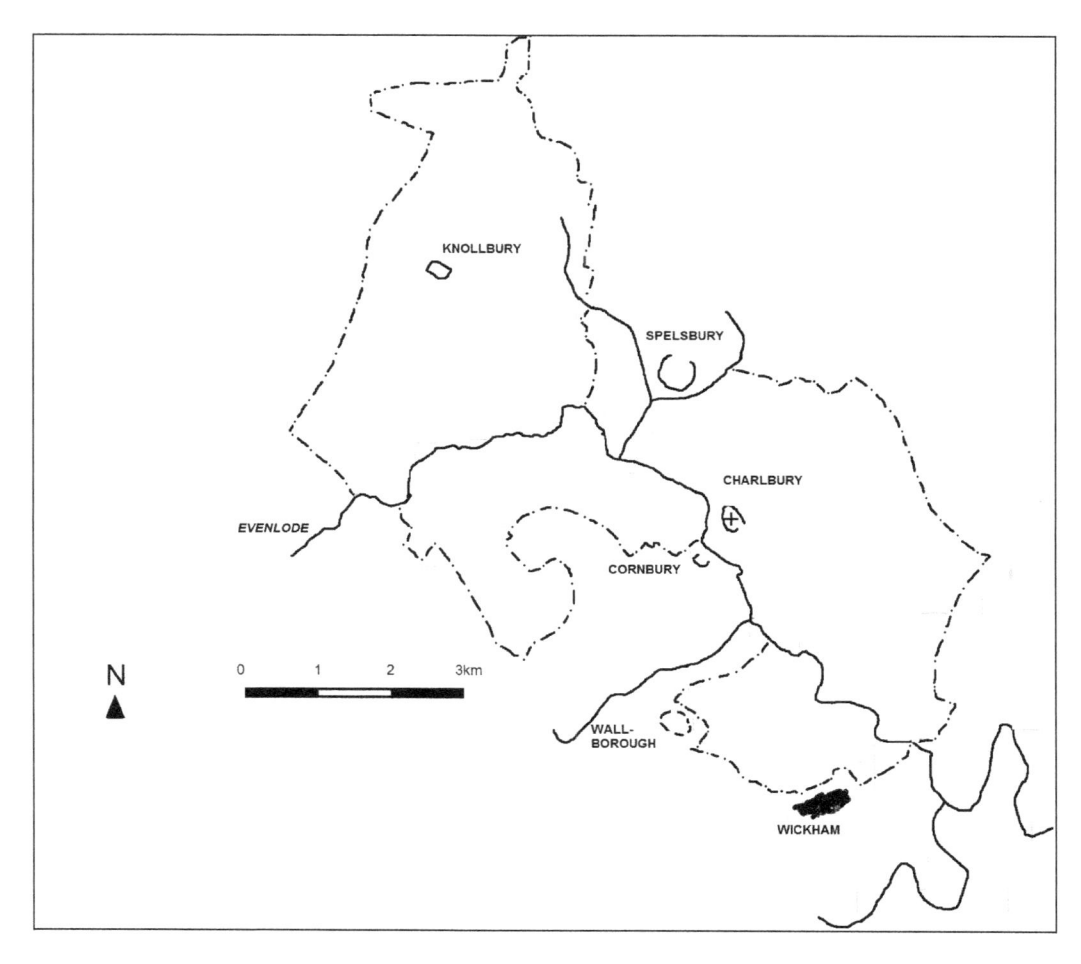

Figure 37: The parochia *of the minster at Charlbury showing the Roman settlement of Wickham and the large prehistoric, and undated, enclosures at Knollbury, Spelbury, Charlbury, and Wallborough (S. Yeates).*

Other photographs show a large enclosure, of Iron Age or Roman date, to the north of Wootton. Akeman Street passes through this territory, as it does with Charlbury, and it is again on the line of this road that the Roman nucleated settlement of Sampson's Platt can be identified. The settlement may have existed prior to the construction of the Roman road, and some realignment may have taken place. There is also evidence in the area for continued occupation into the early medieval period. The major church seems to have been established at Wootton, which seems to have been the earliest centre for what later became the royal Woodstock Estate. The folk-name *Hensingas* seems to have been applied to this group, but the location of the Hen River is not

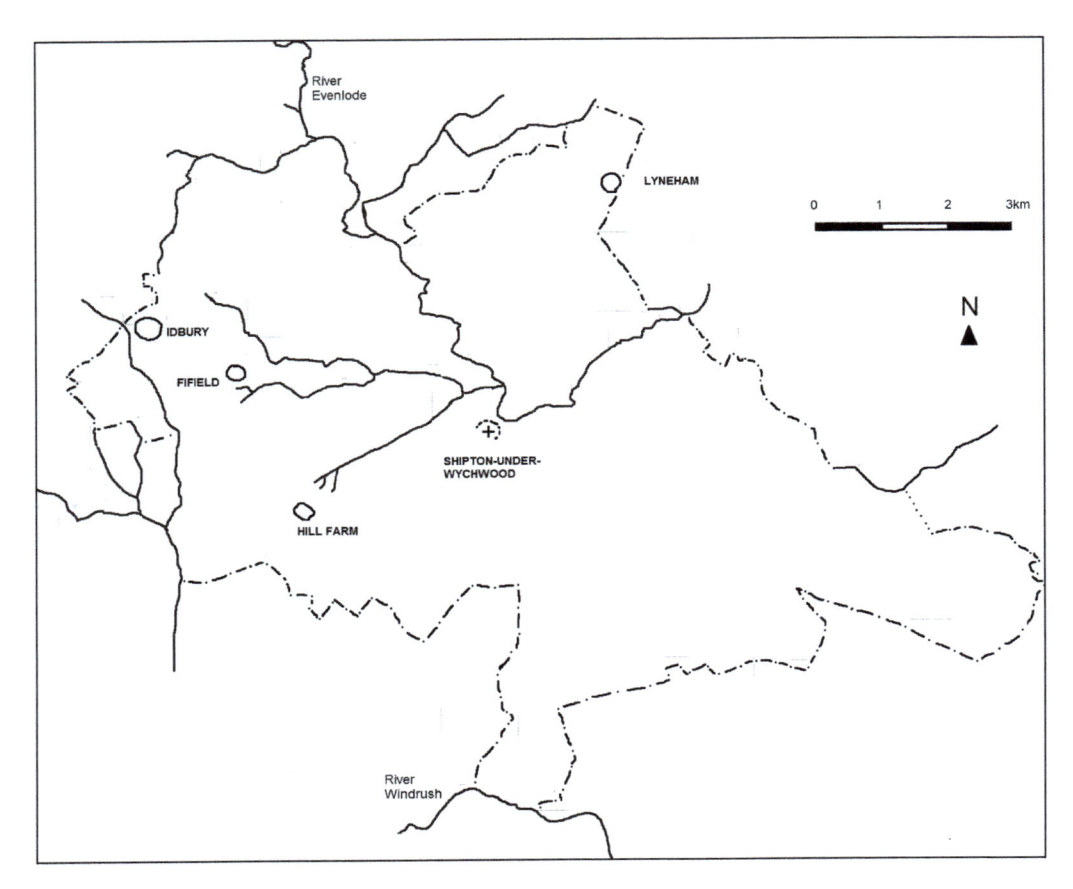

Figure 38: The parochia *of the minster at Shipton-under-Wychwood, which shows the location of a number of large enclosures at Lyneham, Idbury, Fifield, Hill Farm, and Shipton. The nature of these enclosures has not been determined (S. Yeates).*

known. A similar arrangement can be seen at Shipton-under-Wychwood, see Figure 38.

If one accepts that it is not the hill-fort, the Roman nucleated settlements, or the minsters on their own, but the small local region, in which these particular functional sites operated, which acted as the central place, or focus, of a community, then these patterns can be interpreted. Communities that developed alongside each other appear to have developed the same general beliefs and, apparently, built the same types of functional monuments. Even when beliefs and monuments altered the communities retained their folk-names, and their *central place* in a particular river valley.

CONCLUSION

During the period from the Iron Age to the early medieval period a number of events occurred which provide important points for discussion. The two most contentious issues are: the nature of change at the time of the Roman invasion, and ethnic changes which happened after the departure of the Roman legions. A number of the old folk-names that have survived in place-names defy the general interpretations based on the discontinuity hypothesis. These folk-names were, invariably, derived from pre-medieval and sometimes demonstrably pre-Roman river-names. The major settlement evidence, from along the rivers in question, when it has been identified, is mainly Iron Age, and is extensively lowland. It seems that the folk-names that arose derived from the names of the dwellers on the rivers, and incorporated the name of the river, or, in some cases another natural feature, in their name. There are other indications of continuity. The interpretation of hill-forts has been a problem, but there is evidence to indicate that some of these sites were constructed over long periods of time, for seasonal use and with only limited evidence for occupation. By looking at the spatial arrangement of these sites in the landscape it becomes clear that groups of three occurred quite regularly and that there was also, usually, an outlier. Sometimes the clusters may have contained more sites, with evidence of use suggesting variable religious activities.

During the Roman period, nucleated settlements became more evident. At the hearts of these settlements were large enclosed areas, from which evidence can be found for the worship of *genii loci*, the presiding spirits of the local landscapes (rivers and hills) and of the peoples who dwelt there. These spirits were the images of the communities, around which a continuity of identity was maintained from pre-Roman times. The Romans manipulated this process through their diverse concepts of spirits of place, and their ideas of local affiliation and ethnicity. These communities were stable; people could move in and out of them, but the *genius* of the river and their common origin and perception of originating from a shared landscape with common values bound them together. The religious images may have been destroyed, but these deities may not have been lost completely.

When Christianity came to dominate, it also used the folk structure as the initial basis for religious manipulation; hence minsters were founded for groups of people in designated spatial areas, some of whom still retained their British names. They operated as a central place and were a core component which enabled recognition of the manors in later times.

These different types of evidence show examples of changing settlement patterns, from the Iron Age, through the Roman period, and into the early medieval period, which can be seen to overlap spatially. Although they can not be linked together in a clean overall picture of continued meaning, they do demonstrate the importance of local communities and their religion, the significance of place and association, and also possibly, settlement patterns. Over time, despite the huge changes which were brought about by the Roman invasion and later migration, the spatial arrangements of these key sites point towards the existence of stable communities.

Chapter 5

Mining and Minerals: Hill-forts and Temples

In the previous chapter it became apparent that there were underlying structures in the landscape, created and maintained by long lived communities. This was supported by the notion that a number of recorded place-names were pre-Old-English in origin. For this to have happened communities must have been able to create long-lived cohesive groups which were able to preserve the names. One of the archaeological site-types which has been recognised as significant is the Iron-Age hill-forts, or large enclosures. There is some evidence, in quite a number of cases, that enables us to consider how these were used and how Roman religious sites became associated with them. In this chapter the relationship between these archaeological sites, and mineral deposits and mining activity will be considered.

The association between mining and metallurgy with religion and beliefs has been demonstrated by a number of anthropologists; these interpretations might provide an insight into how belief-systems and mining interacted, in the period prior to the Roman invasion (Eliade 1956). Later anthropologists have broken down the cultural elements and, today, mining traditions are considered to consist of three parts, 1) the mineral economy, 2) the social and political structure and 3) ritual and belief (Godoy 1985, 199–217). Mining is a dangerous occupation which recovers a valuable commodity. Therefore, it encourages the development of religious cults, and becomes the focus for shrines and temples (Derks 1998, 77). These observations, on the ritual components of the mining traditions, are revealed in many ways around the world, and these may help us to interpret what occurred in the mining districts of the *Dobunni* territory. Mining traditions are generally associated with two supernatural characters; an earth mother, and a devil, and often also contain accounts of underground libation (Nash 1979; Taussig 1980). An anthropological study of the ochre mines in Tasmania (Sagona and Webb 1994, 133–151) has shown that, because of ochre's special ritual properties, they were owned by clans and subject to social restrictions and rules regarding communal access. Amongst a number of African tribes, for example the Nyoro, the Loikop, and the Dogon, symbolic relationships between mining, kingship and a sky-god, grew up (Childs 1993, 330, 332; Herbert 1984, 33, 39). The reason that these peoples associated a sky-god with mining was because he controlled rain patterns, and therefore, controlled the flooding of the mines and the possible death of the miners.

The use of anthropology enables a much broader understanding, of the information available from ancient sources, to be gleaned. Minerals, such as iron, copper, tin, lead, gold, and silver, have long been prized. Accounts from classical antiquity, and later times, demonstrate that the extraction of minerals, and their processing, was integrated into mythical and ritual activity. Medieval alchemists were aware of some of the names of early metallurgists and, to a large extent, had created myths around the likes of Hermes Trismegistos, Osthanes, and Agathodaemon. It was probably early *scientists*, of this type, who gave rise to the accounts found in Classical sources. Xenophon (von der Lieck 1933), and Pliny the Elder (Rackham 1952, *Nat. His.* XXXIII–XXXV), recognised that mining sites were important and that special properties were given to these sites and the metals they produced, both economically and spiritually. Virgil (Goold 1999, *Aen.* i.66, iii.688) and Ovid (Miller 1921, *Meta.* V.316, VII.204; 1984, *Meta.* XII.810, XIV.713) provided further insight into this developing belief system, making reference to the living rock (*vivum saxum*) which was fed by a root (*radix*). In these works are references to rocks, minerals, and salt-pans, not as dead matter but as living organisms, which could be harvested and which could replenish themselves. The ram and gold were linked in the Greek legend of Jason and the Argonauts, in the form of the golden fleece of the constellation *Aries*. Strabo (Jones 1917, I.2.39; 1928, XI.2.19) claimed that the tradition derived from the Caucasus Mountains, where gold-dust was collected from rivers on fleecy skins. This assertion is supported by an assessment of early sluicing practices, where gorse and fleeces were used to filter gold nuggets from water courses (Craddock 1995, 91). These beliefs resonate with what has already been recognised by anthropologists; that there was an important ritual component to mining traditions. This explains why there should be temples and shrines on mineral sites. It also explains why votive objects, or coin hoards, were often deposited at mining locations. There is also significant evidence that the images associated with mining, and metallurgical traditions, were common in the pre-Christian religious sculpture of north-west Europe (Aldhouse-Green 2002, 8–19). That such a veneration of mining and metallurgy was taking place is, perhaps, also demonstrated by the existence of Irish craft-gods, amongst whom metalworkers can be recognised (O'Rahilly 1984, 308–316).

THE MALVERNS, ARDEN, AND WYRE

The geology of these forests is, in general, extremely diverse. The oldest deposits are found in the Malverns (Barclay, Ambrose *et al.* 1997, 4–44; Worssam, Ellison *et al.* 1989, 2–7), and much of Herefordshire is covered by the Old Red Sandstone sequences (Brandon 1989, 3–19). In the Malvern hills are a number of recognised mineral deposits which could have been important in the past; these include lead, zinc, copper, gold, silver, and garnets (Barclay, Ambrose *et al.* 1997, 122–123; Worssam, Ellison *et al.* 1989, 2–4). Testing has been carried out on both the gold and silver deposits; the results have been variable. The mining of the deposits in the Malverns has not been proved, and research in this area may be required. There is, however, a place-name, the Gold-Mine, to the north of Wych Cutting (Barclay, Ambrose *et al.* 1997, 123). With this particular mineral even if the deposits were not accessible there would still have been attempts to mine the ores. Knowledge about the extraction of other minerals; for example: silver, copper, and even garnets, is equally obscure.

In the northern forests of Arden and Wyre there are igneous outcrops (Mitchell, Pocock *et al*. 1961, 3–6; Whitehead and Pocock 1947, 2–6, 178) and, as in Herefordshire, much of the area is covered by the sequence of Old Red Sandstone deposits. Coal is the main economic component in the rock strata and has been mined in both forests. It is known, from tests made on coal deposits recovered from archaeological sites, that coal was being extracted from these regions as early as the Roman period (Webster 1955, 199–217; Dearne and Branigan 1995, 71–105; Smith 1996, 373–389; 1997, 297–324).

THE FOREST OF DEAN

In the south and west of the area are a series of Palaeozoic rocks (Welch, Crookall *et al*. 1948, 1) which occur in the Forest of Dean, in Kingswood, and in the Forest of Mendip. They are particularly complex (Trotter 1942, 12–13; Welch and Trotter 1961, 59–83; Green and Welch 1965, 1–4) and contain numerous mineral deposits which have been exploited over a number of centuries, even millennia. In the Forest of Dean, a number of important minerals have been found, including gold, silver, ochre, iron, and coal (Welch, Crookall *et al*. 1948, 2; Trotter 1942, 9; Welch and Trotter 1961, 49–58, 86–105; Earp, Hains *et al*. 1971, 78–79; Worssam, Ellison *et al*. 1989, 16–20, 42). The gold and silver occur in the conglomerates found around the edge of the forest. The iron and ochre deposits can be found in the limestones which are also found around the edge of the plateau. The coal deposits occur across the central area of the forest, see Figure 39.

The date at which minerals were first extracted in the Forest of Dean has not been proven categorically, but a number of hammer-stones have been found, at a site interpreted as a probable prehistoric ochre mine, on the eastern edge of the forest near some scowles at Drybrook Quarry (G.SMR 20829). The associated tools have been dated to the Bronze Age or Neolithic (Hughes 2001, 23; Bowen 2003, 16). Evidence has been found to suggest that iron mining was taking place in the Forest of Dean in the middle Iron Age. This was determined by an analysis of metal used in an Iron-Age currency bar recovered from Beckford, Worcestershire (Britnell 1975, 6; Ehrenreich 1994, 16–18). Iron, and presumably ochre, continued to be extracted throughout the Roman period, from both the east and west sides of the forest (Walters 1999, 90–105, 111–115). It is considered that there was an expansion of the iron industry in the second century AD. Production then peaked and went into decline by the third century AD. By the middle of the third century production had stabilised, and continued into the fourth century AD. It is believed that, at some sites, metalworking and occupation continued into the fifth century AD. Along the northern edge of the Forest of Dean is evidence of copper and lead working during the Roman period; for example from the Mount at Lower Lydbrook, which has produced copper ores (Walters 1999, 6). As in other areas in the region, it is known that coal was mined in the Roman period, due to analysis of finds from archaeological sites (Smith 1996, 373–389; 1997, 297–324). There is textual evidence that gold and silver mining occurred in the Forest of Dean in the

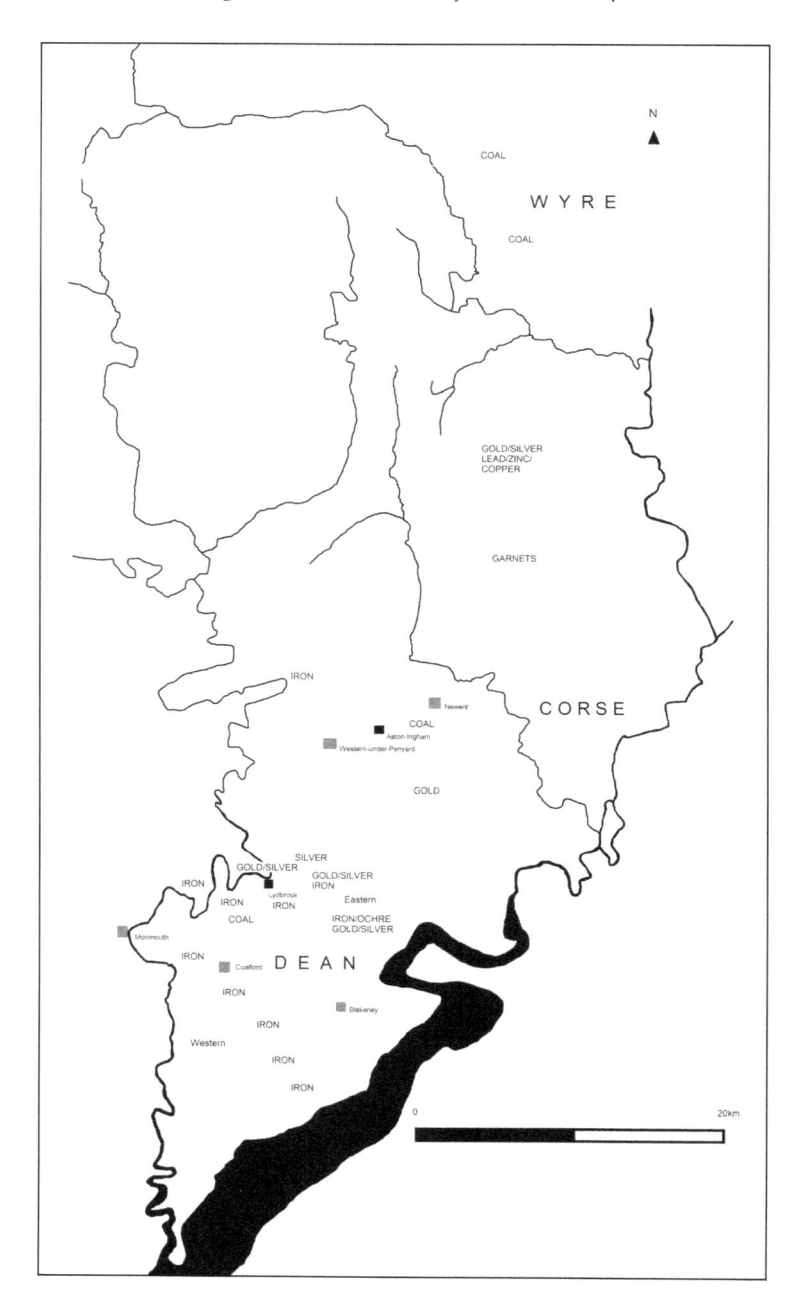

Figure 39: A map showing the mineral locations in the Forest of Dean and the Malvern region. The grey squares indicate major Roman iron production centres and the black squares copper production sites (S. Yeates).

medieval and post-medieval periods (Hart 1944, 98–104), but it is not known if these ores were worked in the later prehistoric and Roman periods.

The grandest Roman temple identified within the Forest of Dean is the Temple of *Nodens* at Lydney Park. It lies in the remains of an Iron-Age hill-fort, which was constructed in, at least, the middle Iron Age. Evidence of earlier and even sub-Roman activity has come from dating the construction of the banks. The remains include a rectangular temple with a cella and ambulatory and three ancillary structures: a courtyard building, a long building, and a bath house (Wheeler and Wheeler 1932). Three, and possibly four, dedications to the god *Nodens* have been found on the site (RIB(I) 1995, nos. 305–307; Collingwood 1932, 100–104; RIB(II:4) 1992, no.2448.3). The first of these was to D(eo) M(arti) NODONTI; the second, on a plaque, mentioned DEUO NODENTI, and referred to the temple as TEMPLUM [NO]DENTIS; and the third, also on a plaque, recorded the name DEO NUDENTE. The likely fourth dedication relies on the interpretation of the writing on the mosaic in the *cella*. The second inscription, which mentioned *Templum Nodentis*, has provided the oldest recorded place-name in Lydney Parish, and it informs us that the temple was the location of a cult dedicated to the god *Nodens*. However, no sculptural relief of *Nodens* has been recovered, although assumed images of his dog-familiar have been. The first attempt at an interpretation of the god's name suggested the meaning *Abyss* (Bathurst 1879, 39–40), although most later suggestions believe that it is derived from **neud-**, *to acquire possession of* (O'Rahilly 1984, 495–496; Tolkien 1932, 132–137). The phrase *to acquire possession of* could be aptly applied to a god of mining. One place-name of particular interest is Nustles, which was recorded in AD 1565 as *Nothehalles* (Smith 1964, 256). It seems to refer to the nook of land on which the temple of Nodens stands, and could be derived from the god's name.

Initially, the temple of Nodens was associated with the cult of Aesculapius, a healing cult (Bathurst 1879, 13–14); an assumption which was generally accepted but has little supporting data. Sites such as this one were normally associated with springs, while the remains at Lydney Park have no spring, only a cistern (Wheeler and Wheeler 1932, 54–55) filled by an unrecognised water source. The temple was built over the remains of iron mines, which it is thought, would have gone out of use before construction of the temple was considered. This assumption can not, however, be sustained as it is apparent that there is a place in the temple where liquid offerings were given directly to the ground, and also, amongst the finds, there is a votive pick axe. These types of structures and finds indicate that the temple users were aware of the activities and the traditions in the area, and it was probable that this was one of the major reasons for the temple being located where it was. It has already been noted that mining sites became the focus for ritual activity on the continent. Perhaps the baths built in the temple complex were related to activities other than pilgrimage, and that the shrine was associated with Forest miners and their ailments. Roman mining sites in Spain are known to have had bathing establishments as part of the complex (Elkington 1976, 188–189).

Other evidence found around Lydney Park, and in the Forest of Dean generally, which may exemplify the veneration of minerals includes the deposition of coin hoards

(Bagnall-Oakeley 1889, 356–358). Some thirteen coin hoards have been found in the Forest (Bagnall-Oakeley 1882, 107–122; Walters 1992, 107–108; Cooke 1882, 217). Of these almost two thirds have been identified as coming from mineral-rich mining sites. Two of the hoards were from Lydney Park; one from under the floors of the temple, the other at the end of a mine. In Perry Grove, near Coleford, in 1848, three jars, containing 3,000 coins, were found, placed at the base of a quarried out scowle. Another coin hoard was found at the Iron Works at Park End, while a further, significant, coin hoard was found in the iron-working site at Bishop's Wood. It has often been said that this votive activity started in the Roman period; however, this can be questioned, as Celtic coins have been recovered from the iron mining scowles at Bream (Walters 1989, 9–29).

Lydney Park can be put in a wider context by considering the earlier anthropological assessment of the mining industry and the references found in ancient European sources. The building of religious sites on mineral rich deposits was a common development. There was often a development in the traditions of a male devil and a female earth mother. For the temple at Lydney Park it is apparent that the god *Nodens* was associated with a female consort. The association of *Nodens* with *Nudd* or *Nuada* means that the god has been interpreted as a sky or storm god (O'Rahilly 1984, 67). The god shows the classical mining god attributes: storm deity, flooded mines, and life. It is also known that offerings were given underground to the deity and that it was believed that the minerals were living and could replenish themselves. If all of these components are taken into account it is evident that the construction of the temple at this location can be explained. *Nodens,* being a god of mining and his name meaning *to acquire possession of,* fits into ideas concerning wealth deriving from mining. In the scowles, at Bream, there is evidence that the idea that coins should be deposited in a scowl (iron mine) actually started in the late Iron Age. The sites' importance and their pre-Roman origins may be indicated by the earlier prehistoric structure under the temple and the siting of the temple in the Iron-Age hill-fort.

A second temple in the Forest of Dean has been excavated at High Nash (Walters 1992, 93–94); also in an iron mining settlement. The temple was rectangular with an apse and made of a beam-slot construction. This building, which was founded in the third-century AD, was removed in the fourth century AD and replaced by a four-post shrine on the same site.

There was probably a third Roman shrine associated with Iron working traditions at Bishop's Wood, where a rectangular enclosure, that was part of a major mining complex covering 22 ha, once existed. The significant coin hoard was found when stone was quarried from a bank, forming a rectangular enclosure (Bagnall-Oakeley 1895, 399–420). It has been thought that the structure was a Roman building but of unknown purpose. The deposition of the coins in or under the bank has the appearance of a votive deposit, perhaps associated with a shrine. The site's location, although not in an Iron-Age hill-fort, seems to have parallels with the location of the mining complex at Lydney Park.

The Roman settlement at Weston-under-Penyard is located on the plateau lying below the bluff on the northern edge of the Forest of Dean. Little is known of the religious activity at the site, but religious sculpture and bronzes, from the time when the settlement was destroyed, have been recovered (Fosbrooke 1821, 36). These included statuary heads and arms, along with quantities of bronze and coins. The account also mentioned that one of the objects found was a large bronze head with ram's horns. The finding of a god with ram's horns is of interest because the site lies on the plains in an area below the gold bearing rocks of the Forest of Dean. It is also known, from classical traditions, that sheep fleeces were associated with panning for gold. The association is intriguing, but as yet no evidence has been found to indicate that gold working was being carried out on the site.

THE KINGSWOOD

Similar types of mineral deposits to those found in the Forest of Dean are to be found in the Kingswood area. Deposits include iron, ochre, coal, lead, tin, and copper (Welch, Crookall *et al.* 1948, 93; Kellaway and Welch 1993, 66–67, 153–155; Rudder 1779, 663; Rudge 1803, 368; Gardner 2004, 65–74, 67). The iron ores can be found in the sandstone near Iron Acton and Frampton Cotterell, and in the conglomerates around Clifton; while iron and ochres occur in the limestone deposits of Wick near Pucklechurch, and at Long Ashton. Tin ores were mined at Berry, near Siston; while the lead ores were found in the rock strata between Westbury-on-Trym, Almondsbury, Cromhall, Yate, and Sodbury. Copper deposits are found at Moorgrave Wood, see Figure 40.

The earliest identified extraction of iron ore in the Kingswood is from the Roman period; excavations have uncovered a shallow Roman mine at Longwell Green (Burnham, Keppie and Esmonde Cleary 2000, 423). Coal mining is known to have taken place in the area, during the Roman period, in the Coal Pit Heath basin (Smith 1996, 373–389; 1997, 297–324). Lead and silver mining were also carried on in the region in the Roman period as the remains of cupulation de-silvering equipment has been uncovered at Rodway (Gardner 2004, 67). Some of the lead ingots from the Mendip region may have come from the Kingswood Forest. Later lead mining was mentioned in the Anglo-Saxon charter of *c.* AD 883 for Stoke Bishop, Westbury-on-Trym (Grundy 1936, 228–231), while copper was mined in Gloucestershire, during the medieval period, in 1462 (Hart 1944, 98–104).

The area around Bristol also has some sites associated with mining traditions, but the information is not as outstanding as for the Forest of Dean and the Temple of *Nodens*. One thing which does become more apparent is that the hill-forts in this area seem to have played an important role in the mining traditions, as both the one recognised temple site and the other probable site are located in hill-forts; Bury Hill, Winterbourne, being located on a hill with iron ore deposits. It is suspected that some of the interior of the camp had been mined prior to the construction of a podium, on which a simple square shrine stood (Davies and Phillips 1926, 8–25).

At Wick the information is more circumstantial but, here also, there seems to have been a shrine or temple in an Iron-Age hill-fort. Antiquaries described the location of two hill-forts which lay either side of the river Boyd. These hill-forts were located on some of the richest ochre supplies in the region (Welch, Crookall *et al.* 1948, 93;

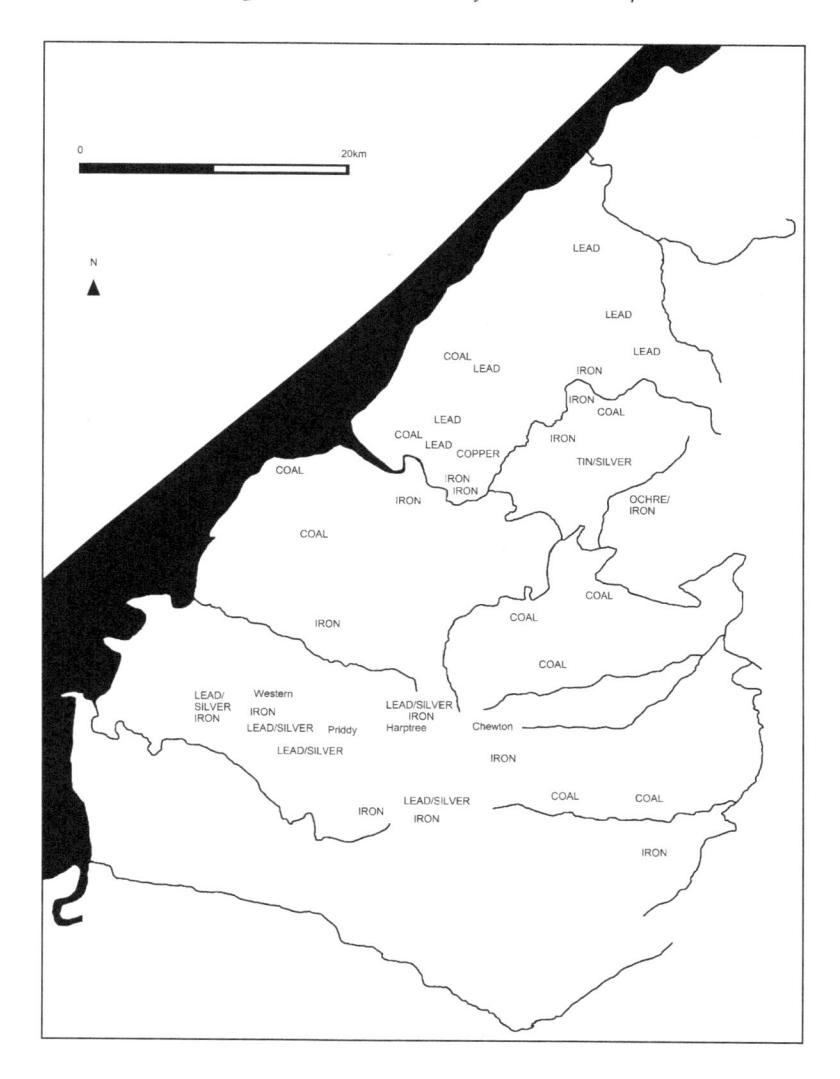

Figure 40: A map showing the mineral locations of the Mendip and Kingswood areas. The four divisions of the Mendip Freeminers are marked as Western, Priddy, Harptree, and Chewton (S. Yeates).

Kellaway and Welch 1993, 153–154) and it is for this reason that the sites no longer exist. From the camp on the Doynton side of the river, was found the remains of a sculptured cornice, as well as, what has been interpreted as, a sacrificial knife. The combination of important mineral deposits, the establishment of two hill-forts, and the recovery of a cornice, provide circumstantial evidence that Wick was another temple site, but the information is too imprecise to go further. What seems to be apparent is that certain, but not all, hill-forts may have, before the Roman period, been associated with the mining traditions of the region and that they were both industrial and ritual. How these sites may have been used in the pre-Roman period will be discussed later when the social structure of the Forest of Dean and the Mendip Forest is considered.

THE MENDIPS

The main mineral deposits of the Mendips include: lead, silver, zinc, iron, and coal (Welch, Crookall *et al.* 1948, 94; Green and Welch 1965, 163–165; Kellaway and Welch 1993, 153–155; Dewey 1921, 4–5, 60–62; Cantrill, Sherlock and Dewey 1919, 28–30). Lead, silver, iron, and zinc ores occur in the Carboniferous rocks at Priddy, Charterhouse, Saint Cuthbert's Without, Banwell, East Harptree, and Nunney. There is also a major iron lode in the pennant sandstone at Temple Cloud fault, and coal measures are found at Nailsea, Corston, Pensford, Clutton, Nettlebridge and Mells, see Figure 40.

The date at which the mines of the Mendips were used has not been ascertained properly, but it is apparent that mining of lead started in later prehistory (Gough 1930, 19). Finds of lead objects, such as fishing weights and lumps of lead ore, have come from archaeological sites and indicate that the mining of this metal may well have taken place in the middle to late Iron Age (Coles and Minnitt 1995, 141). Excavations at two rakes on the west side of Charterhouse have demonstrated that the mining of lead and silver probably took place in that area during the late Iron Age and the early Roman period (Todd 1996, 1–18; 2001, 151–154). It is possible that the silver used to produce *Dobunnic* coinage came from the Mendip region. The distribution of *Durotrigan* coins and East Midland Iron-Age pottery in the region (Todd 2003, 53–55), suggests that the ores were traded with those areas. During the Roman period lead pigs were produced in the Mendip area (Dewey 1921, 60; RIB(II:1) 1990, 2404.1–2404.24). A group of four from Rookery Farm, Green Ore, Wells, shows that the lead was produced free of silver. There is also some evidence that zinc ores were being worked at Charterhouse during the Roman period (Todd 1996, 1–18). Coal was also mined in the Mendips in the Roman period, as analysis of finds from archaeological sites indicate that sources in the Farrington-Radstock, in the Clutton-Temple Cloud, and in the Nettlebridge formations were used (Smith 1996, 373–389; 1997, 297–324). Lead and silver mining probably continued into the middle ages (Gough 1930, 48–69). In the late Anglo-Saxon period there was a concentration of mints in the area which were probably being supplied by Mendip silver (Todd 1996, 1–18).

In both the Forest of Dean and Kingswood hill-forts, Roman shrines and temples were constructed at sites associated with mining traditions; for example at Lydney Park, and Bury Hill. A second type of mining temple could have been constructed in settlements, for example that at High Nash. The evidence for site types from the Mendips is similar. The hill-fort at Whorlebury lies on a spur overlooking the Severn Estuary. It has been excavated and is known to have been the site of many quarry pits.

A significant number of coins have been uncovered, and it has been suggested that this was the location of a probable shrine (Rippon 1997, 90–91, 107); this is, however, impossible to confirm. Nevertheless, an enclosure associated with mining and quarrying, and the later construction of a Roman temple, could explain some of the factors which have been observed at the site.

One of the most important mining settlements in Britain was located in the Mendips, at Charterhouse (VCH(So1) 1906, 334–339). Survey work and new analysis of the area has shown that one of the enclosures did contain a building believed to be a temple (Faulkner 1998); no dedication, however, is known. A small pick, this time made of lead, interpreted as a toy but surely a votive object, came from the Charterhouse Roman settlement (VCH(So1) 1906, 337). A comparable object, associated with a mining temple, has already been noted at Lydney Park. One other possible temple site in the area is what is described as a Roman fortlet, a description which is unconvincing. It has more of the appearance of a late prehistoric enclosure or hill-fort. The site sits above mines and rakes which were started in at least the late Iron Age. A second enclosure, built over the irregular shaped earlier one, seems a suitable candidate to be a *temenos* boundary. If one thinks about the site it is possible to draw major comparisons between it and the one at Lydney Park. Both have an Iron-Age hill-fort, the later reuse of a temple or possible *temenos*, and the major mineral working area.

Other objects from the area are votive in nature and must have been associated with the ritual activity of the mining industry. These include: the remains of a votive mattock, approximately 0.22m long, which was found at the temple on Lamyatt Beacon (Leech 1986, 295–296); and the remains of a coin hoard with two silver ingots, which came from the Harptree area (Scarth 1888, 21–28; Thompson Watkin 1888, 26). This find could be a votive deposit from a mine or rake, but could also indicate the close proximity of a temple. Both possibilities seem plausible. The addition of the votive ingots may indicate the latter; because, as seen in the mine deposits of the Forest of Dean, coins have been found on their own, but votive objects are usually found only at temple sites. A systematic survey of the locations of the coin hoards of the Mendips has not yet been carried out, but just by scratching the surface it has become apparent that parallels with what has been observed in the Forest of Dean, would be found.

THE COTSWOLDS

The Mesozoic rock series of the Cotswolds includes the Jurassic rocks which underlie part of the Severn Valley and the Cotswold Hills. These are formed by rock strata dipping gently towards the east (Richardson 1929, 5–10; 1933, 6–7; Edmonds, Poole *et al.* 1965, 3–7, 118–119; Horton 1987, 21–99; Williams and Whittaker 1974, 3–5). In the east of the Cotswolds there is a lower estuarine series, which include the iron bearing Northampton sands. Iron ores also occur in the eastern Cotswolds, in the marlstone rock beds near Wroxton, and in the Burton Dassett Hills.

Ironstone quarries now scar the landscape around Burton Dassett, Wroxton, Bloxham, and Hook Norton, in the eastern Cotswolds. The date at which ore mining commenced in the area has not been established, but analysis of currency bars has shown that the adjacent Northamptonshire sources were being exploited from late prehistory onwards (Ehrenreich 1994, 16–18). It was not until far later, however, that some historians consider this to have happened in Oxfordshire. The Ragstone of the Braydon Forest may also have once contained some mining activity, but not on the scale seen elsewhere in the area. Medieval iron mining has been recognised on Nash Hill (Wi.SMR ST96NW461) to the South of Chippenham.

The archaeology from the east Cotswolds belies the theory that mining extraction originated at a late date. A relief of the god Vulcan, the blacksmith, has been found at, or near, Ilbury hill-fort, in the vicinity of Ironstone Hill (Henig 1993, no. 90); this must have been linked to the mining of iron ore in the region, and its subsequent smelting and manufacturing. Once again there is an association with a mining cult and a possible shrine or temple, associated with mining, being located within or just outside a camp. This association is persistent, but on the other hand may mean that there is an important underlying association between the hill-fort, the later temple or shrine, and the mineral economy.

SOCIAL STRUCTURE AND BELIEFS: THE USE OF SOME HILL-FORTS AND TEMPLE COMPLEXES

From the Forest of Dean there is evidence that mining probably started for the extraction of ochre, in the Neolithic or Bronze Age. Ochre is a colouring agent and, as such, was used in ritual processes. It is known to have been used in Europe to colour the body, for burial processes, in the Paleolithic. Australian anthropology has shown that access to such mining sites was controlled by family groups or communities. This may provide an underlying context for understanding how some of the hill-forts in the mineral rich *Dobunnic* area were being used.

In both the Forest of Dean and the Mendips, and possibly Kingswood, there were groups who were called free miners. The Forest of Dean was divided into Eastern and Western divisions; each of which had free miners, a tradition which can be dated, by texts, to at least 1282, by which time it had already been established that they could dig for coal and iron on the approval of the gaveller (a mining official, usually the king) (Trotter 1942, 1). The medieval sources also describe who could own, and who could work, a mine. This was restricted to those people born within certain areas of the forest (VCH(Gl5) 1996, 328, 331). It was only in 1775 that the first *foreigners*, those people born outside the Hundred of Saint Briavels, were first accepted as mine-holders. This was a very contentious issue amongst the locals (Hart 2000, 63–66). The laws of the mining community were kept in a book called the Book of Dennis, probably a corruption of Dean. The tradition of free mining was important because, in many ways, it parallels what has been described as happening in Australia; that the mines were controlled by the community and that membership of that community, and possibly even gender, may have determined who could go into the mines.

Like in the Forest of Dean, the Mendip miners were classed as free miners and mining was controlled by a legal framework. The Mendips were divided into four divisions or lordships, which were marked on the Waldegrave Old Map of Mendip, of Chewton Mendip, and are identified as West (around Charterhouse), Priddy, Chewton, and Harptree (Gough 1930, 55, 255). Between AD 1461 and 1483, 10,000 people gathered at Forge Barrow in Rodney Stoke to discuss Mendip mining law (Grinsell 1987, 20). The mining laws of the royal forest of Mendip were described by Lord Chocke as ancient customs (Gough 1930, 69–74). Of the customs described some are considered to be, in essence, *primitive*. That there were similar types of tradition in the Forest of Dean and the Mendips is of interest and it indicates that there was an important series of extremely old customs; both districts operating mining activity which lay outside the rights of medieval manors. This in itself implies that these traditions and rights were established before the medieval manor system came into being, and that strong community action was protecting these rights. There is evidence in the region that in the Roman period manufacturing guilds existed (RIB(I) 1995, no. 141), and it is possible that each of these ancient recognised divisions had its own guild.

The god *Nodens*, the one who *acquires possession of wealth*, was, apparently, a mining god of the Forest of Dean, but it is not apparent if this same mining god was recognised and worshiped in the Mendips and in Kingswood. The mining temple that has been identified in the Kingswood area was of a different design, which may indicate a different cult. The bathing complex at Lydney Park was not the size of a Roman spa bath complex, but could have been a focus for the mining community, which was used for the healing of the ailments of the miners. *Nodens* was the devil to whom libations were given, in the temple and under the ground at the end of the mine shafts, to the ground. The Dean miners, like their Bolivian counterparts, gave this deity a compatriot, a bountiful earth mother, who probably shared the votive material.

Most of the temples were located in Iron-Age hill-forts and it is this which provides an indication of the possible use of some of these sites and the cultural focus and activity which would have been carried out in them. One could argue that there was a break between the Iron Age traditions and those carried out in Roman times, but this is probably incorrect as mining would have been a dominant factor either side of the invasion, and it would be easier to leave communities and their social practices bound together. The hill-forts probably acted as locations for gatherings, perhaps seasonal, and were probably built on mineral rich deposits as a statement of control, restriction, access, and belonging, relative to the mineral resources; the display of a defined community who controlled a specific area. Mining complex hill-forts occurred at: Lydney Park, Bury Hill, Doynton Camp (Wick), Whorlebury, Charterhouse, Nash Hill, and Ilbury, to name a few. There were, undoubtedly, many others but many of them have probably been destroyed and will never be known through anything other than surviving place-names.

Chapter 6

The Gods of War

For some time it has been apparent that there was an unusual relationship between temples and hill-forts in the pre-Roman period (Ross 1967, 69–70; Woodward 1992, 22–26). The previous chapter, although it noted an association between the two site types with respect to mining practices, did not contextualise the phenomenon fully. This association was far more widespread than first thought and most religious artefacts have been found at hill-forts that were not located on mineral deposits. Artefacts found at hill-forts include the remains of altars, reliefs, and other votive material, most notably coins.

The second group of hill-forts which we need to consider is those concerning aspects of war. In many old societies the activity of war was highly ritualised and much more symbolic. Hill-forts, due to their very nature, were considered initially to be defended towns or places of refuge in a war-ravaged Britain. The repetitive patterns which underlie land-unit or *parochia* development hint, however, that this assumption is, at least partly, wrong.

On the continent there are a number of shrines which have been recognised as having a direct association with the act of war. These sites often contained: deposition of weaponry, fragmentary remains of burials in ditches and ramparts, and disarticulated burials in pits. All of these seem to have been part of a common phenomenon. Though the Gallic deposits are very different to any yet found in Britain, one could draw some parallels with those found at Gournay-sur-Aronde (Brunaux, Meniel *et al.* 1985; Brunaux and Rapin 1988) and Ribemont-sur-Ancre (Cadoux 1986, 203–210; 1991). The latter site developed into a large and impressive Roman sanctuary. Their focus as religious sites started as early as the middle Iron Age, with deposits of weaponry. At Gournay-sur-Aronde the swords had been broken deliberately before being placed in ditches. At Ribemont-sur-Ancre mass deposits of human bones, heaped and disarticulated, were found in a religious enclosure; skulls, however, were totally absent from the site.

THE DEPOSITS OF WEAPONRY

The date at which weaponry was deposited at certain hill-forts has not been proven categorically but there are examples where such activity must have commenced in the Bronze Age. From the hill-fort on Nottingham Hill a Bronze-Age weapon hoard has been recovered; it may be the earliest known for this type of activity. What is not known about this deposit is whether it predated the construction of the hill-fort; or, if the deposition occurred when there was already some form of enclosure around the site. Further weapon deposits have been recovered from hill-forts such as Madmarston, and the Ditches, to name but a few. In the Madmarston example the deposits were in the defences' ditch.

Further features found at certain hill-forts are described in various manners as wells, pit, or even a dwelling. The pits are usually large and circular, with diameters of some 3–4m. They are often stone-lined and too large to be associated with grain storage. In some cases there may be more than one. It has been claimed that a number of these features existed on Meon Hill, although only one is described as having been excavated. This was a stone-lined pit which had iron objects deposited in its lowest fill. At Midsummer Hill some of the earliest excavation reports describe a stone-lined circular feature of about the same size. The material used for the lining was Llandovery sandstone from Bronsil Hill. A similar large pit with a stone lining was found in a fragmentary form cut into one of the disused ramparts of the earliest fort at Croft Ambrey. There is also a large well, as described by early antiquaries, at Leckhampton Hill. Perhaps the most significant find was at Painswick Beacon, where a large pit, up to 6m across and 2.5m deep surrounded by a bank, was uncovered; it is called the Devil's Well. In the base of this pit a spearhead and a sword were recovered. The iron objects produced from these pits tend to imply that these were broad votive shafts used for the deposition of weaponry. The Painswick example, though from an early report, seems to indicate that these sites had religious significance. Medieval charters and early post-medieval descriptions refer to other examples; at Barmoor in Warwickshire, and at Wychbury, in north Worcestershire. Whether the hill-fort with the ritual shaft for weapon deposition was purely a *Dobunnic* trait has not yet been demonstrated, but it does seem to represent an important feature at many of the hill-forts.

The deposition of human bones at hill-forts may have occurred at a number of sites, and for a number of reasons. The evidence for this will be returned to later, when burials are discussed. There may have been two distinct activities occurring at these locations, only one of which was associated with the ritual activity of warfare. There are perhaps three sites where activity falls outside the general practices described. At Sutton Walls the chance find of a burial in the base of the rampart was made. The burial was deposited as a votive offering during the construction of a phase of the hill-fort rampart. Other aspects of display are not to do with ritual burials; such as those identified at Bredon Hill, and it may be that what occurred at Sutton Walls was the dumping of mutilated bodies in the ditches around the gates. At Cadbury, near Congresbury, there is evidence of the display of human bones, as a skull, dated to *c*. 500 BC by radiocarbon dating, was recovered from a fifth century AD context. This implies that the skull may have been on display at the site for a thousand years. These deposits, presumably, were war trophies and, in some way, parallel what has been found at the French sites. It is also apparent that the activity was not on the same scale as it was at the Gallic shrines.

There is further evidence, from two hill-fort sites in the region, that there were military shrines associated with hill-forts. A worn figure of Mars, holding a shield and a spear, was found at Cadbury, Tickenham (Burrow and Bennett 1979, 1–5), while another warrior relief, showing a crude figure holding a spear, comes from Stow-on-the-Wold (Henig 1993, no. 130). These reliefs may have come from martial shrines.

Painswick Beacon, near Gloucester, has also produced evidence of a well with deposits of weapons. However, no significant Roman remains have been ascribed to it and it seems, therefore, that the site, although impressive, was abandoned in some way. This may have been because Painswick Beacon has, to a large extent, been used for quarrying. Alternatively, it may have been that, due to the process of development at Gloucester, the importance of Painswick diminished. To the north of Gloucester an auxiliary fort was built in the first century AD. This later became the focus of a martial shrine. The reliefs found at the site contain images of Mars, but there are also dedications to Mars and the *genius* of a military cohort. This development or apparent relationship between Painswick Beacon and Kingsholm seems to be two parts of a process which can also be seen at Cadbury, near Tickenham, and Stow-on-the-Wold. The implication from this is that, not only was the site at Painswick deemed to be no longer necessary with its activities being run down, but also that the functions of votive well and weapon deposition, apparent at this and other sites, could then be developed inside what was a Roman auxiliary fortress. The older activities were probably still carried on but at other locations, and mainly for symbolic reasons.

The images of a number of war gods have been identified in the area, but none have, as yet, provided the type of inscription which would give them a name. It is, perhaps, possible that the names of some of these gods have survived in place-names, but to contextualise these sites it would be necessary to draw parallels with recorded Irish mythologies. In Ireland there is a god named *Coca*, recorded in the tale of *Bruiden Dá Choca* (fort of the god *Coca*), whose association is with a fort, a war god, and the tradition of fostering (O'Rahilly 1984, 136–137). The site of *Bruiden dá Choca*, now *Bruidean Mór*, *Breemore* or *Brinemore*, lay in West Kilkenny (Hogan 1910, 131), where two ring-forts are located (RMP(I) 1996, 023–3). The suggestion is that this name may have been linked to the Welsh word *Coch* meaning **red**, or the Irish *Coic*, which has the same meaning, thus associating *Coca* with the god *Cocidius* (Ross 1967, 467–468), a martial god worshipped in Northern Britain (Rivet and Smith 1979, 468; Charlton and Mitcheson 1983, 143–153).

In the *Dobunnic* and *Hwicce* area there are a number of hill-forts called Cockbury. The oldest recording of this name is *Coccanburh* from AD 769–85, which was derived from the name *Cocca* (Smith 1964, ii.90), see Figure 41. It is the recorded name of the hill-fort on Nottingham Hill, from where weapon deposition occurred in the Bronze-Age. The name also occurred as an old name of Chase Wood Camp to the south of Ross, and on the west edge of the Forest of Dean, where the presence of a hill-fort is suspected. Another Cockbury is at Chaceley, near the river Severn, where, again, no hill-fort has yet been identified. The old recording of the site at Nottingham Hill, the association of that site with weapons, and the derivation of the name, indicate an association with the Irish god *Coca*, and his associated attributes of war, the fort, and fostering. The name is found also in Wales, which implies that there was once a war god called *Coca*, worshipped in Ireland, Wales, and parts of England. From the information available it is possible to say that these sites may only have had seasonal activity, but it is also possible that they operated as military camps, where children, presumably boys, were taken away from their families and taught the art of warfare. Such sites would have left evidence of more permanent occupation, and the associated finds would be horse fittings and other Iron Age military artefacts. It may be that associations with horses can also be seen.

The three Cadburys in Somerset have all produced evidence of shrines within the forts. For the Tickenham example it is known that the shrine was to a war god. For that near Congresbury a shrine has been claimed, and a further shrine is suspected. At South Cadbury, outside the area under study, the robbed-out remains of a cruciform building, thought to have been a temple, has been found (Barrett, Freeman and Woodward 2000, 176–178). Saint Clair Baddeley (1913, 35) suggested that the name derived from *Cada's* fort, with which Watts (2004, 108) agreed. Burrow (1981, 52) suggested that the name may have been derived from the Celtic *Catu-*, **battle**, but this has not yet been accepted. The name seems to have a distribution pattern across the south-west of Britain and it is possible that, if there was an association like that with *Coca*, the distribution may be important. Alternatively, it may indicate that more than one war god was recognised amongst the people called the *Dobunni*. The sub-Roman activity at the Congresbury Cadbury, and the apparent continued display of human material, suggests that warfare, as a cult, continued into the sub-Roman period. It has

Figure 41: The hill-fort of Cockbury at Nottingham Hill (S. Yeates).

been argued (Sims-Williams 1990, 7–8, 20–21, 32) that each Anglo-Saxon kingdom existed in a social and psychological sense, but that regional loyalties were more easily inferred than demonstrated. Sims-Williams also argued that a process of interchange occurred across communal and political boundaries, and that the exchanges of associated weapons were related, not with ethnicity, but with the assertion of warrior values. This was an important shift from the earlier antiquaries' writings.

CONCLUSIONS

Hill-forts were an important part of the landscape and can not simply be seen as a single function central place of the community; it is evident that they were places for social gathering for many purposes. These gatherings seem to have been associated with a number of social and seasonal aspects such as; the mining of metals, the act of warfare, and fostering. That warfare was considered to be a seasonal activity is implied by the Roman tradition. Campaigning took place in the summer and during the winter the soldiers bunkered down in winter camps. By combing place-name evidence and Irish mythology, it becomes apparent that an explanation can be suggested for the activities carried out in certain hill-forts. They were not designed for permanent occupation but had more to do with creating an effective fighting unit or enabling group integration.

These traditions undoubtedly changed in the Roman period as concerns shifted from the neighbouring folk-group or tribe to fitting into a structured empire. This meant that the ritualisation of such sites occurred. When this did not happen it was probably because a new site had been created to take its place.

There are indications that at the Congresbury Cadbury site the warfare cult was re-established and that some of the sites again become important in the new emerging warrior culture of the migration period.

Chapter 7

The Hunter God and the Sacred Grove

In Chapter 2 the deification of the landscape was discussed on a broad scale. It was determined that there was evidence for the deification of the Cotswolds and, even though evidence was sparse, it was apparent that traditions probably once existed that could be compared with continental examples. These landscapes were, in the Roman period, designated as *silva*, while, in the early medieval period, some became wolds; in the Norman period the term forest was applied. In order to understand the use of the term *silva*, it is necessary to refer to the *nemeton* or sacred grove.

Sacred groves have been recognised, in Roman ethnographic sources, for some time but there has been a real lack of understanding of how these features can be identified archaeologically. When Caesar (Edwards 1963, VI.14) discussed the customs of the Gauls, he described the druids, a cult which, it was claimed, originated in Britain. Pliny (Rackham 1968, XVI.95.249–250) discussed the fertility ritual carried out by the druids which involved cutting the mistletoe from the sacred oak tree with a golden sickle. Lucan (Lucan 1928, Pharsalia I.444–446) mentioned the gods *Taranis*, *Teutates* and *Esus*, a triad of gods who demanded human sacrifice. Later commentaries on this poem, probably dating to the ninth century AD, described the victims as being stabbed and hung from trees (Ross 1967, 317–318). Meanwhile, Tacitus (Hutton, Ogilvie *et al.* 1970, *Germ.*39) recorded that the *Semnoni*, a Germanic people, gathered annually in a holy wood (sacred grove) that was associated with ancestral beliefs and the belief that the soil in which it stood was the native soil of the tribe; such a soil would have been untouched by the plough and not developed in any way. These areas may well have been called *Nemeton*, and may have been associated with the deification of the landscape.

When referring to antiquaries' sources it becomes apparent that they knew that, in the pre-Roman and Roman periods, sacred groves or *nemetons* existed. However, there always seem to be contradictions in their views and a lack of understanding of what these places were. Rudder was well aware of the comments of Caesar and Strabo in his discussions of Cirencester. The Latin quote was;

Oppidum autem Britanni vocant, quum silvas impeditas vallo atque fossa muneriunt:

and his interpretation:

the Britons call that a town, when they have surrounded and fenced about their thickest woods with a bank and ditch. What passed under the terms of cities according to Strabo was none other than groves. (Rudder 1779, 345)

He determined, therefore, that Cirencester was a Roman town because it had evidence of proper building foundations. The idea of the **city of trees** was also recognised by the first and subsequent editors of the *Gentleman's Magazine*, and used as a pseudonym throughout its years of production. The pseudonym was *Sylvanus Urban*, **the wooded city**. The big problem here is how this relates to the archaeology of north-west Europe and to this region in particular. A distribution of the known groves and possible sacred groves in the area is shown on Figure 42.

EVOLUTION OF THE WOODLAND LANDSCAPE

To understand this it is essential to return to the *silva* landscapes of Britain, see figures 3 and 42, and discussed earlier, and account for how the woodlands of Britain developed up to the historic period. The science of palaeobotany has enabled an evaluation of how landscapes changed on broad scales (Bell and Walker 1992, 96–101). In the Mesolithic the land of Britain was covered by woodlands in which hunter gatherers operated. Around 10,000 BP the area of the Severn Valley, and much of Britain, was dominated by birch forest, while the Thames Valley and the land to the south were covered by mixed deciduous woodland. By 9000 BP, the beginning of the mesocratic stage of the interglacial, the Severn Valley and large parts of Britain had become dominated by mixed deciduous woodland in which hazel, oak, elm, and lime dominated. By 8000 BP these trees became complemented by alder and ash. The coverage of these woodlands had peaked by 5000 BP when further changes caused the development of heath, grasslands and blanket mires; features which are seen as evidence of widespread anthropogenic activity.

During the Neolithic period farming was introduced to Britain (Darvill 1987, 48–74); it was also at this time that the first monuments were built (Bradley 1984, 6–37). It seems inconceivable that the hunting activities of the primordial woodlands should have ceased altogether; more likely, the perceived absence is probably due to academic habits of categorisation rather than a description of the more complex realities on the ground at the time. The trends evident in the Neolithic continued into the Bronze Age, a period during which Britain saw major changes in the landscape; these changes are interpreted as shifts from ritual and monument to settlement and boundaries (Darvill 1987, 75–107). In the late Bronze Age the landscape of southern Britain was divided up with large linear boundaries (Hingley 2001, 98–100; Bradley, Entwistle *et al.* 1994; Cunliffe 1991, 372–378). This changing landscape was dominated by agriculture and pastoralism with archaeological sites becoming specialised in their use, a factor which resembles the specialisation of the individual manors of the medieval multiple estates. Although the role of hunting in these societies has been addressed it is understood poorly as most domestic sites from these periods produce the bones of only domesticated animals, apart from deer. This lack of evidence in the Iron Age seems at odds with the later ethnographic *topoi* of sacred groves, and hunting iconography.

From Chapter 2 it is evident that forest-names are stratified and that some of them contain pre-Old English names. These *silvas* were defined topographic territories. In the medieval period these woodlands became broken up and new forests, using

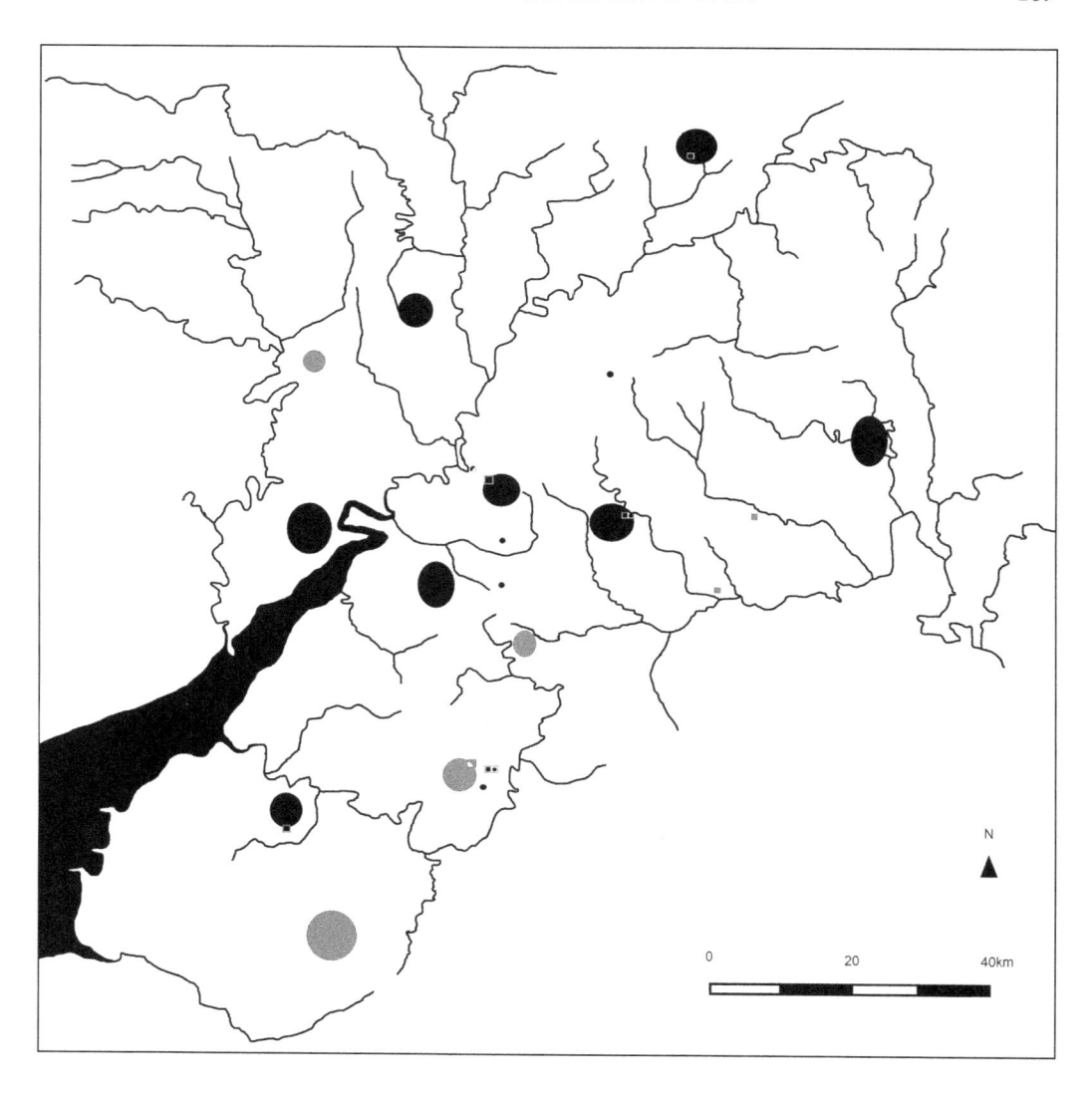

Figure 42: A map showing the distribution of the nemeton. The large black circles represent known late prehistoric linear ditches which are associated with woodland landscapes and qualify for the status of nemeton or sacred grove. The large grey circles represent probable locations. The black squares represent the locations of known hunting temples, while the grey squares possible temples. The small black circles represent known sculpture finds associated with the hunter god Cunomaglos. The black and white circle at Gloucester represents the recovery of a plaque showing the hunter god (S. Yeates).

manorial names, were created. It is apparent, from certain Anglo-Saxon charters, that certain parts of these old forests contained enclosed areas of land, for example in AD 956 at Kemble (Gover, Mawer and Stenton 1939, 60). The enclosures in this particular Forest have not been dated, but they must have existed in the early medieval period. Other enclosures, or bank systems, in woods have been dated to the late prehistoric period.

THE CULT OF THE HUNTER GOD

Images of the hunting god have been found in the *Dobunnic* territory. This has been discussed cogently in the past and the outline of the cult images and shrines set out (Boon 1989, 201–217; Henig 1996, 97–103; Merrifield 1996, 105–113). The earliest debates concentrated on the coherent use of imagery representing the hunter-god across the region and also on some images found outside it. These reliefs were of a male figure, now called **the Cotswold hunter-god**, standing and wearing a tunic, a cloak, and a pointed Phrygian cap, and accompanied by a dog, a stag, and a hare, see Figure 43. The second important factor is the shape of the temple, which is octagonal. Such a temple has been found at a number of sites, and there may have been an evolution from a circular design to the octagonal one at some time in the second or third century. The god also seems to have had a recognised name. A dedication to DEO APOL/LINI CVNO/MAGLO was inscribed upon an altar in the shrine at Nettleton, Wiltshire. This was a locally-named divinity whose name was interpreted, by Jackson, as meaning **Hound Lord** (Wedlake 1982, 53). The association of the god *Cunomaglos* with hunting images is evident in the surviving tales incorporated in the Mabinogion. The name has survived in Welsh as *Cynfael*, which occurs in the Mabinogion as the name of a river (Jones and Jones 1974, 69). By this river a huntsman,

Figure 43: The Cotswold hunter-god, from Chedworth, who can be equated with the god Cunomaglos (photograph Martin Henig).

with his hounds, overcomes a stag and kills it. This is possibly a survival of an extremely ancient tale. When discussing the *silva* regime, and the large banks and ditches in these areas, it becomes apparent that there is a specific type of religious monument not recognised previously in archaeology, and associated with *Cunomaglos*. The known examples covered many hectares.

THE ARDEN *NEMETONS*

In the Forest of Arden, in the upper stretches of the Alne valley, are the remains of a late Bronze-Age ditch system which is known collectively as the Hobditch causeway. The site has been interpreted as being that of a possible oppidum, but there is no evidence of major settlement in the area. The banks and ditch lie around Arden Hill, and it is this name which is known to be a pre-Old English Forest name. The bank systems here are extremely large; in some cases there are three banks, see Figure 44. Their construction has been dated to the early Iron Age. Integrated into the bank layout are at least two large enclosures; one at Oldbury, the other at Harborough Banks. These seem to be integral to the system, and it is possible there was a connection between the larger ditch system and the enclosure. Near Oldbury enclosure the remains of a Roman site have been identified. This has a platform cut into the bank on

Figure 44: The Hobditch bank system which once formed part of the main nemeton of the Forest of Arden (photograph S. Yeates).

which a polygonal shaped building, interpreted as a shrine, was constructed. Sculpture, from a funerary monument, was also recovered from the area. No sculptural images of the hunter-god were recovered but it is apparent that the temple was polygonal in shape; which, in the *Dobunnic* area, was associated with the hunter cult of *Cunomaglos*. The proximity of this site to the enclosure at Oldbury, which seems to have been integrated into the bank system and is presumably a valley fort, should not be ignored.

THE COTSWOLD *NEMETONS*

In the eastern part of the Cotswolds is an area called Wychwood where there is a large Iron-Age linear ditch system which has defied interpretation, see Figure 45. It is usually claimed to be the location of an oppidum, a tribal boundary, or a holding area for cattle; none of these are convincing. The banks have been assessed and are considered to have been built in two phases (Copeland 1988, 277–292). It has also been noted that Celtic and Roman field systems were abundant outside the banks, yet very few features have been detected within the bank system (Copeland 2002, 67). The reason for the construction of these banks is not known, but it is known that Wychwood was woodland, and a recognised hunting ground of the Saxon and Norman nobility. There

Figure 45: The Grim's Ditch in the Forest of Wychwood, which forms part of one of the Cotswold nemetons (photograph S. Yeates).

is evidence from antiquaries' accounts and place-names that two camps were associated with the Wychwood bank system; at Model Farm and at Wallborough. There is, as yet, no indication of the presence of the cult of the hunter god at any of these sites.

There is place-name evidence for a further *nemeton* on the west side of the Cotswolds, in an area of woodland containing undated banks. Nympsfield is securely placed on the west edge of the Cotswold Hills; it was recorded as *Nymdesfelda* (AD 862) which is thought to be derived from **nimeto-feld*, the open country of the shrine or holy place (Smith 1964, (b), ii.243–244). The usual interpretation of **nemeton*, however, is sacred grove (Rivet and Smith 1979, 242). The name has been associated with a shrine at Uley, which had a single standing post, but this seems unlikely as the term grove implies a collection of trees. There are some accounts of undated linear banks in the area and, from the Woodchester charter, it is known that the area was extremely wooded and that other communities believed that they had rights in the area. The extension of this woodland from Woodchester to Wotton-under-Edge is implied by the names. Throughout the *Dobunnic* area there are villas which have in them what are termed Orpheus mosaics. On one hand this is an Empire-wide motif, but on the other it seems to have been conflated locally with the idea of the hunter cult and the lord of the animals (Boon 1989, 201–217; Henig 1996, 97–103; Merrifield 1996, 105–113). The standard image is that of a figure, playing a Lyre and wearing a Phrygian cap, in a central roundel accompanied by two animals, one of which is a dog. The largest example of this type of mosaic was found at Woodchester Villa (Lysons 1797). The juxta-position of the elaborate villa at Woodchester, with its Orpheus Mosaic, to the apparent *nemeton* may well be important.

It is also possible that a nemeton once existed between Rendcomb and Chedworth. The reason for considering this is that there is a recognised prehistoric bank without any known function. Above the villa at Chedworth there is also evidence of a circular temple associated with the hunter-god. The image of the hunter-god on this sculpture is complete, and he is again accompanied by a dog, a stag, and a hare (Henig 1993, no. 110). Other evidence for the presence of a hunting cult at Chedworth includes two other sculptures. One is the torso of a draped figure with a V-shaped strap, to which is attached a quiver. The base and the feet of the other statue wearing sandals have been identified as representing Diana (Henig 1993, nos. 21, 22), but too little of it remains to be able to ascribe it to that goddess confidently; interestingly, the hunter god on the votive relief also has bare legs. This sculptural evidence in itself points to a hunting temple in the vicinity. Meanwhile, further up the Coln valley at Withington, one of the mosaics recovered by Lysons was an Orpheus Mosaic, and this site may also have had a villa associated with the wooded area.

Four other, similar, votive reliefs have also been found in the Cotswold area: at Stancomb Wood near Winchcombe, at Bisley church, at Cherington (Henig 1993, no. 113) and at Box in the south Cotswolds. The Box relief (Cunliffe and Fulford 1982, no. 122) is in an area where undated linear banks can be found. Further mosaics of the Orpheus type have also been found at Barton (Fox 1951, 51–53), and Cirencester (Zeepvat 1979, 65–73).

THE MENDIP *NEMETONS*

There were possibly at least two nemetons located in the Mendips. One of these was in the vicinity of Winford and Chew Stoke. The temple at Pagans Hill was an octagonal temple which has been completely robbed out, and, consequently, the only sculptural piece, recovered from the well, was of a dog from a cult statue. The statue fits into the general pattern and style of the hunter-god, *Cunomaglos*. The temple site at Chew Stoke lay over the remains of a linear Iron-Age ditch (ApSimon, Rahtz *et al.* 1958, 97–105). This pattern of activity parallels that at Blunt's Green and the Oldbury site on the Hobditch causeway, in that the boundary ditch running under the temple site was part of the sacred enclosure of a *nemeton*, flattened in one place for the construction of a temple. There are claims of a *nemeton* place-name associated with this area.

In the central area of the Mendips, around Mendip Beacon, are two hill-forts, Measbury and Mearhead. These lie at either end of a large linear ditch. The area to the north of this is considered, from place-name evidence, to have been woodland, and the Beacon is described as being the heart of the Mendip Forest. Much has been claimed about the Beacon, but little has been identified categorically. In the east Mendips are two villas which contain examples of Orpheus Mosaics, near Nunney and at Newton Saint Loe (Russell 1991, 2–23).

THE CORSE *NEMETON*

In the valley near Gloucester is further evidence of such a site, as excavations along the Portway have identified the remains of an octagonal temple. This has produced a relief of a deity wearing a Phrygian cap. The presence of a wooded landscape in the Twyver valley is also indicated by the place-names Wotton and Barnwood. At the Portway site the Octagonal temple lay alongside another unidentified building.

THE DEAN *NEMETON*

Place-name evidence and medieval traditions indicate that there was probably a nemeton in the east part of the Forest of Dean, around Cinderford. The place-name recorded as *Metambala* occurred in the *Ravenna Cosmography* in what has been considered to be a corrupted form of **Nemetobala* (Rivet and Smith 1979, 424). The meaning attributed to it is **nemeto-*, **sacred grove** and the Celtic **balma*, **pointed rock**, or **peak** or *bal*, **steep beach**, or **steep slope**. The name has been reassessed as *Nemetovala* (Breeze 2002, 49–51), the last syllable of which has been interpreted as *gwawl*, derived from *fala*, **rampart**. This seems more appropriate. It has been claimed that the name was associated with Lydney Park camp, but this is extremely unlikely as there is no real indication that Lydney Park complex was ever associated with a sacred grove or tree cult. In the East Dean area there are numerous undated banks which, it could be argued, formed the boundaries of the sacred nemeton. Historically, this area is also recognised as a royal hunting ground and, in the Mabinogion, it is recorded that

Arthur came to the Forest of Dean to hunt the white stag, examples of which, interestingly, can still be seen in the area.

THE MALVERN *NEMETON*

There is evidence for a further *nemeton* to the west of the Malverns in and around Mathon and Cradley. In this area two large linear banks, crossing the valley, have been identified. It has also been recognised that the original construction of the Shire Ditch, which runs along the line of the Malvern Hills between two hill-forts, must also be Bronze Age, as the earliest bank lies under one of the hill-fort ramparts. This area has, to a large extent, been associated with the Malvern Chase, which originated as an area of Royal Forest. Again, in the case of the *nemeton* at Mathon, there are indications that hill-forts were created as part of the bank system. Sometimes this may have been coincidental or fortuitous but in others it was probably integral to the activities and function of the fort.

THE *NEMETON* AND SILVA

When studying the landscape one cannot but arrive at the same conclusion as Derks; which was that upland or distinct topographical regions were deified. Through place-name evidence, both Roman and medieval, it is possible to identify certain topographical areas as *silva*, or woodland. The name may have originally described a wooded landscape, but in many places became symbolic, in much the same way that *wald* did for the Cotswolds. The *silva*, however, represented only one aspect of this culture; the other aspect is the *nemeton*. It seems that the *nemeton* were an integral part of the pre-Roman deification of the large topographical areas and each of them covered many hectares. To identify the *nemeton* is to re-examine and redefine some of our most familiar monuments; the large bank systems of Bronze and Iron Age date which apparently have no centre of occupation. These bank systems have two other components, an association with longstanding forests, used for hunting, and the bank systems that link the Iron-Age enclosures built into or onto the systems. In the case of Oldbury and the juxtaposition of the later hunting temple it is possible to surmise that there was a relationship between the enclosures and woodland banks, and that the enclosures or hill-forts may well have operated as a social location for the gathering of a community, or an elite, for the carrying out of certain actions associated with the woodland area or *nemeton*. It is possible then that certain hill-forts may have been involved with hunting traditions and that these can be recognised. If this type of activity was being earmarked as an important event in a natural cycle it is probable that other activities, such as fishing, may also have been associated with the construction of such sites.

If these areas contained an area of woodland in historic times it is highly probable that they did so far earlier and one can then see these as the sacred groves recorded by the Roman ethnographers. These sacred groves may well have been associated with the worship of the topographical area, thus integrating the deification of geographical determinism with a ritual social action. If this was so, then it would imply that the deification of the large topographical areas, which can be recognised epigraphically in the Roman period, originated as the deification of large areas of enclosed primordial woodland. Although it is possible that this was happening it is difficult to prove definitively. If this was the case it implies that the forest regimes, and their use by the hunting social elite, may have started at a far earlier date than is now thought.

In the Roman period shrines, originally circular and later octagonal, were constructed on platforms built into the banks of the *nemeton* or over a levelled part of the bank. These shrines were associated with the hunter god, who was portrayed in a tunic and accompanied by his three compatriots, the hare, the stag, and most importantly, the dog, which gave him his name. It seems that the deity had his origins in the territory of the *Dobunni* and, from the reference in the Mabinogion, must have originated as the deity of a river called *Cunomaglos*. Only later would he have become a deity of social action and hunting, in a form in which he could be exported from the *Dobunnic* territory. It is, using *Cunomaglos* perhaps, possible to give a first hint at a process of evolving folk-tradition. The woodland banks had temples constructed on them to this god. During the early medieval period the name Grim's Ditch was used for the Wychwood banks. Grim was another name for Woden, who carried out a mythical hunt across the landscape in search of the souls of the dead. This may mean that Wansdyke is a variation of this name. The Hobditch causeway also fits into this idea of an evolving folk-tradition, as Hob was the name of the devil. The name of the deity may have changed but the landscape themes remained the same. The *nemeto were developed in the Iron-Age landscape as areas of forest which were held to be sacred. They bore the names of the presiding deity, yet were also associated with a god that represented interaction with the natural world. In these landscapes the concept of *domus* and wildwood were inverted, and the wilderness became enclosed. In essence, the *nemeton* represented the soul of the *silva* in which they were located and enabled the communities to focus their ritual activity in one place.

Chapter 8

Tree Shrines

An assessment of the archaeological evidence and ancient sources has indicated that sacred sites may have taken a number of different forms. Hill-forts seem to have had a limited but important focus, which could possibly be assessed from the typological and artefactual evidence at each site. This could include religious and economic evidence, as well as information concerning: fostering, warfare, relationship to sacred woods or *nemetons*, barrows, and small satellite enclosures (see Chapter 9); diverse features which were probably used seasonally. It is apparent that there were clusters of hill-forts and that each member of the group probably had a separate religious function.

Very few examples of religious sites dating from before the Roman invasion have been discussed, although there is some evidence that Roman style shrines were being developed from the late Iron Age in various parts of the country; for example on Hayling Island, Hampshire, outside the *Dobunnic* territory. The *nemetons* were probably the largest religious sanctuaries ever constructed in Britain and Gaul and covered many hectares (see Chapter 7). The use of the sacred grove is only one aspect of the worship of trees and plants, the other being the deification of individual plants.

From the Continent there are a number of examples of these tree or post sanctuaries, most notably those excavated in Germany, for example at Goloring and Goldburg (Green 1989, 151–155). Religious inscriptions and sculpture have also been found throughout Gaul and it is evident that trees were venerated right across north-west Europe in a singular and, in some cases, a dual form. There is further evidence that standing columns were used in the Roman world and that the Jupiter columns had their surfaces carved like the bark on a tree (Bauchhenss 1976, abb.41).

These traditions have also been seen in early medieval Germany, other parts of Britain, and in Ireland. In Germany, the Irminshul, a sacred post marking the centre of the territory of the Saxon peoples, was cut down by Charlemagne; the cutting down of the Gaesmere Oak in AD 772 may have had a similar significance (Wilson 1992, 42). Ross (Ross 1967, 59–65) identified named sacred trees as a focus for religious activity in Irish and Welsh medieval mythology. She discussed the importance of specific trees; for example, from Irish mythology: Omna, Tortu's Tree, Eo Rosa, Éo Magna, and Dath-í (an ash); and from Welsh mythology: the marvellous oak of *Lleu* the eagle. There is evidence, from the Irish sources, that these trees were used for seasonal gatherings. Even though the enclosures did not have the characteristics of the Iron-Age hill-forts they probably served a similar purpose.

There is some evidence that Christian standing crosses may have been a development from the Roman Jupiter column or votive column, and that the image of one god was simply replaced by the image of another (Henig 2004, 11–28). It is apparent that in the *Hwicce* territory the high crosses of the early medieval period would also have been established in enclosures or religious precincts. The argument can also be addressed through the use of the carved imagery on the crosses, much of it is interlacing, reminiscent of entwined branches, while Adam and Eve motifs are also a common theme on many of the surviving sculptures.

SHRINES OF TREES

The standard Greco-Roman and Romano-Celtic temples are not the only types of religious structure which require consideration. Natural imagery connected to the *Dobunnic* area has been found, most notably that on their coinage. Symbolically, it falls into two major types: a branch emblem, and a triple-tailed horse (Allen 1961, 75–149). The *Dobunnic* branch emblem has been compared with classical images, such as the palm branch, and laurel spray. The image has many similarities with the stylised conifer trees found on Romano-Gallic sculpture, especially in Aquitaine and the Belgic areas. In Britain a similar design has also been recognised on a Roman ring found in London; it has also appeared in graffiti at the military sites at Gellygear, South Wales, and Camelon, Scotland, and the civilian site at Barnsley Park, Gloucestershire (Webster and Smith 1982, 134, 173). At the military sites the emblem was possibly an allusion to victory and may represent a laurel wreath, but the civilian site of Barnsley Park is considered to have preserved an image which had some religious significance to the owners who were *Dobunni*. If this was so then it may well have something to do with images displayed on earlier tribal coinage.

The designs on Iron-Age coinage, it has been claimed, were adapted from those on early Roman and Macedonian coins, gemstones and other small objects. The images on the coins have been considered to have used specific types of tribal emblems; the branch for the *Dobunni*, the wheat ear for the *Catuvellauni*, and the vine leaf for the *Atrebates*. The coins are also believed to have imitated Roman traditions and were being used in a process of propaganda. If this is right, British leaders must have been using coins to project both themselves and their tribe, and to compete with other groups.

Dobunnic coins bearing the name EISV have been found; this term may refer to a legendary *Dobunnic* king. A pan-Gallic context can, however, be identified for the name, the Gallic god, *Deo Esus*, who was associated with human sacrifice and sacred groves. The name was recorded in a gloss on Lucan's Pharsalia, and was also inscribed on an altar from Paris. In the associated image, *Esus* is depicted chopping down a willow tree. An altar from Trier carries the same image but has no inscription (CIL 1899, no. 3026; Espérandieu 1915, no. 4929). That a god of this name may have been worshipped in the *Dobunnic* area is also perhaps indicated by the name of the river Isbourne, which has been interpreted as being derived from *Esa*. How individual trees or tree species were associated with this tradition is not known, and would be difficult to determine.

The persistent use of tree images on coins from the area is of interest because it relates to other archaeologically identifiable activities. A number of middle and late Iron-Age sites consisting of a single post or tree within an enclosure have been located in the lands of the *Dobunn*ic area. Excavations at Bubbenhall Quarry, Warwickshire, in 2005, uncovered the remains of a middle Iron-Age settlement (400–100 BC) containing the remains of an enclosure 20m across. It had been re-dug at least six times, and contained a single tree or standing post. The site has been interpreted as having been part of a ritual or ceremonial centre (Yeates 2006, i.68). A similar site, called the Ring, a circular bank and ditch in a similar location at the head of a combe, exists on Cleeve Hill (RCHME 1976, 107–108), but no research has been carried out on this site.

A similar site, set in the same type of location on a plateau at the head of a valley is that of the Uley Shrine (Woodward and Leach 1993, 13–32). Excavations at West Hill uncovered the remains of a Neolithic ditch, forming a U-shape. This had been adapted, reused, and developed, in the late Iron Age, into an enclosure in which there was a large central pit, believed by the excavators to have been the location of a tree or post. Due to the hypothetical interpretation of a long barrow it has been argued that the site was associated with ancestral beliefs. The significance of the tree may have survived in some folk tradition, as the sacred tree of Uley may have been the yew which forms part of the village place-name.

At Custom Scrubs, Bisley, the remains of a sacred enclosure was partially quarried away in 1799 (Saint Clair Baddeley 1925, 87–90). The site has, nevertheless, produced three Roman period votive reliefs. The recess of one of these houses the figure of a standing god, dressed in a tunic. He holds a *cornucopia* in his left hand and a *patera*, above an altar, in his right. The inscription accompanying this figure is now no longer visible, due to weathering, but has been recorded as MARTI OLLVDIO, see Figure 46. The name has been translated as **the great tree**. A god with a similar name was worshiped in southern Gaul, at *Ollioules*. There are a number of important things to note about the shrine of *Olludios* at Custom Scrubs; the first of which is its location on a plateau area at the head of a valley river system. In all of these sites there is uniformity of location; what this means, however, is not as yet apparent.

Also interesting is the name of the nearest farm to the shrine at Custom Scrubs Wittantree Farm. The earliest references are actually to a Wittantree Quarry, probably the nearest quarry to the farm, which was on the Roman religious site. The Wittantree is believed to have been the meeting place of the hundred (Smith 1964, i.128), hence hundred courts and other activities would have been held around the tree in the Anglo-Saxon period at least. In both the Roman and the early medieval periods the site would have been associated with a sacred tree where specific, if as yet unknown, activities took place. The images from both sites were strikingly similar despite being from different periods and it is probable that the functions were also similar.

A shrine has been excavated at Lansdown, above the head of the valley of the Lam Brook (VCH(So1) 1906, 302–303; Bush 1905, 57–61). Little is known about it, but it seems to have the basic layout as the sites discussed previously.

A number of hill-fort sites have small outlying circular enclosures; the vast majority of these have never been investigated, but they must have served a specific purpose.

One of these sites, that at Kingsdown Camp, has had its banks and ditches excavated (Saint George Gray 1929, 100–104), but not its interior. It dates from the late Iron Age, but was reworked in the early Roman period. The finds have included numerous human bones from infant burials. Place-name studies have also associated a significant number of hill-forts with trees from historic times. These include the Yew-burh, and Plum tree-burh, to name but two.

Similar sites, with a post in an enclosure, were located in lowland valleys, close to places of settlement. During the late Iron Age, an enclosure was constructed at Longford (Atkin 1990, 2–13; Atkin and Garrod 1990, 185–192; Frere 1990, 347; Wacher 1995, 163). At the centre of this enclosure was a post or tree pit. Although the shape of the enclosure may not have been the same, the similarity in organisation indicates that the site's function was probably similar.

Figure 46: The relief of Mars Olludios, from Custom Scrubs near Bisley (photograph used courtesy of Gloucester City Museum).

Excavations in Bath Street and Beau Street in Bath have identified a ditch with a causeway, which although not traced fully, was believed to have enclosed an area with very few structural features, and which saw intensive activity in the first century AD (Davenport 1999, 22–37). In the enclosure were the remains of four post-holes, believed to have been for free-standing posts. Their sequence is unknown, so it is possible that they may have replaced each other rather than have been standing at the same time. The enclosure was located between the three hot springs, which was, at the time, outside the main area of settlement, located on the other side of the Avon. One other way of considering the nature of these sites is by looking at the way in which the settlement and the ceremonial sites relate to the topographical features associated with the tud or folk-group and to the presiding spirit of the Roman town. In the case of Gloucester, the deified river seems to have been Horsebere Brook; on which the

Longford settlement lies. In the case of Bath the goddess's name was shared with the spring's, and the enclosure was located between all three of them.

The sites at Bubbenhall, Uley, Custom Scrubs, Longford, and Bath must be taken as the earliest known sites with an enclosure and post design. Although there are variations in the enclosures' designs the essential components are always present. They were certainly regarded as sites of religious significance. This type of religious site had developed by at least the Iron Age and it can be seen that each had two distinct parts, one at the head of the valley and the other low down in the valley, possibly on a significant river, associated with the folk-group. The sites on the hills seem to have gone through various adaptations during the Roman period; at Uley there was considerable elaboration, and a shrine must have been constructed over the enclosure at Custom Scrubs. Other sites, however, such as those at Longford and Bubbenhall, were abandoned.

Similar symbolic sites were, presumably, created in the hearts of *Dobunnic* towns during the Roman period. A possible later development of this tradition may be detected at Cirencester where the remains of a capital and inscribed base, associated with a Jupiter column, have been found (Henig 1993, no. 18; RIB(I) 1995, no. 103). On the capital, four figures, with Bacchic characteristics, are portrayed. An inscription from a column provides information about the erection of this column, or a similar one, in the fourth century AD. Similar columns, found on the continent, were carved with imbricated surfaces resembling bark and foliage. One can, therefore, assume from this that they represented, in some way, the tree or post at the centre of a tree-veneration cult, as has been discussed. It is not known precisely where the Cirencester column stood, but the capital was found in the area of the forum or the *Capitolia*. Both of these areas would have been enclosed, thus keeping to the basic design of an enclosure and post site. The material representation has, evidently, gone through a technological overhaul which probably corresponded to changes in the underlying ideas. On the other hand the simplest description of an enclosed space, this time with a portico and a single standing column are the same.

It was mentioned above that elaboration occurred at some of the shrines and not at others. In the case of Bath, a major elaboration of the site occurred; the underlying idea of the enclosure or temenos and single standing post or column, however, was maintained. The temple complex contained a quadrangular niched monument and also, what has been interpreted as, a large monumental altar. Doubts have been raised about these interpretations as some of the types of sculpture from this area seem to belong to a votive or Jupiter column (Yeates 2006, i.69). The Jupiter column at Hauser-an-der-Zaber has a quadrangular base section with carved figures set in niches on each of the four sides. It is highly likely that the quadrangular monument may have been part of the base of a column which stood in the religious enclosure.

There are two types of areas, within the Roman towns of Cirencester and Bath, where tree or column images could be found: in the major porticoed enclosures associated with the forum, alongside the basilica, which would have had an *aedes* or shrine to the tribal deity; in the large porticoed areas in which major temples would have been located, for example the probable location of the *capitolia*; and in the *temenos* enclosures of temples. This architectural tradition seems to have occurred in other *Dobunnic* towns; for example a sculpture, apparently showing the image of the Gloucester city *tyche*, is shaped as though it came from one of these standing columns. The nearest open space to the place from where this sculpture was recovered is the open area to the north-east of the forum. At least one temple is considered to have stood here. All of this may imply that there was a folk-group connection with the columns. The site at Longford may have gone out of use but it is possible that the activities carried out at the Iron-Age site may have been moved to an area inside the town, near to the central temple complex. The images and designs seen in these examples may have similarities, but it is always difficult to draw direct conclusions from them.

During the early medieval period the importance of a standing post or tree was still important. Nennius (Morris 1980) offers an important piece of information to support the significance of the sanctity of the trees. He listed as the ninth wonder of Britain an ash tree on which apples grew. It was located on a hill above the estuary of the river Wye. Where this tree or shrine was located is not known, but it is the case that Ashberry and Yewbury are place-names recorded on the Gloucestershire side of the Wye estuary. Many of the sites discussed by Nennius were specialised natural locations on which Roman shrines had been built; these included: Bath, and Droitwich in the *Hwicce*, and the Windcliffe, in Gwent. Even if a shrine had gone out of use by this time it is possible that Welsh historians recorded these facts as traditions, and that the veneration of the sites was maintained, albeit in a less formal way.

There are other early medieval sites at which standing posts or trees have been identified, and there is circumstantial evidence that one site may have continued in use from the Iron-Age into the Roman period. Gravel extraction at Bampton, Oxfordshire, has uncovered a major late Iron-Age settlement (Yeates 2006, ii.295–304), which continued to develop into the Roman period. Investigations at a site called the Beam have identified the remains of a medieval chapel, but from the place-names Beam, which means the **standing post**, and Bampton, **the settlement of the standing post**, it has been hypothesised that there was probably an enclosure at the edge of the Roman-period settlement which had a central standing post (Blair 1994, 64; Gelling 1954, 304). This cannot, however, be substantiated archaeologically. Another medieval place-name, which referred to a standing post, can be found on the Powick charter bounds (Powick is in Worcestershire) where the name *Sylbeame* was recorded in AD 972; this may refer to **the pillar tree** (Grundy 1927, 164–169).

The medieval church at Glastonbury was located inside a large enclosure of unknown date, yet part of the religious tradition included reference to a sacred hawthorn tree (Carley 1988, 181–184). A sacred nut tree is recorded as having existed at Longney, Gloucestershire, in *The life of Saint Wulstan* (Heighway 1987, 120–121). This was a full-bodied tree under which games and feasting were carried out; it was cut down, on the orders of the church, in the eleventh century AD.

Though there are references to sacred trees being cut down, there is also evidence that these sites and images were being reused. The *parochia* of Gloucester covered much of Dudstone Hundred. The name was derived from an area to the north-east of the city, presumed to be in the vicinity of Wotton, where there had been numerous Roman-period enclosures associated with extensive cemeteries. From 144 London Road, in the area, the remains of a large Mercian standing cross were recovered in 1889, during building work (Dobson 1933, 266: GLRCM A2654). Dudstone was the hundred's meeting place and the location of a court. The cross was possibly the stone at which the hundred held its court.

CONCLUSION

There is no single example which shows how such sites developed and were reused, but we do have an example of the repetitive reuse of a theme, for a religious purpose, which dated back to the Iron Age. The post in the enclosure replaced the tree; the wooden post was then replaced by a stone column. These columns were central places, symbolic of the community and its group identity. The columns of the Roman period were then replaced by the high crosses of Christianity, standing in minster enclosures and probably also in enclosures of their own; these, again, would have been established for community activities. This reuse and manipulation of a common theme, evident from the Iron Age, has been exploited by subsequent developing religious beliefs. The traditions that were present amongst the *Dobunni* and *Hwicce* fit into a wider European tradition, and also into a world tradition of sacred trees and standing totem poles. The use of the tree, or wooden post, continues in some traditions, but in some instances there has been a change to stone use, which was first seen in the Roman period and was presumably stimulated by technical developments.

Chapter 9

Religion as a Focus for Burial

An important relationship existed between the hill-forts, temples and, burial sites of the *Dobunnic/Hwicce* area which developed over centuries and even millennia. The region's burial sites, however, pose a problem. In the south and east burials are found but, in the absence of datable artefacts, they are not always contextualised. In the north and west of the region the finding of any skeletal material is remarkable due to the acidic soils. While recognising that there are drawbacks with the surviving information it is still possible to suggest some general trends.

BURIAL ACTIVITY

A number of late Bronze Age settlements and cemeteries have been located, yet as so few are known it is not apparent what the relationship between them is (Yeates 2006, i.76). The only site which has given any information for this is at Eynsham, Oxfordshire, where a large settlement, of 1300–900 BC, has been excavated; to its north there is a possible peripheral cremation barrow cemetery. The second, and slightly later Bronze-Age settlement, at Mead Lane, Eynsham, also has evidence of peripheral cremation burials. These limited examples, however, are not enough to enable a recognisable pattern, which can be transposed across the rest of the area, to be seen. The late Bronze-Age settlements at Shorncote Quarry and Hucclecote seem to have been associated with an area of middle Bronze-Age burials. There is also a late Bronze-Age cemetery at Mathon (Blake 1913, 90–93; 1908–11, 180–181; Jack 1911, 235–236; Hamilton 1938, 120–127), where burials were described as being laid in rows, with burnt bones and urns placed by their heads. Unfortunately, this site was disturbed by sand extraction at an early date. Other burials from this period are isolated, but this may be due to the circumstances of survival.

    Certain Neolithic and Bronze-Age burial mounds are thought to have still been important at the start of the Iron Age, as a number of hill-fort locations were built around promontories or hill-tops, on which a number of the earlier monuments are located (Burrow 1981, 228–230). Examples of this phenomenon include Small Down Knoll, Somerset, where excavations of the Iron-Age hill-fort confirmed that burial mounds there were of Bronze-Age date. The camp at Westbury-sub-Mendip has a Bronze-Age round barrow in a central place, while the northern Priddy Circle, Somerset, is the only one of the Priddy Circles which has round barrows incorporated into the camp (Taylor and Tratman 1957, 7–17; Pevsner 1958, 247). Then there is Maiden Hill in Randwick Wood where there is known to be a Neolthic long barrow and a Bronze-Age round barrow (RCHME 1976, 97).

The site of the Big Ring at Cassington also had a number of round barrows, surrounded by an Iron-Age enclosure (Yeates 2006, ii.744–745), although there is little evidence of Iron-Age settlement until the late Iron Age. At Willersey Hill there is limited archaeological evidence of occupation, but in a central part of the camp there is evidence of a Neolithic long barrow (RCHME 1976, 128–130). On the western edge of the study area there is evidence for a hill-fort on the Doward, where there is also evidence of round barrows located within the enclosure (Pevsner 1963, 135). It is difficult to determine the intent of the builders, but for those which have undergone some form of excavation or salvage work it seems that there is little evidence of occupation. If these sites operated in the same way as other hill-fort locations then it is possible that, as these were the only monuments in the enclosure, they acted as a focus for seasonal gatherings. If this was so, then the tombs must have been significant, possibly for ancestral reasons.

It is also possible that these sites operated as places at which the worlds of the living and the dead came together, and that community gatherings and celebrations took place. These festivals could have been fore-runners of May Day and All Souls, the festivals that, in the medieval period, were considered to take place at the time when the souls of the dead could move between the two worlds. In Ireland, at Cruachan, folk-traditions exist that describe the process of moving between our world of the living and the other world. In local folk-tradition at Churchdown Hill, there was claimed to be a fairy funeral which entered the hill near Mussels Well, which lay near the entrance to the hill-fort gates.

Hill-forts with very little occupation activity may have been built around barrows, but it is not apparent that Iron-Age burials were carried out in these enclosures. The early Iron-Age cemetery of twenty-one crouched pit burials at Christon offers the only major funerary site from this period (Morris 1988, 23–81). There was evidence of the deposition of grave goods, and dogs, placed alongside one of the burials. The location of the cemetery, and its relationship to a settlement, is unknown, but a palisade trench was located at the same time, perhaps indicating a peripheral location to some type of enclosure. The site also lies below the small hilltop enclosure at Elborough.

A number of burial sites of the middle Iron Age have been located. There are at least three cemeteries at Yarnton, near an early to middle Iron Age settlement, which could have been satellite cemeteries (Yeates 2006, ii.741–742). Excavations uncovered some thirty-five burials, concentrated in two groups. The third cemetery, of an Iron Age date, may have been disturbed from 1850–1870, as there are references to an area of considerable deposits of urns and bones. Some of the inhumations are described as crouched and the majority of the finds from the area were Iron Age. At Barnwood (Yeates 2006, ii.815–816), near Gloucester, there is further evidence of middle Iron-Age settlement and of a cemetery, although the information and the surviving data are not good. This site was first used in the early Bronze Age for a Beaker burial, but was also used from the second century BC to the second century AD as a cemetery. Only one burial, a female with an urn as a grave good, has been dated to this time, but other undated crouched burials from the site are recorded. The cemetery is known to have produced at least ten late Iron Age cremations, and continued into the Roman period.

Two major types of Iron Age cemetery site which have been identified, with differently determined foci, either large settlements or large enclosures. The major settlement of the Gloucester area in the late Iron-Age was established at Longford where there is a cemetery peripheral to the settlement (Yeates 2006, ii.817–818). Another significant late Iron-Age to early Roman cemetery is known from Eastington, where over forty inhumations and one cremation were recovered (Chouls 1993, 8–20). Though Roman material was scattered across the field, this was not recovered from the graves. The finds from one grave included a late Iron-Age potsherd, while the cremation was in a late Iron-Age pot.

At Bagendon, some six late Iron-Age cremations in urns were found at the church, in a location peripheral to the Bagendon settlement (Clifford 1961, 155). Other late Iron-Age burials were placed in close proximity to hill-forts; for example: at King's Weston, where six extended burials had late Iron Age pottery in their fills (Tratman 1923, 76–82; 1925, 238–243); and in the Birdlip and Crickley burials which overlook Crickley Hill-fort (Stealens 1982, 19–31). Antiquaries have described the recovery of late Iron-Age urns from Leckhampton Hill (Yeates 2006, ii.523–524), and there is also a square barrow at the site which may be of a similar date. In the hill-fort of Nottingham Hill a burial was uncovered, along with a lance head of prehistoric date (RCHME 1976, 59). It is apparent that burials were occurring in the periphery of large late Iron Age settlements and probably also around hill-forts. This seems to have been part of a wider trend of using settlement and religious sites as the focus for burials. The burials during this period occurred by two distinct methods, cremation and inhumation. What this tells us about society has not been established. It could indicate that there were movements of people in and out of the communities, from other places where alternative methods were practiced. This seems to provide the best explanation, but it also indicates that people attempted to bring in their cultural traditions, when they moved, rather than adapt to those that already existed in a place.

We know that there were peripheral cemeteries around the major Roman towns; evidence has been found for this at Gloucester, Cirencester, and Bath (Yeates 2006, i.77). At Gloucester, burials continued at Barnwood, and Longford; while in the late Roman period further cemeteries were established at Barton, Saint Oswald's, and outside the Southgate. Outside Cirencester there are also a number of cemetery sites, which also conform to general Roman period norms. These are found at: the Silchester Gate, the Bath Gate, the Gloucester Gate, and the Verulamium Gate. Bath also has numerous Roman period cemeteries which were in peripheral locations.

It seems that this was the general practice, as it can also be seen with some of the smaller towns. There is a large cemetery at Cassington which must have been on the edge of a Roman nucleated settlement (Yeates 2006, ii.742–743, 750). The cemetery at Rosebury, under the eastern suburbs of Bristol, is also considered to have been on the edge of a Roman nucleated settlement (Yeates 2006, ii.367–368). The mixture of cremations and inhumations seen in the late Iron Age continued into the Roman period. More evidence for this mixture of practices being due to influxes of people is, perhaps, provided by the finding of a Roman tombstone at Gloucester. It was of a Belgic warrior and was associated with a Roman cremation urn.

In the late Roman period, during the third and fourth centuries AD, burial also occurred by inhumation and cremation but, it seems, there were at least two other burial locations other than the previously described peripheral sites. These are: in the centre of towns, and adjacent to Roman temples. The use of temples for cemetery sites was most notable in the county of Somerset, at a number of its major temple sites. A cemetery was established at Henley Wood temple during the late-Roman period; it continued into the post-Roman period (Watts and Leach 1996). In the fifth century or after, the veranda or ambulatory of the temple had fallen or was taken down, but the burials continued around the central *cella*. At Lamyatt Beacon there is another temple with a satellite cemetery (Leech 1986, 259–328); this activity can also be recognised at Brean Down (Bell 1990). The temple site on Lansdown Hill, near the Granville Monument, has also produced evidence of religious sculpture and a peripheral Roman cemetery (VCH(So1) 1906, 302–303; Bush 1905, 57–61).

In Gloucestershire, evidence for burial activity has been identified around the temple site at Uley (Yeates 2006, ii.488–489). Although this is the only temple site in Gloucestershire where the association between burials and a religious site has been discussed there are a number of other sites in the county where this activity occurred. With most of these sites, as in Somerset, the burials started in the late Roman period and continued into the sub-Roman (early medieval) period. The religious inscriptions and sculpture which have been uncovered at Kingsholm, and the description and drawing of an artificial hill in the Gentleman's Magazine, indicate that there had been a temple site there, as mentioned. The temple seems to have been a martial temple, and it is perhaps this factor which is relevant, as this type of temple would obviously see a lot of burials (Yeates 2006, i.78). The evidence indicates that the cemetery at Kingsholm first became a burial ground in the second century AD, and continued in use into the fifth century AD. Antiquarian sources add further information, referring to thousands of burials being found at the Kingsholm gravel pits during the building of the Victorian suburbs, some of which were 'Anglo-Saxon'. This implies burials with weapons, generally associated with the fifth to seventh centuries AD. No finds are known to have survived from these accounts but it is evident from some of the descriptions, which list swords, spears, and battle-axes, should be given some credence. Lysons described a find of sixty blue glass beads in the cemetery; these are rare in Roman period burials, but common in post-Roman (early-medieval) graves. More importantly, a shield boss, of the sixth or seventh centuries AD, which came from the Kingsholm Close excavations of 1972, may also have been used as a grave good.

There seems to have been enough evidence at this site to consider that burial activity went on in Kingsholm for a period of at least 600 years. There is also evidence that the site was chosen not simply because it was peripheral to the town but also, because there was a war temple. The later burials, described as Anglo-Saxon and associated with weapons, mean that it is possible to see social action and religious cult combining in a way which has not been recognised previously. Other sites in Gloucester where temples were probably located were used for late Roman and sub-Roman burials (Yeates 2006, i.78). There is an antiquaries' description of a raft of stones outside the Eastgate of Gloucester. The size of the feature described means that one possibility is that it is likely to have been the podium of a temple, but alternatively could have been part of a triumphal arch. The Barton cemetery of the third and fourth centuries, although it lies outside the *colonia* wall, seems also to have developed around this site.

Late Roman burials inside the urban centres of towns have been claimed at certain sites; for example Kenchester, and Cirencester, but it is possible that these have not been dated correctly (Yeates 2006, i.79). They could well be later and the pottery found could be residual. The reason for believing that this is the case is that these burials, in the walls of towns, were prohibited under Roman law. They should not be considered to have occurred until the Roman way of life was changing and new ideas concerning religious activity and beliefs were being introduced.

The trends evident in the late Roman period continued into the sub-Roman period. Sub-Roman cemeteries can be recognised in locations peripheral to the Roman settlements at Kenchester; Black Banks near Evesham; Staple Hill, near Bidford; Bidford-on-Avon; and Tiddington (Yeates 2006, i.78–79). The Somerset religious sites of Henley Wood, Lamyatt Beacon, and Brean Down continued to have interments during this period. This tradition can also be seen at Wasperton, Warwickshire, where a shrine was probably founded over the Iron-Age settlement. The site has produced part of a Roman religious sculpture, although the exact location in the settlement was not identified. In the early medieval period, the fifth and sixth centuries, the site became the focus for a cemetery. There was also a sub-Roman period cemetery to the south of the Lower Slaughter Chessels, along the line of the Fosse Way. This cemetery seems to have been adjacent to the sanctuary of *Cuda* at the confluence of the Eye and Dickler. The island shrine located at Hereford also has evidence for significant burial grounds, but the date at which they started is unknown. One of the sites was located around the temple-cathedral while the other was under the castle. One of the early burials uncovered under the castle was described as having the jaw bone deposited between the legs. This particular activity is considered to be either late Roman or sub-Roman. This means that burials commenced in this area at a far earlier date than had previously been thought.

It was probably in the fifth century or later when burial activity occurred in the centre of the Roman towns. Temples in towns acted as major foci for the ritual activity of burying the dead. At Saint Mary de Lode, Gloucester, the site of a substantial building, believed to be a temple, which was associated with fifth century AD human remains (Bryant and Heighway 2003, 97–178). At Cirencester, the insula, to the south-east of the forum, was possibly the site of a Capitoline temple and an undated burial has been recovered from a road-side ditch in this area (Yeates 2006, i.78–79). In the Ashcroft area of the same town, religious sculpture has been recovered. This is also an area of the town where numerous undated burials have been unearthed. When the fortification on Bury Hill, Weston-under-Penyard, was flattened, sculpture, of a religious nature, was recovered, along with numerous burials (Fosbrooke 1821, 36). It is possible that this was the site of a temple in the central complex of the town; around this were late Roman, or more probably sub-Roman, burials.

There is evidence that, in the sub-Roman period, the religious ideas associated with hill-fort sites meant that they started being used in the same way as temple locations. Examples of sub-Roman (early medieval) burials in or outside hill-forts occur all across the region (Yeates 2006, i.79); they include: Idbury, Oxfordshire, where some were found in a peripheral location to the camp; and Lyneham Camp, Oxfordshire, where they were within the site and on its periphery. Sub-Roman burials have also been found at Tadmarston Camp, Oxfordshire, and Willersey Camp, Gloucestershire. The remains of a single sub-Roman burial, dated by artefacts, were recovered from Meon Hill, Warwickshire. Undated burials were also found outside the camp at Tytherington, Gloucestershire. In Herefordshire, burials have been recovered from Walls Hill, near Ledbury, and Ivington Camp; no date, however, has been attributed to these finds. At Norbury, Farmington, is a burial claimed to be Iron Age or Roman in date; evidence to date this precisely, however, is lacking.

To emphasise the religious significance of the sub-Roman period burials there are a number of hill-fort sites which contain both a temple and burials. These indicate that the relationship between the sites and the actions being carried out were relatively complex. A number of dates have been attributed to the crouched pit burials at Sutton Walls, found in the hill-fort (Whimster 1981). The excavation report claims, however, that the burials were late in the sequence and that their grave cuts had been truncated (Kenyon 1953, 1–87). This means that they would be either late Roman or sub-Roman in date. The fact that a Roman temple has been described at the site means that this group of burials, although crouched, fit into the normal pattern of burials in the area for the post-Roman period.

There is also evidence of sub-Roman burial at Stow-on-the-Wold, which has previously been described as the location of a hill-fort and temple (Yeates 2006, i.81). Here again, the hill-fort and temple are probably part of a more complicated arrangement, and, as seen before, the temple seems to have had a military association.

There is also evidence for the reuse of Neolithic and Bronze-Age burial mounds in the late Roman and sub-Roman periods. There is a Roman example at Ivy Lodge, and sub-Roman examples at Chavenage, and Foxhill (Darvill and Grinsell 1989, 39–105; O'Neil and Grinsell 1960, 90). The exact nature of most of these burials is not known because of the early date at which they were disturbed. Further burials have been found in such sites that seem to indicate that they were early medieval executions. These are located at two long barrows in the parish of Swell (Darvill and Grinsell 1989, 39–105; O'Neil and Grinsell 1960, 90; Royce 1883, 74–75), where the digits of the hands and feet were missing and spears were placed in the graves in an unusual position. The digits were found in the excavations on the surface of the mounds, probably indicating that the bodies had once been on display.

The evidence of early medieval (middle and late Anglo-Saxon) burial at the sites described continues the older tradition of sacred space, in this case a place where burials take place, being enclosed. At Worcester, burials from the middle and late Anglo-Saxon periods have been found around the church, and a burial with, a third-century AD potsherd, was found in the fill of the town's ditch, which had been used as the monastic *vallum* (Yeates 2006, i.79–80). At Gloucester, middle to late Anglo-Saxon period burials were concentrated outside the west wall of the Roman town; in the area of Saint Oswald's and under what is now the western cloisters of the cathedral. Burials have been found at Bishop's Cleeve, in a ditch which ran around the edge of the minster precinct. They are essentially undated (Parry 1999, 96–98); although they were classed as Roman. In reality, however, they may date from anywhere between the Iron Age and the twelfth century AD. During and after the middle Anglo-Saxon period burials were becoming focused around religious enclosures or inside them.

Excavations in the Priory area at Warwick have uncovered the remains of cremations and burials of sub-Roman to middle Anglo-Saxon date. These burials, along with the choice of Warwick for a minster, imply that the town was the site of an older enclosure which was used for the foundation of the early church (Yeates 2006, ii.80). Within the *parochia* of Bourton-on-the-Water the only middle to late Anglo-Saxon burials located had been buried in the bank of, and around, Salmonsbury. For this site to conform to the pattern evident elsewhere, one must hypothesise that a minster or major church was founded within it, which gave its name to the earliest estate (Yeates 2006). Perhaps, when the manors were obtained by the abbey of Evesham, the site became excess to requirement and, subsequently, only parish churches were needed in the area.

A major minster was founded at Westbury-on-Trym, yet little evidence for older activity has been found at the current church's site. At the site of Saint Werburgh, Henbury, the remains of a chapel have been excavated, with Roman, sub-Roman, and possibly later burials (Burrow 1981, 300–301; Russell and Williams 1984, 18–26; Rahtz and Cleevedon Brown 1959, 154). This is all supposed to overlie the remains of a temple, the evidence for which is ambiguous. Chapels obtaining burial rights from their mother church at an early date have been demonstrated only at Lower Sapey (Hoverd 1997).

CONCLUSIONS

Conclusions concerning the nature of the burial activity have to be made with great caution as many of the burials are undated, and so it would only be possible to give a general overview. Cemeteries could be described as being peripheral to settlement development, on minimal evidence, in the late Bronze-Age and middle Iron-Age, but this becomes increasingly more apparent for the periods from the late Iron-Age to the sub-Roman (early medieval) period. Although there is some evidence of burials being focused on religious sites during the late Iron Age and in the early Roman periods it is in the late Roman period that this activity becomes important. Burial activity continued around temple sites well into the seventh century. What this actually means is not known; one possibility is that there was a change of religious affiliation, but from the evidence at Kingsholm and Stow-on-the-Wold, this seems to have been unlikely and it is probably the case that these burials were located around a war temple, due to the evidence of the weaponry and warrior cult.

The nature of the burial activity in the region varied over time. In the late Bronze-Age the area was dominated by cremation burials. In the early Iron Age there were crouched burials in pits, of which some had grave goods. In the middle Iron Age there are again crouched burials, of which one or two had grave goods. In the late Iron Age there was a mixture of extended inhumations and crouched inhumations along with cremation burials. The easiest way to understand this apparent continuity is through the limited movement of people into the area. The mixture of burials continued through the Roman period, and it is only in the centres, such as Gloucester, where significant numbers of cremations occurred in the early Roman period. Even then there was not a majority of such burials. In the sub-Roman era there was again a mixture of burial practices; crouched and extended inhumation, and some cremation burials. It is difficult to understand what is happening, but it is fair to say that cremations, although they occurred right across the territory seem to have been more concentrated in certain places, especially in the east. This could indicate continuity if an underlying culture remained dominant.

As explained above, some hill-forts, constructed around hill-tops or slopes, were the location of earlier barrows, either Neolithic or Bronze Age. The exact significance of the barrow chosen is not known, but in some cases there is a single central barrow, such as at Willersey, and in others a group of four, such as at Small Down Camp. Where salvage or excavation has taken place there is little evidence that these sites had much evidence of occupation, and one can only hypothesise that the barrows in the enclosure where designed to be the focus for a religious gathering. Therefore, it could be assumed that ritual, and/or changing elites, appropriated an established sacred site and adapted it for their own use. The two festivals where this would have been most appropriate later became the festivals of May Day (Beltane) and All Hallows (Samain). On these two days it was believed that it was possible to move between the lands of the living and the dead. It is highly likely that many of these sites have not been excavated because they seem sparse in material finds. However, this presumes an evidential certainty that does not exist and medieval texts are only mirrors of the social certainties of desired elites. Therefore, we can not know for sure.

Chapter 10

The Sacred Horse

The horse occurs in the archaeological record of the *Dobunni* in the form of carved and monetary images and as skeletal remains in burials. There has long been a call for a discussion of the significance of the horse in Britain. In north-west Europe, when such artefacts were created, textual evidence does not exist, but still there are indications that, in the Bronze Age, horse fittings were distributed widely. The normal assumption is that the images and burials were related to rider god cults. It is possible, however, that the early horse traditions were associated with the use of the chariot.

The use of wheeled vehicles can be identified across late Prehistoric Europe, including parts of Britain, from burials and in the accounts of later Roman ethnographers. Further evidence indicates that, with Iron-Age enclosures and human burials, the horse seems to have had a ritual association, especially as evidenced by the deposition of horse skulls. On the continent, there are some important Iron Age ritual sites which involve the horse; for example, at Gournay, in Northern Gaul (Brunaux, Meniel *et al.* 1985; Brunaux and Rapin 1988), complete horses were interred. In Southern Gaul, the horse was portrayed in the context of war, for example at the shrines at Mouriès, Bouches-du-Rhône, and Nâges, Gard. Warrior figures and the severed heads of adult men were found at both shrines (Green 1989, 146; 1992, 72–73, 150).

Such debates that have developed on the role of the horse in the Classical world have, in general, only been carried out at a European level (Green 1992; Mackintosh 1995). These have generated ideas associating the rider god with Mars or Jupiter, as well as the widely worshiped goddess Epona. There is a belief that these images and traditions were developed in the Greek world and that they spread out from there. The impression that rider images developed in Greece may, however, only be because of the better survival of artefacts and records.

THE HORSE AMONGST THE *DOBUNNI*

A discussion on the role of the horse in British society was suggested many years ago by Scarth (1854, 49–72), however, even though there is much archaeological evidence connected to the horse, it is still too fragmentary to be able to make any firm conclusions. A number of Iron-Age sites with deposited horse remains, have been found, all thought to have had a religious significance. The first group is those sites associated with enclosures or defended settlement sites (Yeates 2006, i.84). At Crickley hill-fort a quarry pit behind the rampart was known to have had a horse's head deposited in the fill. At Leckhampton hill-fort horse's teeth have been recovered from the make-up of the rampart. At Pembridge, Herefordshire (Arnold 1912, 18), an enclosure has been reported in which masses of human and horse bones and teeth were found. Some twelve late prehistoric, or early Roman, cist cremations containing horse bones, were excavated outside the hill-fort at Kempsey. At Ryeham Field, near Berkeley (Yeates 2006, i.85), seventeenth century and later antiquaries reported unusual finds, including a mound inside an enclosure. From around, or within, the enclosure human burials were recovered, most of them considered Roman. Some of the pottery has been interpreted as pre-Roman, and amongst the finds were the bones of small horses. The exact nature of the site is not known. The mound could have been a burial mound or the podium of a temple. The enclosure could have been a *temenos* for a temple or equally plausibly the location of an Iron-Age hill-fort. The same type of activities as those which took place at the Pembridge site seem to have been carried out here, though the site was recorded at a far earlier date. The fact that pre-Roman pottery is reported may indicate a shrine or tumulus inside an Iron-Age hill-fort or enclosure, at this site on a bluff over the river Doverle. The reference to small horse bones may also point to an earlier date as prehistoric horses were generally smaller.

The deposits at Leckhampton, Pembridge, and perhaps Ryeham, had horse bones and teeth scattered around the site in an arbitrary manner, indicating much disturbance and redeposition. Leckhampton had a well at its centre, which is consistent with a martial tradition. It is possible that the site at Pembridge is of the same type. A pit is also believed to have existed at Wychbury, a site from which horse terrets have been recovered. At Crickley the deposit seems to have been singular and more localised as, in all the years of excavation, this is the only horse deposit that has been recovered.

There are further Iron Age and Roman settlement sites which demonstrate the systematic relationship between human and horse deposition, enclosures, and pits, some of which are clearly religious while others are suspected as showing ritual action alone (Yeates 2006, i.84). At Whitegate Farm, Bleadon, a number of early to middle Iron-Age pits, containing horse skulls, were found. Excavations at the ritual site of Rollright has also produced evidence for an Iron-Age enclosure in which a horse skull was deposited, with stones placed in the sockets of the eyes. There was also a pit containing 12 human skulls. The site of Roman Fields, near Gloucester, produced evidence for an Iron-Age circular building, where two cow skulls, as well as a complete horse burial at its entrance, were found. In Worcestershire, at Beckford, is the site of a late Iron-Age enclosure, where peculiar depositional processes concerning horse skeletons were considered to have been the result of religious practice. Excavations at Worcester have uncovered the remains of an articulated horse burial on the periphery of the Iron Age settlement.

Another group of horse deposits, associated not just with random deposits of human bones but with human burials, may have similarities to some of the sites mentioned above. In the *Dobunnic* area the association of the horse with human burials can be traced back to the early to middle Iron Age. On the site of the Wormington compressor station the remains of a sub-square enclosure, containing a human burial, were found; alongside this was a horse burial (Dalwood 2002, 239; Burnham, Hunter *et al.* 2002, 311).

The use of the horse in ritual activity, from the very earliest part of the Iron Age, in the area of the *Dobunni* can be illustrated in three ways. The first of these is the mass deposition of disarticulated bones dispersed across hill-fort sites. Such deposits are also associated with prehistoric burials. Then there is the deposition of the skull, on its own or with human skulls. It could be considered that all of these sites give evidence of ritual practices; in some cases, perhaps, it could be said that there is evidence for the sacrifice of horses on a large scale, due to the amount of bones reported. Perhaps horses were displayed in the same way that humans were. That the horse was considered a potent image to this Iron-Age tribe is evident from the emblems on the coinage that was struck at the end of the Iron Age. Here, the horse, along with the branch emblem, was used as one of the two most important tribal symbols. The image may have been taken from an earlier Greek prototype, but it was used because it had significant meaning locally. Amongst later images a small bronze horse from Focester Court is very likely a votive object (Price 2000, 57–59).

From the Roman period are other settlements associated with the deposition of both human and horse bones. At 127 Dean's Way, Gloucester, a late first to early second century pit was excavated which contained the remains of a human skull, and the skull and vertebrae of a horse (Sermon 1996, 18; Rawes and Wills 1996, 163–185). The site at Kingsholm contained an auxiliary fort on which a later martial temple was established and around which a cemetery developed. Here, the ritual deposition of the horse may have been associated with the Roman martial temple, and, again, the ritual activity has similarities to that already described for Leckhampton and Pembridge, even though this is a Roman site and the others probably originated in the Iron-Age. The act of sacrificing horses was associated with Mars, as attested to in Rome.

Other Roman sites may point to an alternative tradition, concerned purely with the deposition of horses' skulls. Salvage work at Baginton has produced evidence for a religious site associated with the river Sowe, as discussed earlier. At the Hall pit two wells were uncovered, along with 50–100 pits, and a ditch. One of the wells contained the remains of a horse skull (see Chapter 2 and 3). At the New Police Station site, on the periphery of the small Roman town of Worcester, the remains of a high status site have been identified, from which a horse skull was recovered (Edwards, Griffin and Dalwood 2002, 103–132; Mould 1997, 51; Dinn 2000, 321–331; Burnham, Keppie *et al.* 2000, 406; Mould 1998, 56–142; Dinn 2002, 245–254). On Holt Heath the remains of a Roman period enclosure were excavated, from which the fragmentary remains of a horse skull were recovered (Burnham, Hunter *et al.* 2002, 311; Watt 2002, 142). These sites may all be religious and belong to the Roman period; the deposition of a single skull seems to relate them to the type of site which was identified earlier at Crickley Hill, where the ritual activity concerned simply the deposition. There is, in these cases, no association with human burial. The site of Asthall has produced evidence for a circular building in an enclosure associated with two wells, one of which produced the remains of five dog skeletons and the remains of a horse jaw-bone.

Late Roman and sub-Roman burials have also involved horse bones. At Pembridge (see above), the burials are described as *"stein graves of bric"*, presumably because the graves were lined with ceramic building materials. The date and significance of this enclosure have, as yet, not been determined, but Roman artefacts such as ceramics have been reported. If bricks were used in the lining of the grave then the grave must have been Roman or sub-Roman and made of reused material. The same tradition can be observed at Ryeham Field, where Roman tombstones have been reported. A number of other sites where, unusual depositions of horse bones associated with human burials have been found, have also been dated to the Roman period. At the Weald, a number of human burials associated with horse teeth were uncovered in the nineteenth century (RCHME 1976). The area around Kempsford has produced several Roman burials, associated with horses, including four cremations placed above a horse burial; and, at another site, two human burials were associated with a horse burial (Yeates 2006, i.85). At Syreford Mill, near Wycomb, pits containing ox and horse bones were dug before the site became a human cemetery (Timby 1998).

In Somerset there are three known examples of human burials associated with horses. At Sydney Gardens, Bathwick, outside Bath, in 1866, two stone coffins were uncovered; one of them contained a human burial, the other a horse's skull (Scarth 1876, 28; Norton 1969, 216; VCH(So1) 1906, 266). At the Shute Shelve, in 1879, two burials, associated with horse teeth and boars' tusks (VCH(So1) 1906, 366; Scarth 1879, 335), were found. Two cremations, one human, the other equine, were recovered at Herriott's Bridge, although the human burial was assigned to the late first century AD and the horse burial to the second century AD (Greenfield 1977, 76–77; Rahtz and Watts 1989, 330–371).

In the Iron Age, the image of the horse was portrayed on the tribal coinage, whereas in the Roman period it was placed on reliefs. Roman military reliefs have been recovered from Cirencester, Gloucester, and Bath, while religious reliefs have turned up on three occasions; at Bisley, Gill Mill, and Calcote Barn (Henig 1993). The altar from Bisley was found under the south-west corner of the church tower. The front of the sculpture has sheared away, but the image, of a male deity accompanied by a horse with his face looking towards the viewer, is still clear. In his right hand he has a sword and in his left a shield, while the horse has its left foreleg raised. This image has been associated with a Mars rider-god. The relief at Gill Mill is set into the gable-end of a building and, as the building dates from AD 1853, must have been found before this time. The image is much abraded and the legs of the horse are missing. It is still possible to recognise the horse in profile and see that the rider holds a short sword and a shield. The last relief, from Calcote Barn, was, likewise, set into a later building; it has, however, now been removed and is now in the Ashmolean Museum. This relief depicts a horseman, with his shield and sword, accompanied by other figures. All of these are native images of a deity who probably had a common significance, but on none of these reliefs is the name of the deity given. A rider-god of eastern Britain, at Martlesham in a different tribal area, has been found and is associated with a dedication to Mars (RIB(I) 1995, no.213).

There are possibly other representations of the rider god in the area, but these are more circumstantial. In the towns of Gloucester, Cirencester, and presumably Bath there is evidence for the construction of standing columns, as discussed. On the Continent some of these monuments are known to have been surmounted by a sky-god, Jupiter for example, riding a horse. Below the feet of the horse is the image of a chthonic giant being trampled into the ground. Unfortunately, in the *Dobunnic* territory no sculpture has, as yet, been identified as having come from the top of such a column. In the neighbouring *civitas* of the *Cornovii* at Wroxeter the probable head of a horse from such a monument has been recovered, and indicates, possibly, that British columns were similar in design to their continental counterparts (Henig 2004, no. 1.9). The rider-god can, therefore, be seen in the two ways identified above, he may be associated with Mars as indicated from a relief in eastern England, or he may be a representation of the sky god Jupiter.

There is insufficient evidence to indicate whether the activities first seen in the Iron Age, and which continued into the Roman period, had a great effect on the sub-Roman period. The only example, from this period, of the burial of a man and horse is to be found at Asthall Barrow, where the remains of a seventh century cremation contained the remains of human and horse bones along with grave goods including horse fittings (Leeds 1924, 113–126).

CONCLUSION

The surviving material indicates that the horse was revered in a religious and ritualised way in both the Iron-Age and Roman periods. Much of the ritual action of these periods was similar in nature, but there was a real change in the early medieval period where some of these activities, but not all, stopped. Certain large enclosures, probably all hill-forts, were associated with the finds of numerous horse bones and teeth. What was causing this mass deposition has not been ascertained. There were also smaller enclosures which were associated with the deposition of human skulls and horse skulls. In the Iron-Age horse skulls were placed in enclosures on their own. There are also examples of an enclosure in the Iron Age and one in the Roman period of a whole horse being buried alongside an individual. This is the only horse tradition which has ever been discussed and which also continued into the early medieval period, with the burial at Asthall. The Asthall barrow contained a rich burial and, one would presume that, even in the Iron Age and the Roman period the killing of a horse and its insertion into the grave showed a high degree of wealth wasted. The part of the horse which is most frequently deposited within Roman burials is the head.

Chapter 11

A Goddess for the *Dobunni*

In Chapter 4 it became apparent that there were associations between community and territory, and that these had manifested themselves in the representation of deities and *genii*, which in turn were representations of provinces, *civitas capitals*, *colonia*, and *vici*. Some of these figures, for example, the *genius* of Cirencester, the *tyche* of Gloucester, the *genius* of Dorn, and the goddess of Bath, have already been identified. It is, however, possible to go further than this and identify a cult amongst the *Dobunni* which brought all of these together and bridged the divide between the Roman invasion and the migration period. What holds this argument together is a series of reliefs portraying a goddess whose symbol is a sacred vessel.

THE CULT OF A GODDESS

This book has been concerned with the development of ideas within a society through time. It would be necessary, therefore, to discuss what we know about the Iron Age traditions and fit them into the longer trend of a central native religious cult present amongst the *Dobunni*. The important developments, although it may only have become fully apparent later, had occurred by at least the late Iron Age. Extremely rich burials with vessels, weapons, and mirrors have been found deposited in barrows at Birdlip and Crickley (Stealens 1982, 19–31). Further undated burials of an unusual type have also been reported at Nottingham Hill and Iron-Age cremations have been found on Leckhampton Hill (Yeates 2007a). These burials do not lie in or on the edge of an *oppidum*, but on the boundaries of a large circular valley with a 12 mile (19 kilometer) diameter. From the burial sites there are views into this valley, which lies at the heart of the *Dobunnic* territory. It should also be noted that three of these burials were described as containing the remains of a vessel, with either a bowl, a basin, or a bucket, placed over the face of the deceased. This rite is unusual; the graves were opulent, and used an apparent cult object which may have, in some way, mirrored the valley over which these tombs look, see Figure 47.

Five local Roman period reliefs have been recovered which obviously represent the same religious tradition. These reliefs come from Cirencester, Bath, two from Gloucester, and a further one from Nettleton (Wedlake 1982, 137). The similarities between these reliefs have been noted for some time, but the relationship between them and what they represent has not. Two further reliefs from this area, which also

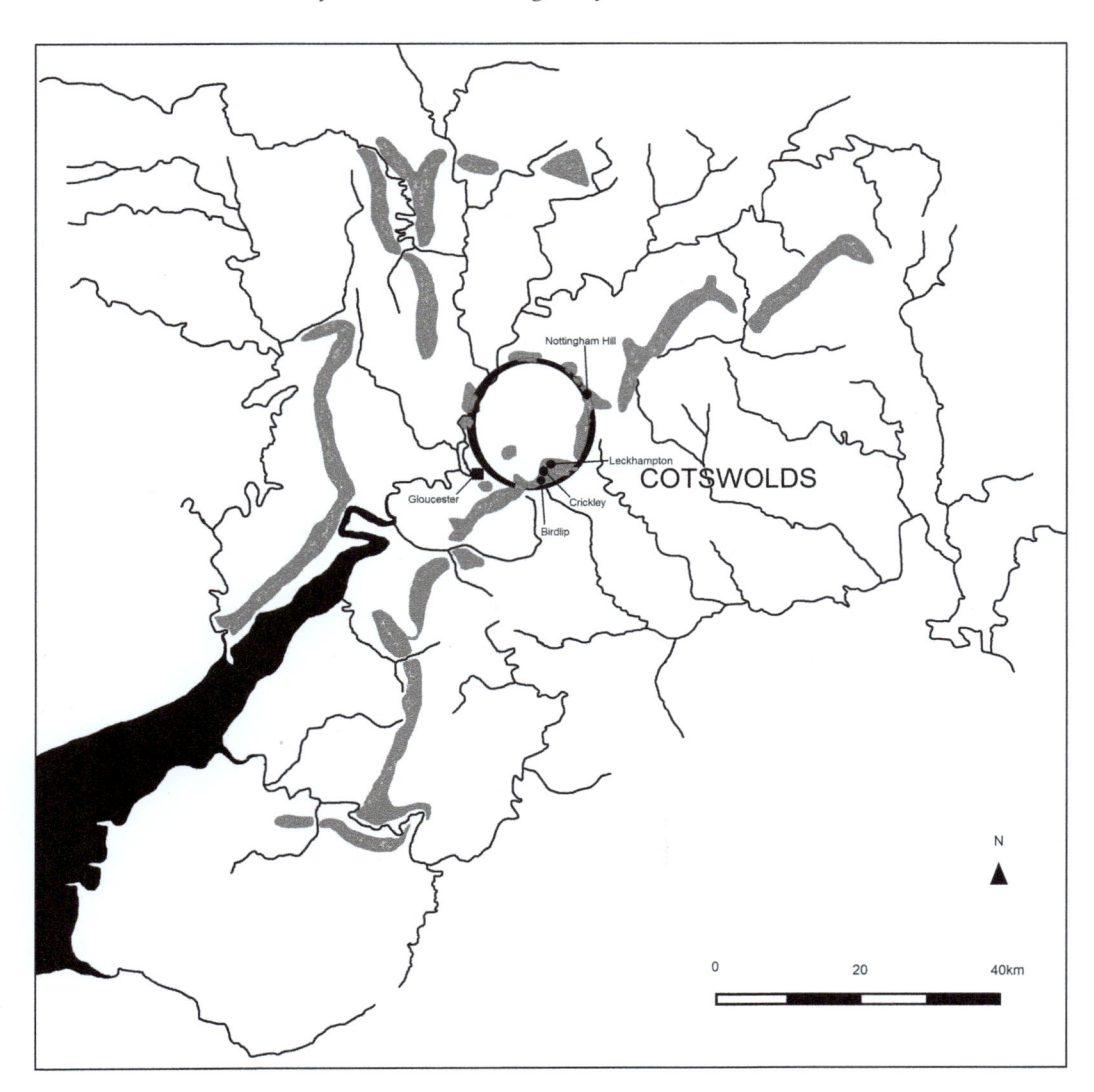

Figure 47: A map of the Severn valley showing the location of the rich late Iron-Age burials at Crickley and Birdlip, and the other unusual but undated burials at Leckhampton Hill and Nottingham Hill. The grey areas indicate the lines of scarp slopes along the Cotswold Edge and outliers, the Forest of Dean, Malverns, Mendips and Wyre Forest. The enclosed circular valley lies to the north-east of Gloucester and is highlighted in black (S. Yeates).

probably have representations of the goddess, have been found at Wellow, in Somerset, and in Aldsworth (Yeates 2007a), see Figure 48.

The only temple in Cirencester that had been described by early antiquaries is a circular temple which was located in an open area, to the south-west of the forum

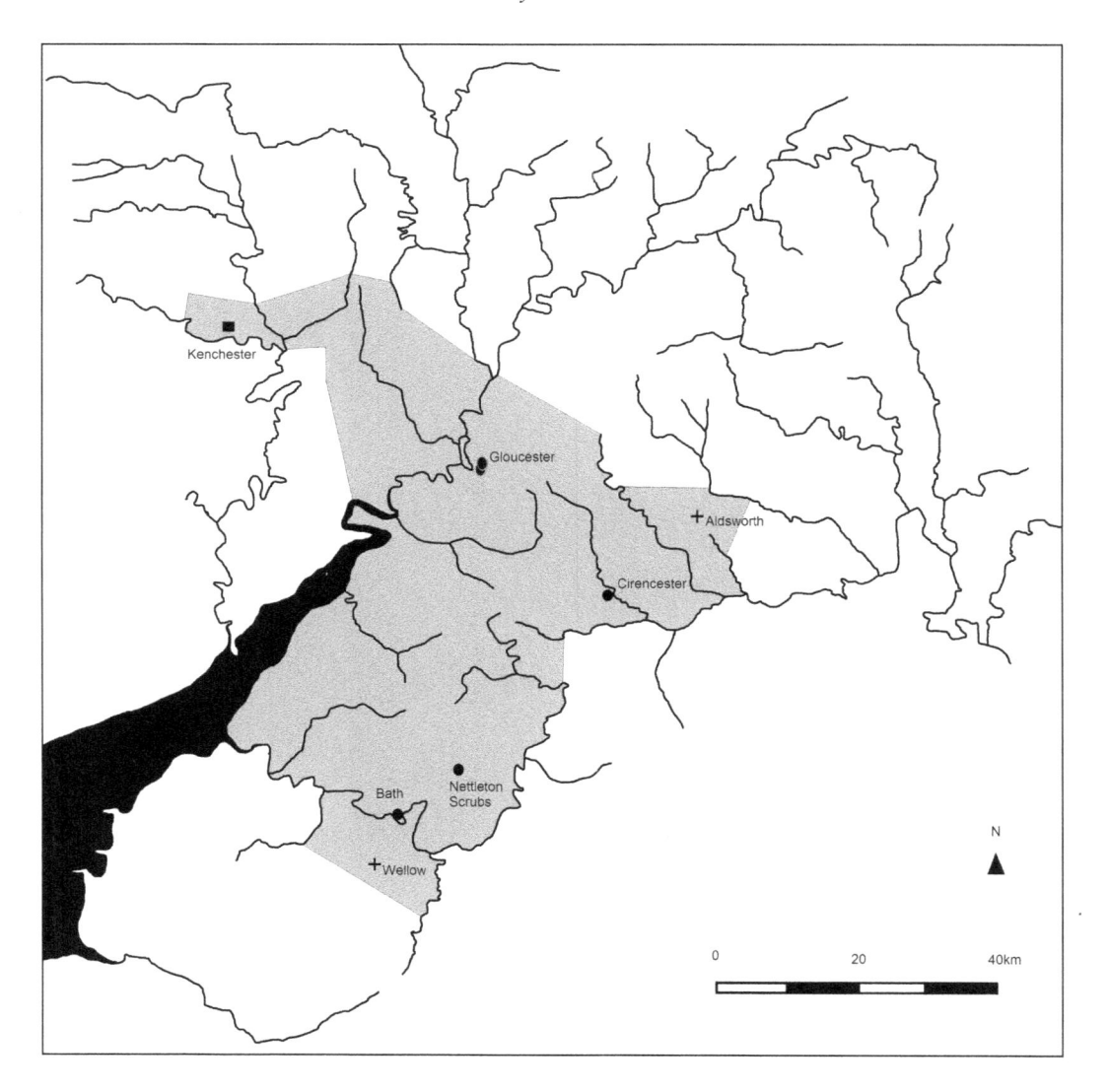

Figure 48: A map showing the distribution of the reliefs showing the mater and Mercury (black circles), which can be interpreted as the mother and father of the Dobunni. The reliefs from Wellow and Aldsworth (crosses) have also been included because they seem to show the same deities. The Kenchester inscription (black square) has also been inserted. The light grey shading indicates territory which was almost certainly part of the Dobunnic territory (S. Yeates).

(Holbrook 1998, 177–188). There is evidence that the temple was dedicated to Mercury and the *Matres* (Henig 1993, nos. 63–64, 70, 81, 118). This dedication is supported by the images recovered from the area. A relief of Mercury, inscribed DEO MERCVRIO, was recovered from the Leauses in 1862. It has Mercury, in his normal guise, standing in an *aedicule*. Further images of Mercury, which must have originated from a shrine to the god on this site, include a head of the god, and a money bag. Another relief from the Leauses was also found in 1862. It is set in a gabbled block and shows the image of three seated mothers wearing long garments with pleats. A further relief with a rectangular recess and gabled top, from the Leauses site and found in AD 1862, depicts Mercury standing alongside a female consort, frequently called '*Rosmerta*' (the inverted commas indicate that this is a local goddess of a *Rosmerta* type, but probably not known by that name). Mercury stands on the left, with the goddess on the right; it is the attributes of this goddess which are important, because, to her right, there is an object, believed to be a tub, see Figure 49. Although the relief is damaged it is possible that the hair style, due to the shape of the head, was the same as that of the *matres* which were recovered from the same site. Hence, it may be that the same goddess has been shown both in a singular and triplicate form, and a standard cultural template was being used.

Similar images can be identified in finds from Bath, and a temple dedicated to the same divinities has been located. To the east of the temple, of Sulis Minerva, and under the site of the abbey, are the remains of a circular temple as at Cirencester (Cunliffe 1989, 59–86). The reliefs recovered nearest to this temple came from the excavation of the great baths in 1878–90 (Cunliffe and Fulford 1982, nos. 24, 39). One relief shows an image of Mercury on his own; the second shows Mercury alongside a female companion accompanied by a tub or vessel, a repetition of the Cirencester relief and also found near a circular temple. At Bath the circular shrine was in alignment with the temple of the presiding spirit of the town, see Figure 50.

Figure 49: The relief showing Mercury and the mother from the Leauses site in Cirencester (photograph by the late M. B. Cookson, photograph held by the Institute of Archaeology, Oxford).

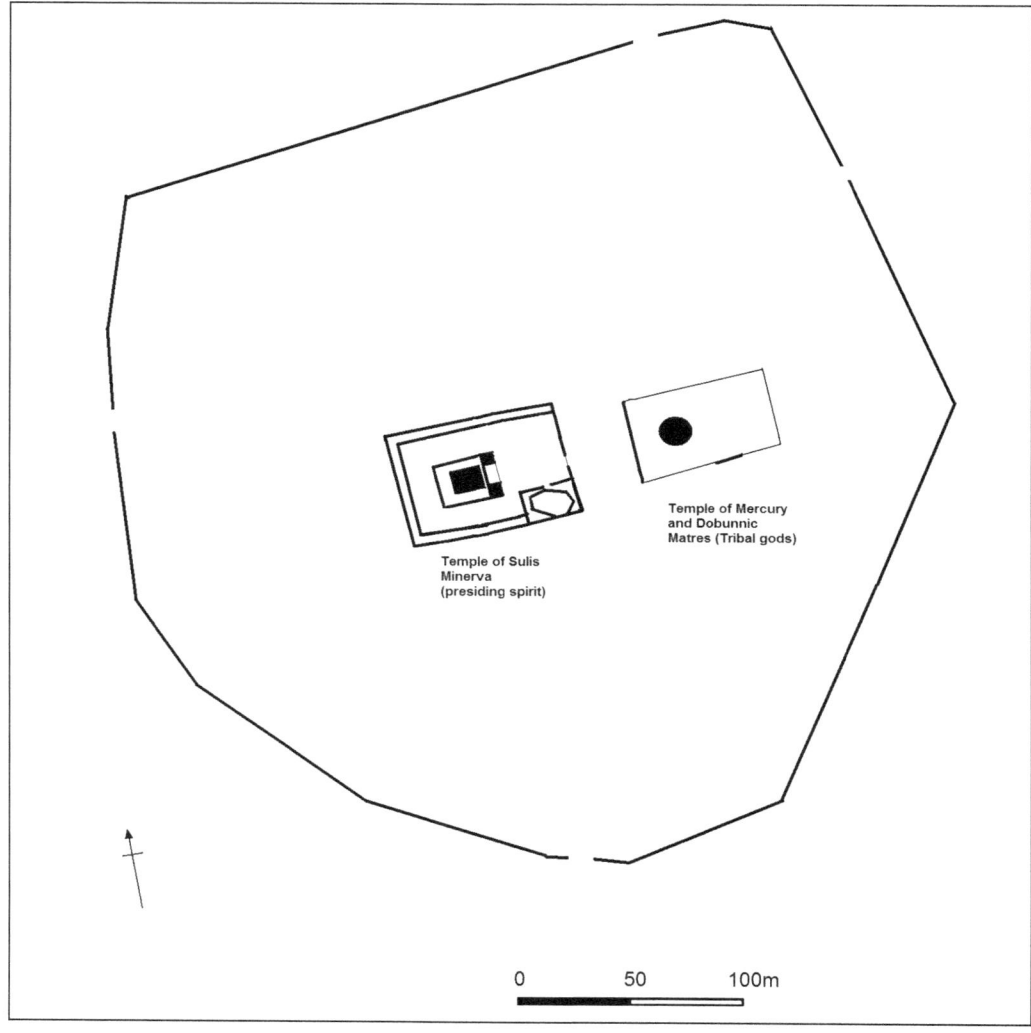

Figure 50: A plan of the city of Bath showing the temple of Sulis Minerva and of the mother goddess of the Dobunni (S. Yeates).

The same image being found in both towns indicates that they were symbols of a widespread cult in the *Dobunnic* territory. The cylindrical object has been interpreted as a bucket or cauldron.

Evidence also exists for the cult of Mercury and the *Matres* at Gloucester, where two reliefs have been recovered (Henig 1993, nos. 78, 79), see Figure 51. The first, and best preserved, was found in 1857 on the site of the Shakespeare Inn, which was presumed, at the time, to come from a nearby shrine. It shows two deities in an *aedicule*, with Mercury on the left and a consort on the right. The consort wears a long tunic, belted at the waist, and carries a sceptre in her left hand and a dipper over a wooden tub in her right one. A second relief was recovered from near The Cross. Here, Mercury is shown alongside a goddess holding a jug, perhaps a replacement for the ladle. The terracotta image of a similar goddess was recovered from the site of the Tolsey. The images on the reliefs are the same as those from Cirencester and Bath. The fact that more images of this deity are turning up within the central enclosure of the *colonia* settlement tends to indicate that the shrine complex lay in an open area to the north-east of the forum. The location of the reliefs indicates, perhaps, that there were two temples, one dedicated to Mercury and the *Mater*, and the other to the city tyche.

The goddess depicted in the reliefs seems to have been associated with a widespread

Figure 51: The relief of Mercury and the mother, found in 1857, from Northgate Street, Gloucester. This has the best surviving image of the mother goddess of the Dobunni who holds a ladle above a bucket or circular vessel (photograph used by kind permission of Gloucester City Museum).

cult amongst the *Dobunni*, which was not only present at an important site in the *civitas* town of Cirencester, but also at a temple aligned with the major temple at Bath, and another in the centre of the *colonia* at Gloucester, in an area to the north-east of the forum. The cult of Mercury and the consort was evidently practised in circular temples, as described by antiquaries at Cirencester and seen through material analysis at Bath.

A similar, but fragmented, relief, from Nettleton in Wiltshire, was found in excavations in 1912 (Cunliffe and Fulford 1982, no. 117). Although the images are less clear, a curly haired male, with his arms at his side, and a robed female, holding a round object or a globe, can be made out. The goddess stands behind an altar or a low platform and there is a cylindrical object, sometimes described as a pillar or casket, between the two figures. The male figure seems to hold a caduceus, a staff with two serpents entwined around it, in his left hand and the remnant of a purse in his right hand. The carving has many of the characteristics of the other reliefs, but the representation is cruder.

The remains of another relief from Wellow show three images, described as Mercury and two consorts (Cunliffe and Fulford 1982, no. 116). The panel can be compared to those from Gloucester, but it is more apparent in this relief that the image of the female on the left hand side is that of the goddess with a tub, as there is clearly a cylindrical vessel alongside the goddess. The central figure, the second consort, may have been a representative of the area around Wellow. There is a relief from Aldsworth (Henig, Cleary *et al.* 2000, 362–363) which shows Mercury alongside Minerva, who is evidently meant to represent his consort. At first it seems as though it doesn't follow completely the pattern seen on the images discussed so far, but it may be that the goddess could appear in a number of guises, and that this was a representation of the tribal goddess as protector.

The goddess has been shown in many of the reliefs as having a tub, a cylindrical cask, a bucket, or a cauldron; a representation of a mythical vessel. She appears to have been associated with fecundity and was worshiped and revered widely throughout the *Dobunnic* area as well as in the *colonia* territory annexed from the *civitas*. She was, therefore, not a goddess confined to a specific topographic region, but was important throughout the area of distribution of the tribal coins associated with the *Dobunni*. Tribal goddesses are known from elsewhere in Britain and it is highly likely that this deity was the mother of the *Dobunni* people. In coming to this conclusion it makes the Iron Age customs of the Birdlip and Crickley burials more comprehensible as the tub, or sacred vessel, was an image associated with the cult of the tribal mother. That these burial sites overlook a large circular valley places them, and the cult, further in context. The circular valley which is now called the Vale of Gloucester, and which was probably once covered by the Corse Forest, was the natural feature which was venerated above all things, and provided the underlying dynamics for the *Dobunnic* religion.

The image of the cult vessel can be projected backwards through its use in these burial practices, probably of the *Dobunnic* elite. The tradition of the *mater* with the sacred vessel can also be projected from the Roman period forward into the early medieval period. The *Hwicce* were the name of the tribe who followed the *Dobunni* in the territory, as discussed previously. This name is used in English texts such as Bede's, however, Bede, in AD 603, implied that these people were still of British origin and not Germanic. The insistence that they were British suggests that the name was not given as a result of migration from the east, although the name used for them is Old English. The name derived from the Old English *hwicce*, for which the etymology is **sacred vessel** (Gelling 1982, 59–78). Therefore, it could be surmised that it is an English name applied to a people whose goddess possessed a sacred vessel. That the tribal goddess had such a vessel can be demonstrated by the distribution of the sculpture and the locations where it turned up in the Roman period towns. There has also been a suggestion that the sacred vessel, which gave these people their name, was none other than the Severn valley, between the Cotswolds and the Malverns.

It would seem that wherever one looks: in elite Iron-Age burial practices; on the reliefs of the tribal goddess of the *Dobunni*; and even in the early medieval tribal name, the central idea is the **sacred vessel**. Whether this is placed over the face, shown by the side of the goddess, or seen in the landscape's morphology. There is, however, more yet to say about the name *Hwicce*. The word is also the root of the Old English *wicce*, which means a female participant in witchcraft, and *wicca*, a male participant in witchcrafts. The *Hw* combination in Old English words soon disappeared becoming *wh* or *w*. The name of the tribe was arguably, therefore, associated with pagan religious action and sacred objects, and could equally have been used to describe the tribe of witches. It seems apparent that the *Hwicce* are the only English or British tribe whose name was associated directly with the pre-Christian religion. The name is not recorded as having been initiated by this tribe, but by others, for example Bede. It is also apparent that when this name was being used, from the sixth and seventh centuries, there was already a large Christian population in the territory (see Chapter 12). Even so, at this time the memories of the mother with her cauldron, and the goddess portrayed in triple form, see Figure 52, must have still influenced the use of language, and the symbolic language. It is also evident that there are some underlying associations here which are still difficult to comprehend fully.

The Roman epigraphic sources may suggest other reasons why an English, once British, tribe should be honoured with the Germanic name for a sacred vessel or a pagan religion. When Caesar talked of the Druids, in the Gallic War (VI. 13), he insisted

Figure 52: The relief showing the **Matres** *from the Leasues site in Cirencester. This shows the consort of Mercury in a triple representation (photograph by the late M. B. Cookson, photograph held by the Institute of Archaeology, Oxford).*

that their religion was founded in Britain and that those in Gaul who wished to study the subject more closely travelled to Britain to learn it. It seems, therefore, that pre-Christian religious beliefs were greatly influenced by Britain, and were exported to Gaul from here. The *Dobunnic* area may have had, therefore, influence in religious matters over a much wider area than that implied in the discussion of the worship of the god *Cunomaglos*. He is seen as part of a cult widespread in their territory, but was also exported, in sculptural form, to London in the second and third centuries AD, and into the Mabinogion texts during the medieval period, at a later date (see Chapter 7). Other associations between cults and the territory can be seen in the Mabinogion, but these will be returned to later. In the list of the wonders of Britain, from the early medieval period, the vast majority of the wonders in the top ten were located in the land of the *Hwicce*, or in the adjacent land of the *Glywysinga/Gwent*.

The reliefs show the goddess in a single and triple form and associate her with a cult or sacred vessel. Often, in English literature, for example in Shakespeare's Macbeth, three witches are shown around a cauldron. This image is believed to have been developed from the Germanic myths of the Wyrd sisters, or Norns; three women who lived at the root of the world tree (Ellis Davidson 1964, 26). This may mean that the name, *Hwicce*, could also have been developing through a process of Germanic *interpretatio*, where a native British goddess in her many forms was linked with similar Germanic deities. This would have paralleled the actions of the earlier Roman culture. If all of these things were true then it would imply that there had not only been a major survival of British people but that there was also an influx of Germanic people, but who may have held senior positions in society, who were trying to comprehend the native religion within their own traditions.

CONCLUSION

It is apparent that in the land of the *Dobunni* there was a widespread cult worshipping a goddess with a cauldron, tub, or sacred vessel, whose temples can be detected in both major and minor settlements. That the cult of this goddess was carried out in the pre-Roman period is evident in the high status burial practices of the elite; that it continued afterwards is evident in the tribal name. That the centre of this cult was a large natural circular valley is apparent from the location of the elite Iron Age burials who fed symbolically from the cult vessel.

There are two main interpretations of this name, both feeding into a common tradition. The simplest explanation of the tribal name is that it describes both the image of the goddess's cult vessel on the reliefs, and also the shape of the landscape. Later, the territory, although becoming Christian, kept its association with the older religious practices, traditions, and symbols. These emphasised an area of Britain being particularly associated with the pagan past, *Hwicce* (sacred vessel), and *Wicce* (the witch, or the people who knew the sacred vessel). The cauldron, in all mythical interpretations, is considered to be the place of creation and knowledge, and of life and death. That the large circular valley which lay at the heart of the *Dobunnic* territory was perceived in this way seems implicit if not provable. Thus, it can be said that the

Hwicce were, not only the people who knew the sacred vessel, but also, the people who were born and who lived in or even sprang from the sacred vessel. To understand their goddess is the closest one can get to understand the creation myths of the *Dobunni* and the *Hwicce*. The tribe believed in a divine father and mother, but the cauldron of the mother, the vessel from whence life sprang, was associated with a specific location.

The names of these two divinities have not been recovered on any inscription, but amongst the *Brigantes* the name of the goddess is a homonym of the tribal name, *Brigantia*. There is a further inscription from Slack to *deus Bregans*, a masculine form of the tribal name *Brigantes*. Although it can not be confirmed it is implicit that a similar tradition may have existed amongst the *Dobunni*.

Chapter 12

The Arrival of Christianity: The Locations of Shrines and Minster Churches

The history of Christianity in Britain can be summarised, using textual sources, as follows. The earliest evidence for Christianity in the Roman period survives mainly in medieval texts, for instance *Gildas*, and refers to saints being martyred, for example Saint Alban (Winterbottom 1978, *History* 10–11; Thomas 1981, 48–49). What value can be placed on these is unknown, but the persecutions were usually placed in the reign of Diocletian. The period of persecution ended with a series of edicts from the Emperor Constantine. The first of these was that of Toleration, or the Galerian, of AD 311 (Bettenson 1943, 21–22; Stevenson 1965, 296). This was followed by the edict of Milan. There are a number of references to Christianity in Britain from the fourth century AD. Amongst these is the inclusion of bishops from Britain in the list of bishops attending the council of Arles in AD 314. Much is made of Constantine's conversion to Christianity in the fourth century AD but most of this tale was probably fictionalised for political purposes. It is probably true to say that the adoption of Christianity by the empire was a much slower process; probably not being achieved until the reign of Constantius II, who adopted Arianism as a means of combining church with state. There is also archaeological evidence for Christianity in Britain at this time, but the degree to which it was accepted is not known; because of this the continuance of a Christian belief system in much of Britain after the departure of the Romans has been questioned (Frend 1992, 121–131; Watts 1991; 1998). In 391 Theodosius closed the temples and banned pagan cults (Watts 1998, 2), but this procedure failed to establish Christianity firmly in Britain and soon after this the province left the Empire.

In the fifth century AD, Britain ceased to have a monetary economy and, in this environment, the villas and temples underwent a long, slow, period of decline. There were a number of Christians in Britain at this time who followed the Pelagian heresy, a doctrine of free will and grace, while Gildas stated that Christianity was flourishing in Britain into the fifth and sixth centuries AD (Morris 1965, 26–60; Cross and Livingstone 1977, 1059; Stevenson 1966, 217–219). It is the only good textual sources which support the idea that Christianity survived in the extreme west of Britain, presumably in Dyfed, West Wales, and that it was reintroduced by Irish monks to other parts of the west from those places where it thrived. The *Hwicce* lay in a part of Britain which was, not only influenced by the development of Christianity in Ireland and Wales, but also by the Roman Church, which had been established at Canterbury in AD 597. The church of Canterbury established the *Hwiccian* See at Worcester in AD 679 (Darlington and McGurk 1995, 137).

Bede's *Ecclesiastical History* (Bede, Colgrave and Mynors 1969, HE I.30, ii.13) included two statements that are relevant to the current argument about the integration of Christianity and pre-Christian beliefs. The first, in AD 601, concerned a letter from Pope Gregory to Bishop *Mellitus*; it claimed that the existing temples were not to be destroyed but that the idols should be and then be replaced with altars and relics; so that the temples, if they were well built, could be converted for use by the Church. The second reference, referring to the years AD 616 × 628, described King *Raedwald* of East Anglia who kept an altar for Christian mass and an *arula* for the old religion. His temple, church, or *fanum* was still standing in *c.* 670 AD and was seen by King Ealdwulf as a youth.

CHRISTIANITY LOCALLY

The development of Christianity in the west of England has been assessed archaeologically, but the surviving data is usually only in the form of small objects (Yeates 2006, i.73). A chi-rho inscription was found at Chedworth Villa, and another was found at Wiggington Roman Villa, on a lead tank. A lead baptismal tank from Bourton-on-the-Water, and a late Roman Christian ring from the Andoversford area have also been found with chi-rho symbols. Some of the objects, claimed to represent the presence of Christianity, are ambiguous. An inscription from Bath complains about the wreckers of the temple, though it does not state that the wreckers were Christian. The remains of a tombstone found at Sea Mills to SPES, "hope" is claimed as Christian. Excavators have also claimed to have found the remains of Christian churches; for example, on Uley shrine, and in the Roman villa at Bradford-on-Avon. Even though the objects may show that Christianity was present in the *Dobunnic* territory, the evidence is often contradictory. The inscription from Bath records the restoration of the temple, the lead tanks at Bourton-on-the-Water were broken, and the stone on which the chi-rho symbol was carved at Chedworth was removed from the *nymphaeum*. These indicate that this was a period when religious views were in flux and that Christianity was not dominant. An inscription of AD 363, from the base of a column from Cirencester, proclaims the reintroduction of the old religion with a dedication to Jupiter, best and greatest. In the Cirencester and Gloucester areas it was probable that the two religions continued alongside each other, and that Christianity, in the fourth and fifth centuries, may have been only a minor religion. The breaking of the lead tanks at Bourton and the burial of the tank at Wiggington may have been due to acts of iconoclasm by Christians to prevent their use for the local *Dobunnic* religion and the cult of the sacred vessel. Lydney Temple has long been noted as a place of the Pagan revival in Britain and, even though the dating of the sequences has been altered, it is still apparent that religious activity continued there, due to the deposition of a late Roman coin hoard. Views on what happened to these temples are changing; instead of having been deliberately dismantled they are now seen as having gone through a period of decline and decay in much the same way as the villas.

The number of Christians in the area is impossible to calculate, but it is probably the case that Christianity was not the official religion for some time despite imperial decrees. That the kingdom, which from AD 603 can be called the *Hwicce*, had local Christian elements can be implied from the writings of Bede. The evidence which survives indicates that the process of Christianisation, or of missionary activity, began in the sixth century AD. The earliest known establishment of a permanent church in the region is at Hereford in AD 540 (Pretty 1989, 171–183). The church at Hereford is known to have been founded over a temple site, which suggests that, at least in this area, there was a replacement process going on, which often led to an amalgamation of ideas between the two religions. Certain medieval documents imply that a church may have been founded at Gloucester at more or less the same time (in AD 536) (Yeates 2006, i.73–74). The claimed site was near the Southgate, which, by chance, was the gate nearest the basilica, a key site for the establishment of early churches in the late-Roman to sub-Roman period. If a church had been established in Gloucester at this time, it was not on one of the major temple sites. Later, a middle Anglo-Saxon minster was founded at Gloucester, which may have replaced an earlier church. It was only with this foundation that the church was, either, founded alongside the imperial temple, or more likely founded within that structure. The joint minster on the Saint Mary de Lode site was also founded on top of what is considered to have been a Roman temple.

The dates of the establishment of churches at sites such as Glastonbury are often controversial; nevertheless, it is possible that a church was founded there in *c.* AD 600. This date can be supported archaeologically by the recovery of a small cast copper-alloy censer in 1986, which was dated to the late sixth to seventh centuries AD (Bradbury and Croft 1989, 157–185; Rahtz 1991, 33). Also, legendary traditions claim that Malmesbury had an early foundation by an Irish monk (Moffatt 1805, 21). At Marden, Herefordshire, a Celtic bell, an object often used by the early medieval British Church, was found (Mahon 1848, 264; Westwood 1849, 169; Fisher 1926, 330). In Worcestershire, the estate of Hanbury was given to an Irish monk in AD 657–674; this predated the foundation of the see of Worcester, in AD 679 (Finberg 1972, no. 195).

A number of place-names contain a word meaning church and, like many place-names, these can be considered to have developed in a stratified manner. The word is the Latin *eclēsia*, which produced the Welsh *eglwys*, and the old-Irish *egliss* (Yeates 2006, i.74). Eccleswall lies on the ancient Ross parish boundary and may mean **the well on the boundary of the Welsh church's community** (see Figure 53), but the church at Ross had a complicated arrangement with that at Linton. Exhall was a chapel of Salford Priors; it lies close to the parish boundary and may mean **the hill or nook of land on the boundary of the Welsh church's estate**. A similarly derived name was located on the periphery of the *parochia* of Coventry. If these interpretations are correct then the mother churches of Ross, Salford Priors, and Coventry must also have been founded at an early date. The Eccles Brook lay on the edge of the *parochia* of Worcester Cathedral and it is possibly an indication that a church was in existence prior to AD 679 at Worcester (see Figure 54). This may also have been the case with Eggleton, in Herefordshire, which was an estate held by the ecclesiastical centre at Bishop's Frome, the location of another significant mother church.

The foundations of other minsters are not considered to have occurred until the

Figure 53: The mother church of Ross-on-Wye, Herefordshire (photograph S. Yeates).

beginning of the eighth century AD, among them those at Daylesford and Evesham. At Evesham there was a tradition of a vision of three women; one of whom was the Virgin Mary. The story is considered to mask older traditions, and be a representation of the *Dobunni* triple mother, or a more localised mother. The church is believed to have been established on a temple site, and stonework from a Roman building has been recovered in the area (Yeates 2006, ii.722–724). This tradition implies two things; first, that there was an interplay and a readjustment of practices between the old and new religions; and second, that the foundations of these churches started in AD 540 and continued until *c.* AD 730 or later.

It is apparent, from earlier studies, that communities had complex social systems and that many ancient sites, or their localities, were reused for similar purposes. The hill-forts, standing posts or trees, and *nemetons* all had a religious component, as did the Romano-Celtic temples. This means that there was a diverse range of sites on which the developing Christian religion had to focus on and reuse for the establishment of the minsters or mother churches. The key feature of these sites was that they possessed a boundary wall to act as a monastic vallum. This feature can be identified for temples and also hill-forts. That temples were a particular target for conversion into early Christian sites is implied from what has already been discussed for Hereford, Gloucester, and Evesham; but a number of other mother churches in the area are also known to have been established on religious sites. Mother churches are known to lie on certain types of site; these can be placed into five groups: large late Bronze-Age settlements, large Iron-Age settlements, large Roman settlements, Iron-Age hill-forts,

Figure 54: The cathedral church of Worcester (photograph S. Yeates).

and Roman-period temple sites. In many cases it is known that the large settlements, either of Bronze Age, Iron Age or Roman date, probably had central enclosures which acted as a religious site. It is also known that Iron-Age hill-forts were associated with temples or shrines. There must have been, therefore, a complicated arrangement concerning earlier religious sites. In a number of mother church cases, however, there is insufficient knowledge of the site to say much about this.

The surviving Gloucestershire evidence, from the Vale of Gloucester and the Cotswolds, is that many of the sites chosen have evidence of earlier activity (Yeates 2006, for all listings). The church at Deerhurst, (see Figure 55) was founded on the site of a Roman villa and, it has been hypothesised, was also a shrine. There is some evidence that it may have been the location of a valley fort on the edge of the river Severn. There is evidence of a Roman town under Tewkesbury; the place-name evidence and the settlement's street design indicate that the church lay in a large circular enclosure adjacent to the Roman town. Excavations have also shown that the mother church at Cheltenham lay in a large, possibly late Iron Age, enclosure. At Bishop's Cleeve there is also evidence that the church lay in a large enclosure at the centre of a middle to late Iron-Age settlement. The church at Winchcombe lies in what would seem, from limited evidence, to have been an Iron-Age site, and was probably a valley-fort. The village at Stanway is known, from aerial photographs, to lie over an undated enclosure.

The church at Guiting Power seems to lie in a large defended Iron-Age enclosure which has the appearance of a hill-fort, while the minster at Blockley, (see Figure 56),

Figure 55: The Anglo-Saxon priory church of Deerhurst, Gloucestershire (photograph S. Yeates).

is known to lie over a Bronze-Age settlement. At Bourton-on-the-Water the present church of Saint Lawrence lies over the top of a Roman cemetery, but due to the middle and late Anglo-Saxon burials which are located in and around the fort of Salmonsbury it is likely that the site of the major church has moved. The church of Northleach lies on a spur, across which runs an undated bank, a location where one would expect to see a shrine for the river Leach. The church of Coln Saint Aldwyn is located on a hilltop above a Roman settlement on Akeman Street. The church at Kempsford is believed to lie over the remains of a Roman town, while there are also traditional claims for the presence of a fortification. The minster at Bibury lies in the vicinity of a Roman site, and the place-name element burh means fortification. At Withington, Gloucestershire, there is evidence of earlier undated buildings under the churchyard and rectory garden, while the church sits above a never failing spring, a classic temple location.

The church at North Cerney lies over earlier buildings. The minster at Cirencester was founded in a Roman town. There are indications that at least three Anglo-Saxon churches were built there, of which only a probable late Anglo-Saxon church has been excavated. The village of Kemble has produced material from the Bronze Age to the early medieval period. The place-name Daglingworth indicates that there was once an enclosure on the site. The church of Bisley lies on a probable spring shrine, and reliefs have been found on the site, but from the layout of the village and the scarping to the south of the church the site may have been a hill-fort. The church at Standish lies over,

Figure 56: The minster church of Blockley, Gloucestershire (photograph S. Yeates).

or adjacent to, an Iron-Age settlement of an unknown design and function. The church at Frocester lay in a Roman enclosure which has been associated with a villa, although the plan of any building there has not been fully resolved. The church of Minchenhampton lies in an area of Iron-Age Bulwarks, and there are further ditches under the town which do not conform to the design of those on the common, thus indicating a further probable component of the Iron-Age landscape. The minster at Tetbury is claimed by antiquaries, to have been located in an Iron-Age hill-fort.

In South Gloucestershire the list of early or major churches associated with earlier sites continues. Berkley was the location of a minster, but it is probable that it absorbed earlier *parochia* to gain its late Anglo-Saxon size. The church there lies in a possible prehistoric enclosure called Canonsbury, and the site has produced Iron-Age and Roman material. The mother church of the parish of Cam, which could have been at Cam or Dursley, has not been evaluated properly. Tradition has it that there was a pre-Conquest castle at Dursley. There was also a pre-Conquest castle at Beverstone, which normally means that this would have been the location of an Iron-Age hill-fort. Little is known about the site at Wotton-under-Edge, but a Roman religious relief has been recovered from the town. The minster of Hawkesbury has earlier buildings underneath it, and its name indicates that it is the location of a fortification.

The church of Old Sodbury lies in undated earthworks, while that at Bitton sits on a Roman site, which has produced a votive dog. The church of Pucklechurch has evidence of a Roman site and also an Iron-Age hill-fort. The shape of the village of

Almondsbury, and the place-name, indicate that the church lies in a large undated enclosure. Westbury-on-Trym also has a place-name which indicates a fortification. Olveston lies over a series of undated crop-marks, while the site of Thornbury is, traditionally, claimed as the location of a British town, or fort; this is supported by the place-name.

In West Gloucestershire the same activities can be found. The church of Lydney is located over a Roman site. At Westbury-on-Severn there is a claim of an ancient castle, supported by place-name evidence. The site of Woolaston has not been investigated properly although Woolaston church lies in a circular churchyard. The church at Newent lies on the edge of a Roman settlement, and part of the town has a circular design, implying an older enclosure.

In Herefordshire, the same type of activity can be observed at most sites. The church at Much Marcle may lie in a large undated enclosure; it is possible that this is marked out by some of the roads. The place-name Ledbury, with its use of burh, indicates that there is an enclosure under the town, while Iron-Age and Roman material has been recovered. The village of Bishop's Frome lies over a Bronze-Age settlement, and a Roman bronze statuette has been recovered. The town of Bromsyard lies in a big enclosure, which is indicated by road layout and place-name evidence. The location on a spur over the river may indicate the presence of a hill-fort. Marden lies in an enclosure, as indicated by place-name evidence, while Roman artefacts and settlements have been found on the other side of the river Lugg, and crop-marks on the Marden side. The priory of Leominster lies over a circular building, and is located in a large undated enclosure. The church of Eardisland lies in a Roman enclosure on the banks of the Arrow. Leintwardine is also the location of a mother church and a Roman town, which has recently produced a major Roman religious inscription.

Worcestershire also has a number of churches with similar arrangements. The place-name evidence for Tenbury indicates that it lies in an undated fortified enclosure, as does the circular nature of the settlement. The road layout of Clifton-upon-Teme has also produced evidence to indicate the presence of an older enclosure. Roman pottery was recovered from the graveyard at Kidderminster. The place-name Hartlebury indicates that this was the location of a fortification. The site of the church at Dodderhill, (see Figure 57) lies in a fortification which has produced Iron-Age and Roman artefacts. The cathedral at Worcester was located in the fortifications of a Roman town, while the minster at Kempsey lay in a promontory-fort, and that at Ripple in a probable valley-fort. The road layouts of both Bredon and Pershore indicate older enclosures. The church at Fladbury was located in a large valley fort, and at Inkberrow there is evidence of scarping on the spur on which its church stands besides an Anglo-Saxon period reference to a burh on the site. The church of Hanbury lies in an Iron-Age hill-fort.

The county of Warwickshire has not had its minster or mother churches discussed to any great extent, yet investigation shows that it is no different from the other counties. The church of Coughton was founded over an Iron-Age settlement, and that of Kynwarton has various deposits from the Iron Age to the early medieval period around it, for example burials. The churches at Salford Priors, Welford, and Hampton

Lucy, need further research, while Stratford-upon-Avon minster lies in an undated enclosure. It is possible that the church at Warwick was founded in an Iron-Age hill-fort, while the church at Leek Wootton, according to tradition, is on a Roman religious site. Tradition also claims that Wolston lies in a square camp. The name Harbury, and tradition, indicate that there was a fortification here also, while Burton Dasset church lies in a probable Roman enclosure, possibly a spring shrine. Great Wolford church lies in a partially levelled, but essentially undated, earthwork, which may have been the site of a hill-fort.

Similarly, in West Oxfordshire there is also evidence for minsters located on earlier sites. The church at Cropredy lies in an enclosure, as do those at Adderbury, through place-name evidence, and Bloxham, by inference of

Figure 57: The minster church of Dodderhill, Worcestershire (photograph S. Yeates).

street layout. Shipton-under-Wychwood church lies in an undated enclosure, while place-name and road layout evidence at Charlbury are indicative of this being the site of a large undated enclosure. The church at Eynsham lies in an enclosure at the centre of an extensive Bronze-Age settlement. The church at Stanton Harcourt also lies on an earlier site but one which is ill-defined; the name Black Ditch, however, may indicate a site associated with intensive early occupation. Excavations, and an assessment of the road layout, at Bampton show that the church lies inside a large valley-fort.

In Wiltshire, late Prehistoric and Roman material has also turned up at certain minster locations. There is a Roman town under Cricklade, and Malmesbury is in an Iron-Age hill-fort, as is, probably, Sherston. Chippenham lies in an undated enclosure, while at Bradford-on-Avon a Roman relief has been recovered, perhaps indicating the location of a temple. The church of Calne is claimed to lie in an old fortified site called Kingsbury.

In Somerset both minsters at Bath were located over temples; that of the presiding spirit of the place and a tribal temple. The minster at Keynsham lies on a Roman settlement, perhaps a small town, as do Portbury, and Congresbury. There is a Roman villa under Banwell, and a Roman site under Cheddar. Roman material has been recovered from Wells, while the abbey of Glastonbury lies in a large undated enclosure which has Roman pottery scattered across it. Frome is traditionally claimed as the location of a fortification.

CONCLUSIONS

British Christianity was making inroads into the region by *c.* AD 540, by means of the establishment of religious foundations. However, from what is known about the foundation of the church of Evesham in *c.* AD 700, pre-Christian motifs and temple sites were, apparently, still important. The story of the Evesham foundation contains an account of three women, one of whom was Mary, who might be plausibly interpreted as successors to the *Dobunnic* mothers. This interpretation raises serious questions concerning *Theodore's* foundation of the parochial system and implies that the structure around which the parishes were arranged was a pre-existing social system. It also implies that the acceptance of Christianity was not simply reliant on the imposition of kingship, but was probably achieved through the actions of countless missionaries in every corner of the territory. This process took over two hundred years and was, ultimately, reliant on the incorporation of the local folk-based religions, based on the recognition and personification of each of the folk-groups' characters. In this process the Christianisation of the pagan shrines can be recognised. The *genius* or *tyche*, which was the presiding spirit of each folk-group, had to be absorbed. This ties in with Bede's comments about *Raedwald* and Bishop *Mellitus's* letter.

Why particular sites were chosen for the establishment of the minsters is not known exactly but they must have been chosen for their religious relevance to the folk-groups of the area. Large ancient settlements would have invariably had religious sites in them, and hill-forts must also have had a religious component. It is not the case that one type of site was chosen for the establishment of the church, but all of those sites chosen may have had an underlying spirituality.

Chapter 13

The Never Dying Gods:
Nature Deities in a Christian World

As the influence of Christianity spread the power of the old religion did not die immediately, but rather the deities faded and were absorbed into the histories, traditions, folk-lore and genealogies of the new age (Yeates 2006, i.90–95). This can be deduced from both Welsh and English texts, in place-name evidence, and in recorded genealogies.

That river and tribal deities were being written into genealogies is evident in at least two examples from outside the area, one from the Continent and the other from Wales. The first of these examples dates from the third century AD and concerns a Belgic chieftain called Viridomix who claimed decent from the god of the Rhine (Saint Clair Baddeley 1924, 27); possibly copying the imperial Roman habit of using gods as ancestors, part of liminal sanctification. The Welsh example implies that the tribal deity of the *Demetae* was being incorporated in to the genealogical lists as the founder of the royal line. Dumville (1977, 72–104) has noted that the royal line of Dyfed claimed descent from *Dimet*; presumably, an eponymous ancestral divinity, whose name was derived from the personification of the *Demetae*. The recording of the name DEMETI on an early medieval stone at Saint Dogmael's, in the form HOGTIVIS FILI DEMETI, shows a tribal name being used as a personal name; again, the reference is probably not so much to a person but to the presiding deity of the people.

Early medieval royal lines in Britain also claimed descent from gods. The Mercian royal family claimed descent from Woden, *Icel, Cnebba, Cynewald, Crida, Pypba*, and *Penda* (Brooks 1989 159–170, 162–164). This group were called the *Icelingas*. *Icel* is thought to have been a historical figure but this has not been proven. In an assessment of early tribal names across the kingdom of Middlesex it became apparent that some of the folk-group names (Bailey 1989, 108–122), for example *Beningas*, were derived from natural features; in this case, the etymology is **people of the river Beane**. The place-name *Gumeninga hearh*, modern Harrow, means the **pagan sanctuary of *Guma's* people**. The interpretation may be slightly misleading as *Guma* may have been the local deity. It is apparent, therefore, that the genealogies that developed in the Later Roman period and in the post-Roman world incorporated the names of deities of rivers and gods of tribes amongst their founders.

Certain medieval and pre-medieval texts were often constructed using a mixture of ideas from a number of sources. Academic approaches to such tales and texts have evolved over time. The oldest European texts are those of Greece, for example Homer's, which are seen as stratified tales mentioning places and artefacts which were lived in or used at different dates in history (Sherratt 1992, 145–165). There are also Irish texts which have been thought of in similar ways, some of which have already been encountered. Initially it was thought that the tales could be projected back into the Iron Age, but it is now apparent that they are a more complicated mix using assumed or desired material from the past and also some from the time in which they were written (Aitchison 1994).

A similar approach could be used with the Welsh tales, but this has not been done to any great extent. The group of eleven tales referred to now as *The Mabinogion* is a relatively recent compilation. The stories have survived in the form of two medieval Welsh texts (Gantz 1976, 29–33): The *White Book of Rhydderch*, compiled in *c.* 1325, and the *Red Book of Hergest*, of *c.* 1400. It has not been resolved whether the White Book was the first transcript or whether both were transcribed from an earlier, but now lost, document. The two texts are not considered to have been well known in Wales until their translation into English in 1849, by Lady Charlotte Guest. Of the other translations that have been undertaken, the most notable are the translations of the White Book; by Evans, in 1907; and by Jones and Jones, in 1948; and the translation of the Red Book, in 1927, by Ellis and Lloyd. The only significant study of any of these tales was carried out on the tale of Bran. When assessing such tales archaeologically a number of aspects have to be scrutinised, including locations, the nature of the dwellings, the people's dress, the modes of combat, and the weaponry involved; to this can be added religious sculpture.

THE *DEITIES*, *GENII* AND *MATRES* OF THE *DOBUNNI* THROUGH TIME

Many legends have been written about the foundations of the minsters and abbeys of Britain, and it is possible that, in a number of cases, there may be some idea or concealed knowledge which can be deciphered. The legendary cycle for the foundation of Glastonbury Abbey is one such tale and combines many of the ideas which have been discussed on a general European level. The story describes how a Swine herder called *Glast* followed a wandering sow to an apple tree, which later became the site of the abbey. The story has been dismissed as medieval pseudo history, but this does not explain many of the problems which underlie the tale (Thornton 1991, 191–203). *Glast* is a name associated with a place-name and as *glass* or *glast* it may also be a river-name, while the mythical character is also the ancestor of a folk-group which also shares its name with Glastonbury. This figure bears all the characteristics of a *genius* who had been manipulated by newly emerging religious forces. The images associated with him may have been added to later or may already have existed since the Roman period or before.

A second account concerns the foundation of the abbey of Evesham, see Chapter 2. Here again, there is a swine herdsman, called *Eoves*, who follows a sow and comes across three women. The story has been described previously, but we have Evesham and *Eoves*, creating a tradition of folk-beliefs and developing place-names.

The Welsh traditions claim that there was a mythical character of the fifth century called *Glywys*, who was the ancestor of the *Glywysinga* (Savory 1984, 317). An alternative suggestion, however, that has been made is that *Gywysinga* was derived from *Glevensis* and that the name parallels *Erging*, which was derived from *Ariconium*. If this was the case then it is apparent that *Glywys* must be the eponymous deity of the city of Gloucester, which then re-emerged in the Welsh traditions of South Wales in a genealogical list. Gloucester had a city *tyche*, but *Glywys* is accounted as masculine (Yeates 2006, i.91). There is the possibility that this deity also existed in a masculine form.

The goddess *Cuda* was identified as a deity with shrines in the Cotswolds, yet in the eighth century, when this name was used it was as a personal-name, which must indicate a local association with a recognisable personification. This possibly means that the deity may have developed into a folk-tradition or genealogical character who emerged to provide the origin for certain names. Further examples, in the Cotswold area, of natural features associated with so-called personal names may include: Colesborne, Dowdeswell, Isbourne, and Crudwell. These must have fitted into a folk process which gave the presiding spirits a persona with ancestral origins, with the reality eventually becoming subsumed and lost. There must have been a cultural interplay causing confusion between places, a system of homonyms, and later back formations which are now difficult to disentangle; by using the place-name, sculptural, and textual evidence, and the theories underlying them, we can now attempt to untangle these.

The Mabinogion was brought together in its present form in the high middle ages. There are references to Gloucester that referred to what was going on in two of the recognised temple complexes in the city (Gantz 1976, 165–166; Jones and Jones 1974, 123–126). In the first extract, from *How Culhwch won Olwen*, Arthur's followers or warriors, are looking for *Mabon*, son of *Modron*, **the son of the mother**. The searchers asked, in succession: an ousel, a stag, an owl, an eagle and a salmon, about his whereabouts. *Mabon*, they were informed by the salmon of Llyn Llyw, was taken away from his mother after three days and imprisoned, most cruelly, at *Caer Loyw* (Gloucester). References to *Mabon* and *Modron* can also be found in Roman-period inscriptions. *Mabon* can be equated with the 'Celtic' god *Maponus* (a god recorded on religious inscriptions in northern Britain, for example at Corbridge, and on a place-name in Gaul, *Mabono Fonte*, the well of Mabon). *Modron* can be associated with the 'Celtic' goddess *Matrona* (the goddess of the river Marne, France). These characters can, therefore, even before the location of the tale is considered, be associated with a series of older ideas. Archaeological evidence for the cult of Cybele and Attis in Britain is present for Gloucester (Lewis 1966, 117). The location of the temple has, however, not been determined. In the Roman period native gods were associated with Roman deities, and there has been a suggestion that the god *Maponus* was associated with the god Attis, although on minimal evidence.

In *Peredur, son of Evrawg*, the story mentioned a fortress called Gloucester, which was inhabited by a group of nine hags, and their father and mother. It was they who taught Peredur the art of horse riding and how to handle arms. At the end of the tale Peredur went back to Gloucester and killed the hags. The legend of Peredur does not mention a sacred vessel or cauldron at Gloucester specifically, but it does mention a large circular valley and the nine hags. The significance of the nine hags, maidens, or damsels has long been a point of discussion. Much of this is based on the poem *The spoils of Annwn*, written *c*. AD 900, which can be found in *the Book of Taliesin* (Nash 1858, 210–216). In the second verse is a reference to a cauldron, warmed by the breath of nine damsels. Such examples have given rise to the association of the nine women with a large water vessel. This seems to be a reference to the *Dobunni Mater*, whose symbol was a cauldron or sacred vessel. Hence, the nine maidens or hags (priestesses) were known to live with their mother (*Mater*) and father (Mercury), and to look after the sacred vessel (the tub or Vale of Gloucester).

In the Mabinogion, the River *Cynfael* is also mentioned, see chapter 7, the name is a reduced form of *Cunomaglos*, a deity only recorded in the *Dobunnic* area and part of a widespread cult. He is described in the text as 'a hunter killing stags'; this also describes aspects of the local Cotswold hunter god cult. Here also, there are traditions of a *Dobunnic* origin which were being reused in the Mabinogion. These may only be small fragments of the tales but it is apparent that images used and current in the second to fourth century in the Gloucestershire and Wiltshire areas were re-emerging in the thirteenth century as short extracts explaining aspects of the religion in the Vale of Gloucester and the surrounding area. How this occurred probably had something to do with *Glywysinga* and *Glevensis*, and perhaps an elite band which moved from Gloucester into South Wales.

There are also later medieval accounts of presiding spirits. *William Worcestre* (Neale 2000, nos. 55–56, 64), in the late fifteenth century, described a giant called *Ghyst*, associated with Clifton Camp, and the hot spring at Hotwells which was described as being placed below Ghyston Rock. It can be hypothesised that this spring would have had a presiding spirit in the Roman period. It is not now apparent, however, how all of this fitted together, how much of it is medieval pseudo-history, and how much of it derived from traditions associated with the pre-Christian religion. Other mythical giants have also been reported in the Somerset area. The most notable example is *Merk*, associated with Maesbury Castle. This story's origins are unknown, but it may have been a late development, as the name was derived from an Old English place-name. However, this tradition does show that the concept of the presiding spirit persisted, with examples being created or reworked well into the fifteenth century.

CONCLUSIONS

It seems that the presiding spirits and other deities did not disappear quietly, and, as in other Christianised kingdoms, the *Hwicce* combined their old traditions with the new. The presiding spirits of place, the symbols of their communities, were written into their genealogies and folk-lore. Of the temples that existed at Gloucester, it is also apparent that their traditions, images and knowledge influenced certain paragraphs in later texts, as these were being grafted into more complex arrangements. The cult of *Maponus* and *Matrona*, the cult of the divine couple with the sacred cauldron, and also the cult of the hunter-god *Cunomaglos*, had all been reawakened from their temple slumber to be talked of in the halls of kings and nobles.

The questions raised at the start concerned the relationship of the *Dobunni* and the *Hwicce*, the significance of the latter name, and how religion was used within their communities is a complex matter. Hopefully, this has provided some answers to these sweeping questions. The landscape was deified on all levels of its topography, both rivers and hills. Sacred enclosures, groves and standing posts were established. The folk-groups had a long development; and some of the pre-Old English groups left their impression on medieval names. Many archaeological features can be recognised which tie into these communal groups as places of social action. That the *Dobunni* and the *Hwicce* were one and the same people is possibly demonstrated most cogently by the recognition of the tribal goddess with her sacred vessel, which emerged as part of a cult; first in burial practices in the Iron Age, as the symbol of a *mater* in the Roman period, and later providing the tribal name in the early medieval period. These deities can be recognised but it also can be seen that they did not fade with the acceptance of Christianity but turned up in medieval traditions, folk-lore, and place-names. Technology may change, invasions and the movement of peoples may occur; but for over a thousand years the *Dobunnic* mother ruled and haunted her tribe of 'witches'.

Bibliography

Aitchison, N. (1994) *Armagh and the royal centres in early medieval Ireland*, Glasgow, Cruithne Press.

Akerman, J. Y. (1857) Some account of the possessions of the abbey of Malmesbury in North Wiltshire, in the days of the Anglo-Saxon kings; with remarks on the ancient limits of the Forest of Braden, *Archaeologia* 37, 257–315.

Alcock, J. P. (1966) Some aspects of Celtic religion in Gloucestershire and the Cotswolds, *Transactions of the Bristol and Gloucestershire Archaeological Society* 85, 45–56.

Alcock, J. P. (1986) The concept of genius in Roman Britain. In, M. Henig and A. C. King (eds) *Pagan gods and shrines of the Roman Empire*, 113–133, Oxford, Oxford University Committee for Archaeology.

Aldhouse-Green, M. J. (1999) Introduction, Aldhouse Green, M. J., ed. *Pilgrims in stone: stone images from the Gallo-Roman sanctuary of Fontes Sequanae*, Oxford, BAR International Series 754, 1–9.

Aldhouse-Green, M. (2002) Any old iron! symbolism and ironworking in Iron-Age Europe. In M. Aldhouse-Green and P. Webster (eds) *Artefacts and archaeology: aspects of the Celtic and Roman world*, 8–19, Cardiff, University of Wales.

Allen, D. (1944) The Belgic dynasties of Britain and their coins, *Archaeologia* 90, 1–46.

Allen, D. (1961) A study of the Dobunnic coinage. In, E. M. Clifford (ed.) *Bagendon: a Belgic oppodum*, 75–149, Cambridge, Heffer.

Allies, J. (1852) *On the ancient British, Roman, and Saxon antiquities and folk-lore of Worcestershire*, London and Worcester, Privately Published

ApSimon, A. M. (1965) The Roman temple on Brean Down, Somerset, *Proceedings of the University of Bristol Spelæological Society* 10 (3), 195–258.

ApSimon, A. M., Rahtz, P. A. and Harris, L. G. (1958) The Iron Age A ditch and pottery at Pagans' Hill, Chew Stoke, *Proceedings of the University of Bristol Spelæological Society* 8 (2), 97–105.

Arnold, T. N. (1912) Pembridge, *Transactions of the Woolhope Naturalists' Field Club* 21, 18.

Atkin, M. (1990) Excavations in Gloucester 1989: an interim report, *Glevensis* 24, 2–13

Atkin, M. and Garrod, A. P. (1990) Archaeology in Gloucester, 1989, *Transactions of the Bristol and Gloucestershire Archaeological Society* 108, 185–192.

Atkyns, R. (1712) *The ancient and present state of Gloucestershire*, London, W.Bowyer (Gloucestershire County Histories 1974 reprint).

Bagnall-Oakeley, M. E. (1882) On Roman coins found in the Forest of Dean, *Transactions of the Bristol and Gloucestershire Archaeological Society* 6, 107–22.

Bagnall-Oakeley, W. (1889) Roman coins found in the Forest of Dean, *Transactions of the Woolhope Naturalists' Field Club* 12, 356–8.

Bagnall-Oakeley, M. E. (1895) Notes on a great hoard of Roman coins found at Bishop's Wood in 1895, *Transactions of the Bristol and Gloucestershire Archaeological Society* 19, 399–420.

Bagnall-Smith, J. (1995) Interim report on the votive material from Romano-Celtic temple sites in Oxfordshire, *Oxoniensia* 60, 177–203.

Bailey, K. (1989) The Middle Saxons. In, S. Bassett (eds) *The origins of Anglo-Saxon kingdoms*, 108–122, Leicester, Leicester University Press.

Barker, P. P. and Ranity, G. F. (2003) *A report for the friends of Leominster Priory on a geophysical survey carried out at Leominster Priory*, Leominster, The friends of Leominster Priory.

Barrett, J., C., Freeman, P. W. M. and Woodward, A. (2000) *Cadbury Castle, Somerset: the late prehistoric and early historic archaeology*, London, English Heritage Archaeological Report 20.

Bassett, S. (1989) Churches in Worcester before and after the conversion of the Anglo-Saxons, *The Antiquaries Journal* 69, 225–256.

Bathurst, W. H. (1879) *Roman antiquities at Lydney Park, Gloucestershire*, London, Longmans, Green and Co.

Bauchhenss, G. (1976) *Jupitergigantensäulen*, Stuttgard, Ges. für Vor.

Barclay, W. J., Ambrose, K., Chadwick, R. A. and Pharaoh, T. C. (1997) *British geological survey: geology of the country around Worcester*, London, Her Majesty's Stationary Office.

Beckinsale, R. P. (1991) The Cotswold Hills: a geographical definition, *Proceedings of the Cotswold Naturalists' Field Club* 40 (1), 20–30.

Beesley, T. (1853) On Roman remains in the neighbourhood of Banbury and on the late remarkable discovery of coins at Evenley, *North Oxfordshire Archaeological Society* 1, 15–24.

Bell, M. (1990) *Brean Down excavations 1983–1987*, London, English Heritage Archaeological Report 15.

Bell, M. and Walker, M. J. C. (1992) *Late Quaternary environmental change*, Harlow, Longman.

Besly, E. M. (1986) The coins, *Britannia* 17, 304–316.

Bettenson, H. (1943) *Documents of the Christian Church*, Oxford, Oxford University Press.

Blair, J. (1994) *Anglo-Saxon Oxfordshire*, Stroud, Sutton Publishing.

Blair, J. (2005) *The Church in Anglo-Saxon society*, Oxford, Oxford University Press.

Blake, J. E. H. (1908–11) At Mathon, *Transactions of the Woolhope Naturalists' Field Club* 20, 180–1.

Blake, J. E. H. (1913) Some remains of the Bronze Age at Mathon, *Proceedings and Transactions of the Birmingham Archaeological Society* 39, 90–3.

Boon, G. C. (1989) A Roman sculpture rehabilitated: the Pagans Hill dog, *Britannia* 20, 201–17.

Boon, G. C. (1992) Traces of Romano-British Christianity in the West Country, *Transactions of the Bristol and Gloucestershire Archaeological Society* 110, 37–52.

Bowen, C. (2003) Pebble tools from the Forest of Dean, *Glevensis* 36, 16.

Bradbury, J. and Croft, R. A. (1989) Somerset archaeology, 1989, *Proceedings of the Somerset Archaeological and Natural History Society* 133, 157–85.

Bradford, J. S. P. and Goodchild, R. G. (1939) Excavations at Frilford, Berkshire, 1937–8, *Oxoniensia* 4, 1–70.

Bradley, R. (1984) *The social foundations of prehistoric Britain: themes and variations in the archaeology of power*, Harlow, Longman.

Bradley, R. (1990) *The passage of arms: an archaeological analysis of prehistoric hoards and votive deposits*, Cambridge, Cambridge University Press.

Bradley, R., Entwistle, R. and Raymond, F. (1994) *Prehistoric land divisions on Salisbury Plain: the work of the Wessex linear ditches project*, London, English Heritage Archaeological Report 2.

Brandon, A. (1989) *British geological survey: geology of the country between Hereford and Leominster*, London, Her Majesty's Stationary Office.

Braudel, F. (1972) *The Mediterranean and the Mediterranean world in the age of Philip II, volume I*, London, Collins.
Breeze, A. (1998) The name of Laughern Brook, near Worcester, *Transactions of the Worcestershire Archaeological Society (Third Series)* 16, 251–2.
Breeze, A. (2002) Plastered walls at Rudchester? The Roman place-names Vindovala and Nemetovala, *Archaeologia Aeliana (fifth series)* 30, 49–51.
Brett, J. (1996) Archaeology and the construction of the Royal Edward Dock, Avonmouth, 1902–1908, *Archaeology in the Severn Estuary* 7, 115–20.
Brewer, R. J. (1986) *Corpus of sculpture of the Roman World, Great Britain volume I fascicule 5: Roman sculpture from Wales*, Oxford, Oxford University Press.
Britnell, W. J. (1975) An interim report upon excavations at Beckford, 1972–4, *Vale of Evesham Historical Society Research Papers* 5, 1–12.
Brooks, N. (1989) The formation of the Mercian kingdom. In, S. Bassett (ed.) *The origins of Amglo-Saxon kingdoms*, 159–70, Leicester, Leicester University Press.
Bryant, R. and Heighway, C. M. (2003) Excavations at Saint Mary de Lode church, Gloucestershire, 1978–9, *Transactions of the Bristol and Gloucestershire Archaeological Society* 121, 97–178.
Brunaux, J.-L., Meniel, P. and Po'plim, F. (1985) *Gournay I: Les fouilles sur le sanctuaire et l'oppidum*, Paris, Revue Archéologique de Picardie.
Brunaux, J.-L. and Rapin, A. (1988) *Gournay II: boucliers et et lances: dépôts et trophées*, Paris, Revue Archéologique de Picardie.
Burnham, B. C., Hunter, F. and Fitzpatrick, A. P. (2002) Roman Britain in 2001, 1 sites explored, *Britannia* 34, 276–354.
Burnham, B. C., Keppie, L. J. F. and Esmonde Cleary, A. S. (2000) Roman Britain in 1999: 1, sites explored, *Britannia* 31, 372–423.
Burrow, I. (1981) *Hillfort and hill-top settlement in the first to eighth centuries AD*, Oxford, British Archaeological Reports (British Series) 91.
Burrow, I. and Bennett, J. (1979) A Romano-British relief from Cadbury Camp, Tickenham, Avon, BookA Romano-British relief from Cadbury Camp, Tickenham, Avon, Bristol, *Bristol Museum and Art Gallery Monograph* 2, 1–5.
Bush, T. S. (1905) Preliminary exploration in the second field east of the Grenville Monument, Lansdown, June, 1905, *Proceedings of the Bath Branch of the Somerset Archaeological and Natural History Society*, 57–61.
Cadoux, J.-L. (1986) Les armes du sanctuare gaulois de Ribemont-sur-Ancre (Somme) et leur contexte. In, A. Duval and J. Gomez de Soto (eds) *Actes du VIIIe coloque surles Ages du Fer en France non-Méditerrane'enne, Angoul, 1984*, 203–210, Aquitania Supplement I.
Cadoux, J.-L. (1991) Organisation spatiale et chronologie du sanctuaire de Ribemont-sur-Ancre. In, J.-L. Brunaux (ed.) *Les sanctuaire Celtiques et le monde Méditerrainéenne*, Paris, Dossiers de Protohistoire 3.
Cantrill, T. C., Sherlock, R. L. and Dewey, H. (1919) *Special reports on the mineral resources of Great Britain IX: Iron ores, sundry unbedded ores of Durham, East Cumberland, North Wales, Derbyshire, the Isle of Man, Bristol district and Somerset, Devon and Cornwall*, London, Her Majesty's Stationary Office.
Carley, J. P. (1988) *Glastonbury Abbey: the holy house at the head of the moors adventurous*, Woodbridge, The Boydell Press.
Charlton, D. B. and Mitcheson, M. M. (1983) Yardhope: a shrine to Cocidius, *Britannia* 14, 143–153.
Childs, S. T. (1993) Indigenous African metallurgy: native and culture, *Annual Review of Anthropology* 22, 317–337.

Chouls, W. H. (1993) The Whitminster, Eastington and Frampton-on-Severn areas, *Glevensis* 27, 8–20.
CIL (1869) *Corpus Inscriptionum Latinarum: inscriptiones Hispaniae Ltinae, volume 2, part 1*, Berlin, Berolini apud Georgium Reimerum.
CIL (1872) *Corpus Inscriptionum Latinarum: incriptiones Galliae Cisalpinae Latinae, volume 5, part 1*, Berlin, Berolini apud Georgium Reimerum.
CIL (1899) *Corpus Inscriptionum Latinarum: incriptiones trium Galliarum et Germaniarum Latinae, volume 13, part 1, fasciculae 1, Aquitania, Provincia, Lugudunensis*, Berlin, Berolini apud Georgium Reimerum.
Clifford, E. M. (1961) *Bagendon, a Belgic oppidum: excavations 1954–1956*, Cambridge, Heffer.
Coates, R. and Breeze, A. (2000) *Celtic voices, English places: studies of the Celtic impact on place-names in England*, Stamford, Shaun Tyas.
Coles, J. and Minnitt, S. (1995) *Industrious and fairly civilized: the Glastonbury lake village*, Taunton, Somerset County Council Museum Services.
Colgrave, B. and Mynors, R. A. B. (1969) *Bede's Ecclesiastical history of the English people*, Oxford, Clarendon Press.
Copeland, T. (1988) The North Oxfordshire Grim's Ditch: a fieldwork survey, *Oxoniensia* 53, 277–292.
Copeland, T. (2002) *Iron-Age and Roman Wychwood: the land of Satavacus and Bellicia*, Charlbury, The Wychwood Press.
Coplestone-Crow, B. (1989) *Herefordshire place-names*, Oxford, British Archaeological Reports (British Series) 214.
Collingwood, R. G. (1932) Inscriptions, Wheeler, R. E. M. and Wheeler, T. V. (eds) *Report on the excavation of the prehistoric, Roman, and post-Roman site in Lydney Park, Gloucestershire*, London, Reports of the Research Committee of the Society of Antiquaries of London IX, 100–104.
Collinson, J. (1791) *The history and antiquities of the county of Somerset, collected from authentick records, and an actual survey made by the late Mr. Edmund Rack adorned with a map of the county, and engarvings of Roman and other reliques, town-seals, baths, churches, and Gentlemen's seats, volume 1*, Bath, R. Cruttwell.
Cooke, W. H. (1882) *Collections towards the history and antiquities of the county of Hereford: in continuation of Duncumb's history, volume III*, London, John Murray.
Corney, M. (2001) The Romano-British nucleated settlements of Wiltshire. In, P. Ellis (ed.) *Roman Wiltshire and after*, 4–38, Devizes, Wiltshire Archaeological and Natural History Society.
Cox, D. C. (1979) A currency bar hoard from Harrow Hill, Middle Littleton, *Vale of Evesham Historical Society Research Papers* 7, 31–38.
Craddock, P. T. (1995) *Early metal mining and production*, Edinburgh, Edinburgh University Press.
Cross, F. L. and Livingstone, E. A. (1977) *The Oxford dictionary of the Christian Church (second edition corrected)*, Oxford, Oxford University Press.
Cunliffe, B. (1989) The Roman tholos from the sanctuary of Sulis Minerva at Bath, England. In, R. I. Curtis (ed.) *Stvdia pompeiana and classica, in honour of Wilhelima F. Jashemski, volume II: Classica*, 59–86, New York, Orpheus Press.
Cunliffe, B. (1991) *Iron Age communities in Britain (third edition)*, London, Routledge.
Cunliffe, B. and Davenport, P. (1985) *The temple of Sulis Minerva at Bath, volume 1(I) the site*, Oxford, Oxford University Committee for Archaeology Monograph 7.
Cunliffe, B., W. and Fulford, M. G. (1982) *Corpus of sculpture of the Roman World, volume I fascicule 2: Great Britain, Bath and the rest of Wessex*. Oxford, Oxford University Press.

Dalwood, H. (2002) Archaeology in Worcestershire (outside Worcester) 2000–2001, *Transactions of the Worcestershire Archaeological Society (Third Series)* 18, 235–243.
Darlington, R. R. and McGurk, P. (1995) *The Chronicle of John of Worcester*, Oxford, Clarendon Press.
Darvill, T. (1987) *Prehistoric Britain*, London, Batsford.
Darvill, T., C. and Grinsell, L. V. (1989) Gloucestershire barrows: supplement 1961–1988, *Transactions of the Bristol and Gloucestershire Archaeological Society* 107, 39–105.
Davenport, P. (1999) *Archaeology in Bath: excavations 1984–1989*, Oxford, British Archaeological Reports (British Series) 284.
Davies, J. A. and Phillips, C. W. (1926) The Percy Sladen memorial fund excavations at Bury Hill Camp, Winterbourne Down, Gloucestershire, 1926, *Proceedings of the University of Bristol Spelæological Society* 3 (1), 8–25.
Dearne, M. J. and Branigan, K. (1995) The use of coal in Roman Britain, *The Antiquaries Journal* 75, 71–105.
Derks, T. (1998) *Gods, temples and ritual practices: the transformation of religious ideas and values in Roman Gaul*, Amsterdam, Amsterdam University Press.
Dewey, H. (1921) *Special reports on the mineral resources of Great Britain XXI: Lead, Silver-lead and Zinc ores of Cornwall, Devon and Somerset*, London, His Majesty's Stationary Office.
Dinn, J. (2000) Archaeology in the city of Worcester, 1997–99, *Transactions of the Worcestershire Archaeological Society (Third Series)* 17, 321–331.
Dinn, J. (2002) Archaeology in the city of Worcester, 2000–2001, *Transactions of the Worcestershire Archaeological Society (Third Series)* 18, 245–254.
Dixon, P. (1994) *Crickley Hill, volume 1: the hill-fort defences*, Nottingham, Crickley Hill Trust and University of Nottingham.
Dobson, D. P. (1933) Anglo-Saxon buildings and sculpture in Gloucestershire, *Transactions of the Bristol and Gloucestershire Archaeological Society* 55, 261–276.
Drinkwater, J. F. (2000) A review: Gods, temples and ritual practices: the transformation of religious ideas and values in Roman Gaul, by T. Derks, Amsterdam, 1998, *Britannia* 31, 458–459.
Dumville, D. N. (1977) Kingship, genealogies and regnal lists. In, P. H. Sawyer and I. N. Wood (eds) *Early medieval kingship*, 72–104, Leeds, The school of History, University of Leeds.
Durkheim, E. (1964) *The elementary forms of religious life*, London, Allen and Unwin.
Earp, J. R., Hains, B. A., Pocock, R. W. and Whitehead, T. H. (1971) *British regional geology: the Welsh borderland (third edition)*, London, Her Majesty's Stationary Office.
Edmonds, E. A., Poole, E. G. and Wilson, V. (1965) *Memoirs of the geological survey of Great Britain: England and Wales: geology of the country around Banbury and Edge Hill*, London, Her Majesty's Stationary Office.
Edwards, R., Griffin, L. and Dalwood, H. (2002) Excavations on the site of the New Police Station, Castle Street, Worcester, *Transactions of the Worcestershire Archaeological Society (Third Series)* 18, 103–132.
Ehrenreich, R. M. (1994) Ironworking in Iron Age Wessex. In, A. P. Fitzpatrick and E. L. Morris (eds) *The Iron Age in Wessex: recent work*, 16–18, Association Francaise, D'Etude de L'Age du Fer and Trust for Wessex Archaeology.
Ekwall, E. (1928) *English river-names*, Oxford, Oxford University Press.
Ekwall, E. (1960) *The Oxford dictionary of English place-names (fourth edition)*, Oxford, Oxford University Press.
Eliade, M. (1956) *The forge and the crucible: the origins and structure of alchemy (second edition)*, Chicargo, University of Chicago Press.

Elkington, H. D. H. (1976) The Mendip lead industry. In, K. Branigan and P. J. Fowler (eds) *The Roman West Country: Classical culture and Celtic society*, 183–197, Newton Abbot, David and Charles.
Ellis Davidson, H. R. (1964) *Gods and myths of Northern Europe*, Harmondsworth, Penguin.
Espérandieu, É. (1910) *Recueil Général des bas-reliefs, statues, et bustes de la Gaule Romaine (tome troisième): Lyonnaise, première partie*, Paris, Imprimerie Nationale.
Espérandieu, É. (1915) *Recueil Général des bas-reliefs, statues, et bustes de la Gaule Romaine (tome sixième): Belgique, deuxième partie*, Paris, Imprimerie Nationale.
Espérandieu, É. (1918) *Recueil Général des bas-reliefs, statues, et bustes de la Gaule Romaine (tome huitième): Germanie Supérieure*, Paris, Imprimerie Nationale.
Espérandieu, É. (1922) *Recueil Général des bas-reliefs, statues, et bustes de la Gaule Romaine (tome huitième): Gaule Germanique, deuxième partie*, Paris, Imprimerie Nationale.
Espérandieu, É. (1925) *Recueil Général des bas-reliefs, statues, et bustes de la Gaule Romaine (tome neuvième): Gaule Germanique, troisième partie*, Paris, Imprimerie Nationale.
Everitt, A. (1977) River and Wold: reflections on the historical origins of regions and pays, *Journal of Historical Geography* 3 (1), 1–19.
Faulkner, D. P. (1998) *Charterhouse: a reappraisal of a Roman small town, Bristol: unpublished dissertation for MA landscape archaeology*, University of Bristol.
Feuerbach, L. (1957) *The essence of Christianity*, New York, Harper.
Finberg, H. P. R. (1955) *Roman and Saxon Withington: a study in continuity*, Leicester, Leicester University Press.
Finberg, H. P. R. (1972) *The early charters of the West Midlands*, Leicester, Leicester University Press.
Fisher (1926) The Welsh Celtic bells, *Archaeologia Cambrensis* 81, 324–334.
Fosbrooke, T. D. (1807) *Abstracts of records and manuscripts respecting the county of Gloucester; formed into a history correcting the very eroneous accounts, and supplying numerous deficencies in Sir Robert Atkyns, and subsequent writers, volume 2*, Gloucester, Joseph Harris.
Fosbrooke, T. D. (1821) *Ariconensia or archæolgical sketches of Ross and Archenfield illustrative of the campaigns of Caractacus: the station of Ariconium, and with other matters*, Ross, W. Farror.
Fowler, P. J. and Miles, H. (1971) Excavation, fieldwork and finds, *Archaeological Review* 6, 11–49.
Fowler, P. J. and Miles, H. (1972) Excavation, fieldwork and finds, *Archaeological Review* 7, 12–65.
Fox, A. (1951) The date of the Orpheus mosaic from the Barton, Cirencester Park, Gloucestershire, *Transactions of the Bristol and Gloucestershire Archaeological Society* 70, 51–53.
Fox, H. S. A. (1989) The people of the wolds in English settlement history. In, M. Aston, D. Austin and C. Dyer (eds) *The rural settlement of medieval England: studies dedicated to Maurice Beresford and John Hirst*, Oxford, Blackwell, 77–101.
Frend, W. H. C. (1992) Pagans, Christians and the 'barbarian conspiracy' of AD 367 in Roman Britain, *Britannia* 23, 121–131.
Frere, S. S. (1990) Roman Britain in 1989: 1, sites explored, *Britannia* 21, 304–364.
Frere, S. S. (1991) Roman Britain in 1990: 1, sites explored, *Britannia* 22, 222–292.
Frere, S. S. (1992) Roman Britain in 1991: 1, sites explored, *Britannia* 23, 256–308.
Gantz, J. (1976) *The Mabinogion*, Harmondsworth, Penguin.
Gardner, K. S. (2004) Avon: an imperial pagus> a discussion paper, *Bristol and Avon Archaeology* 19, 65–74.
Geertz, C. (1975) *The interpretation of cultures*, London, Hutchinson.
Gelling, M. (1953) *The place-names of Oxfordshire: part 1*, Cambridge, Cambridge University Press.

Gelling, M. (1954) *The place-names of Oxfordshire: part 2*, Cambridge, Cambridge University Press.
Gelling, M. (1969) A note on the name Worcester, *Transactions of the Worcestershire Archaeological Society (Third Series)* 2, 26.
Gelling, M. (1973) *The place-names of Berkshire: part 1*, Cambridge, Cambridge University Press.
Gelling, M. (1978) *Signposts to the past: place-names and the history of England*, Chichester, Phillimore.
Gelling, M. (1982) The place-name volumes for Worcestershire and Warwickshire. In, T. R. Slater and P. J. Jarvis (eds) *Field and forest: an historical geography of Warwickshire and Worcestershire*, Norwich, Geo-Books, 59–78.
Gelling, M. and Cole, A. (2000) *The landscape of Place-names*, Stamford, Shaun Tyas.
Godoy, R. (1985) Mining: anthropological perspectives, *Annual Review of Anthropology* 14, 199–217.
Goold, G. P. (1999) *Virgil's Eclogues, Georgics and Aeneid libri i–vi*, London, Leob Classical Library.
Gough, J. W. (1930) *The mines of Mendip*, Oxford, Clarendon Press.
Gover, J. E. B., Mawer, A. and Stenton, F. M. (1936) *The place-names of Warwickshire*, Cambridge, Cambridge University Press.
Gover, J. E. B., Mawer, A. and Stenton, F. M. (1939) *The place-names of Wiltshire*, Cambridge, Cambridge University Press.
Green, G. W. and Welch, F. B. A. (1965) *Geology of the country around Wells and Cheddar*, London, Her Majesty's Stationary Office.
Green, M. J. (1986) *The gods of the Celts*, Stroud, Alan Sutton.
Green, M. J. (1989) *Symbol and image in Celtic religious art*, London, Routledge.
Green, M. J. (1992) *Animals in Celtic life and myth*, London, Routledge.
Green, M. J. (1993) A carved stone head from Steep Holm, *Britannia* 24, 241–242.
Greenfield, E. (1977) Herriott's Bridge. In, P. A. Rahtz and E. Greenfield (eds) *Excavations at Chew Valley Lake, Somerset*, London, Department of the Environment Archaeological Report 8, 69–82.
Grinsell, L. V. (1987) Somerset Barrows: revisions 1971–87, *Proceedings of the Somerset Archaeological and Natural History Society* 131, 13–26.
Grundy, G. B. (1927) Saxon charters of Worcestershire, *Transactions of the Birmingham Archaeological Society* 52, 1–183.
Grundy, G. B. (1928) Saxon charters of Worcestershire, *Transactions of the Birmingham Archaeological Society* 53, 18–131.
Grundy, G. B. (1932) The Saxon charters of Somerset, *Proceedings of the Somerset Archaeological and Natural History Society* 78, 161–192.
Grundy, G. B. (1933) Saxon Oxfordshire charters and ancient highways, *Oxfordshire Record Society Series* 15.
Grundy, G. B. (1936a) The ancient woodland of Gloucestershire, *Transactions of the Bristol and Gloucestershire Archaeological Society* 58, 65–155.
Grundy, G. B. (1936b) Saxon charters and field names of Gloucestershire, Gloucester, Bristol and Gloucester Archaeological Society.
Hadley, D. M. (2000) *The northern Danelaw: its social structure c. 800–1100*, Leicester, Leicester University Press.
Hamilton, W. G. (1938) A Bronze-Age burial site at Southend, *Transactions of the Woolhope Naturalists' Field Club* 29 (3), 120–127.
Hannan, A. (1993) Excavations at Tewkesbury 1972–74, *Transactions of the Bristol and Gloucestershire Archaeological Society* 111, 21–75.

Harding, D. W. (1987) The Iron-Age and Romano-British site at Woodeaton, Oxfordshire, excavations, 1965–66, Harding, D. W. (ed.) *Excavations in Oxfordshire, 1964–66*, 27–56, Edinburgh, University of Edinburgh, Department of Archaeology Occasional Paper 15.

Hart, C. E. (1944) Gold in Dean Forest, *Transactions of the Bristol and Gloucestershire Archaeological Society* 65, 98–104.

Hart, C. E. (2000) Verdict of the three foreign hundreds in the Forest of Dean (c. 1244), *The New Regard* 14, 63–66.

Hawkes, C. F. C. (1954) Archaeological theory and method: some suggestions from the Old World, *American Anthropologist* 56, 155–168.

Heighway, C. (1987) *Anglo-Saxon Gloucestershire*, Gloucester, Alan Sutton and Gloucestershire County Library.

Henig, M. (1984) *Religion in Roman Britain*, London, Batsford.

Henig, M. (1993) *Corpus of sculpture of the Roman World, Great Britain volume I fascicule 7: Roman sculpture from the Cotswold Region with Devon and Cornwall*, Oxford, Oxford University Press.

Henig, M. (1996) Sculptors from the West in London. In, J. Bird, M. Hassall and H. Sheldon (eds) *Interpreting Roman London: papers in memory of Hugh Chapman*, Oxford, Oxbow Monograph 58, 97–103.

Henig, M. (1998) A relief of a *mater* and three *genii* from Straton, Gloucestershire, *Transactions of the Bristol and Gloucestershire Archaeological Society* 116, 186–189.

Henig, M. (2004) *Corpus of sculpture of the Roman World, Great Britain volume I fascicule 9: Roman sculpture from the North West Midlands*, Oxford, Oxford University Press.

Henig, M. (2004) Murum civitatis, et fontem in ea a Romanis olim constructum: the arts of Rome in Carlisle and the civitates of the Carvetii and their inflence. In, M. R. McCarthey and D. Weston, (eds) *Carlile and Cumbria: Roman and medieval architecture, art, and archaeology*, 11–28, London, British Archaeological Association Conference Transactions at Carlisle 2004.

Henig, M., Cleary, R. and Purser, P. (2000) A relief of Mercury and Minerva from Aldsworth, Gloucestershire, *Britannia* 31, 362–363.

Herbert, E. W. (1984) *Red gold of Africa: copper in precolonial history and culture*, Madison, The University of Wisconsin.

Hingley, R. (2001) Iron Age archaeology in the West Midlands region: overview of the discussion points, *West Midlands Archaeology* 44, 98–100.

Hogan, E. (1910) *Onomasticon Goedelicum: Locorum et tribuum Hiberniae et Scotiae: an index with identifications, to the Gaelic names of places and tribes*, Dublin, Four Courts Press.

Holbrook, N. (1998) The shops in insula II (the possible macellum): excavations directed by J. S. Wacher, 1961. In, N. Holbrook (ed.) *Cirencester: the Roman town defences, public buildings and shops*, 177–188, Cirencester, Cirencester Excavations V.

Holbrook, N. (2003) Great Witcombe Roman villa, Gloucestershire: field surveys of its fabric and environs, 1999–2000, *Transactions of the Bristol and Gloucestershire Archaeological Society* 121, 179–200.

Hooke, D. (1985) *The Anglo-Saxon landscape: the Kingdom of the Hwicce*, Manchester, Manchester University Press.

Horton, A. (1987) *British geological survey: geology of the country around Chipping Norton*, London, Her Majesty's Stationary Office.

Hoverd, T. (1997) *Old Saint Bartholomew's church, Lower Sapey, Worcestershire: a re-interment*, Hereford, Archaeological Investigations Limited Hereford Archaeology Series 326.

Hurst, H. (1977) The prehistoric occupation on Churchdown Hill, *Transactions of the Bristol and Gloucestershire Archaeological Society* 95, 5–10.

Jack, G. H. (1911) Prehistoric burials, *Transactions of the Woolhope Naturalists' Field Club* 19, 235–236.
Jack, G. H. (1922) Excavations on the site of Ariconium: a Romano-British smelting town, situate in the parish of Weston-under-Penyard, South Herefordshire, *Transactions of the Woolhope Naturalists' Field Club* 23 (2), Addition 1–44.
Jones, G. and Jones, T. (1974) *The Mabinogion*, London, Dent.
Jones, H. L. (1917) *Strabo's The geography (I) libri i–ii*, London: Leob Classical Library.
Jones, H. L. (1928) *Strabo's The geography (V) libri x–xii*, London: Loeb Classical Library.
Kellaway, G. A. and Welch, F. B. A. (1993) *Geology of the Bristol district*, London, Her Majesty's Stationary Office.
Kenyon, K. M. (1953) Excavations at Sutton Walls, Herefordshire, 1948–1951, *The Archaeological Journal* 110, 1–87.
Lawrence, W. L. (1863) Excavations at Wycomb, *Proceedings of the Society of Antiquaries (second series)* 2, 302–307.
Lawrence, W. L. (1863) Excavations at Wycomb, Gloucestershire, *Gentleman's Magazine (New Series)* 15, 627.
Leech, R. (1986) The excavation of a Romano-Celtic temple and a later cemetery on Lamyatt Beacon, Somerset, *Britannia* 17, 259–328.
Leeds, E. T. (1924) An Anglo-Saxon cremation-burial of the seventh century in Asthall Barrow, Oxfordshire, *The Antiquaries Journal* 4, 113–26.
Leeds, E. T. (1930) A bronze cauldron from the River Cherwell, Oxfordshire, with notes on cauldrons and other bronze vessels of allied types, *Archaeologia* 80, 1–36.
Lewis, M. J. T. (1966) *Temples in Roman Britain*, Cambridge, Cambridge University Press.
Lewis, S. (1845) *Topographical dictionary of England, comprising the several counties, cities, boroughs, corporate and market towns, parishes, and the Islands of Guernsey, Jersey, and Man, volume 2 (fifth edition)*, London, S. Lewis and Co.
Lysons, S. (1797) *Account of Roman antiquities discovered at Woodchester*, London, T. Bensley.
Mackintosh, M. (1995) *The divine rider in the art of the Western Roman Empire*, Oxford, British Archaeology Reports (International Series) 607.
Maclean, J. (1885) *Smyth's The Berkeley manuscripts, volume III: a description of the hundred of Berkeley in the county of Gloucester and its inhabitants*, Gloucester, John Bellows.
Macray, W. D. (1863) *Chronicon Abbatiæ de Evesham*, London, Chronicles and memorials of Great Britain and Ireland during the Middle Ages.
Mahon (1848) Thursday, May 11th, 1848, *Proceedings of the Society of Antiquaries of London* 1 (13), 262–264.
Marshall, E. (1873) *The early history of Woodstock manor and its environs: in Bladon, Hensington, New Woodstock, Blenheim*, Oxford, James Parker.
Marx, K. and Engels, F. (1957) *On religion*, Moscow, Progress.
Mattern, M. (2001) *Corpus Signorum Imperii Roman: Corpus der skulpturen der Römischen Welt Deutschland, band II, 12 Germania Superior*, Bonn, Rudolf Habelt GMBH.
Mawer, A. and Stenton, F. M. (1927) *The place-names of Worcestershire*, Cambridge, Cambridge University Press.
Mawer, A. and Stenton, F. M. (1938) *The place-names of Hertfordshire*, Cambridge, Cambridge University Press.
Merrifield, R. (1996) The London hunter-god and his significance in the history of Londinium. In, J. Bird, M. Hassall and H. Sheldon (eds) *Interpreting Roman London: papers in memory of Hugh Chapman*, Oxford, Oxbow Monograph 58, 105–113.
Miles, D. and Palmer, S. (1982) *Figures in a landscape: archaeological investigations at Claydon Pike, Fairford/Lechlade, an interim report 1979–82*, Oxford, Oxford Archaeological Unit.

Miller, F. J. (1921) *Ovid's Metamorphoses (I) libri i–viii*, London: Leob Classical Library.
Miller, F. J. (1984) *Ovid's Metamorphoses (II) libri ix–xv*, London: Leob Classical Library.
Mitchell, G. H., Pocock, R. W. and Taylor, J. H. (1961) *Memoirs of the geological survey of Great Britain: England and Wales: geology of the country around Droitwich, Abberley and Kidderminster*, London, Her Majesty's Stationary Office.
Moffatt, J. M. (1805) *The history of the town of Malmesbury and its ancient abbey*, Tetbury, J. G. Goodwyn.
Moore, J. S. (1982) *Domesday Book: Gloucestershire*, Chichester, Phillimore.
Moore, T. (2001) An archaeological assessment of Hailey Wood Camp, Sapperton, Gloucestershire: a Roman temple complex in the Cotswolds? *Transactions of the Bristol and Gloucestershire Archaeological Society* 119, 83–93.
Morris, E. L. (1988) The Iron-Age occupation at Dibble's Farm, Christon, *Proceedings of the Somerset Archaeological and Natural History Society* 132, 23–81.
Morris, J. (1980) *Nennius' British History and the Welsh Annals*, Chichester, Phillimore.
Morris, J. R. (1965) Pelagian literature, *Journal of Theological Studies (New Series)* 16, 26–60.
Mould, C. (1997) Reports: West Midlands archaeology in 1997, *West Midlands Archaeology* 40, 22–114.
Mould, C. (1998) Reports: West Midlands archaeology in 1998, *West Midlands Archaeology* 41, 56–142.
Nash, D. W. (1858) *Taliesin; or the bards and druids of Britain, a translation of the remains of the earliest Welsh bards, and an examination of the bardic mysteries*, London, John Russell Smith.
Nash, J. (1979) *We eat the mines*, New York, Columbia University Press.
Neale, F. (2000) *William Worcestre: the topography of medieval Bristol*, Bristol, *Bristol Record Society Series* 51.
Norton, A. B. (1969) Burials. In, B. W. Cunliffe (ed.) *Roman Bath*, London, Report of the Research Committee of the Society of Antiquaries of London XXIV, 212–218.
O'Neil, H. E. and Toynbee, J. M. C. (1958) Sculptures from a Romano-British well in Gloucestershire, *Journal of Roman Studies* 48, 49–55.
O'Neil, H. and Grinsell, L. V. (1960) Gloucestershire barrows, *Transactions of the Bristol and Gloucestershire Archaeological Society* 79 (1), 5–149.
O'Rahilly, T. F. (1984) *Early Irish history and mythology*, Dublin, Dublin Institute for Advanced Studies.
Palmer, R. (1994) *The folklore of Gloucestershire*, Tiverton, Westcountry Books.
Parry, C. (1999) Iron Age, Romano-British and medieval occupation at Bishop's Cleeve, Gloucestershire: excavations at Gilder's Paddock 1989 and 1990–1, *Transactions of the Bristol and Gloucestershire Archaeological Society* 117, 89–118.
Pevsner, N. (1958) *The buildings of England: North Somerset and Bristol*, Harmondsworth, Penguin.
Pevsner, N. (1963) *The buildings of England: Herefordshire*, Harmondsworth, Penguin.
Pike, A. (1990) A review: South Midlands archaeology, *South Midlands Archaeology* 20, 81.
Pike, A. (1991) A review: South Midlands Archaeology, *South Midlands Archaeology* 21, 102–107.
Pretty, K. (1989) Defining the Magonsæte. In, S. Bassett (ed.) *The origins of Anglo-Saxon kingdoms*, 171–183, Leicester, Leicester University Press.
Price, E., G. (2000) *Frocester: a Romano-British settlement, its antecedents and successors, volume 2: the finds*, Gloucester, Gloucester and District Archaeological Research Group.
Pryor, F. M. M. (1991) *The English Heritage book of Flag Fen: prehistoric Fenland centre*, London, Batsford.

Rackham, H. (1952) *Pliny the Elder's Natural history (IX) libri. xxxiii–xxxv*, London, Leob Classical Library.
Rackham, H. (1968) *Pliny the Elder's Natural history (IV) libri. xii–xvi*, London, Leob Classical Library.
Rahtz, P. A. (1971) West Midlands archaeology: fieldwork, *West Midlands Archaeological News Sheet* 14, 6–38.
Rahtz, P. A. (1991) Pagan and Christian by the Severn Sea. In, J. P. Carley (ed.) *The archaeology and history of Glastonbury abbey: essays in honour of the ninetieth birthday of C. A. Raleigh Radford*, 3–37, Woodbridge, Boydell Press.
Rahtz, P. A. and Cleevedon Brown, J. (1959) Blaise Castle Hill, Bristol, 1957, *Proceedings of the University of Bristol Spelæological Society* 8 (3), 147–171.
Rahtz, P. A. and Watts, L. (1989) Pagans Hill revisited, *The Archaeological Journal* 146, 330–371.
Rawes, J. and Wills, J. (1996) Archaeological review no.20, 1995, *Transactions of the Bristol and Gloucestershire Archaeological Society* 114, 163–185.
RCHME (1932) *An inventory of the historical monuments in Herefordshire II: east*, London, His Majesty's Stationary Office.
RCHME (1976) *Ancient and historical monuments in the county of Gloucester, volume 1: Iron Age and Romano-British monuments in the Gloucestershire Cotswold*, London, Her Majesty's Stationary Office.
RIB(I) (1995) *The Roman inscriptions of Britain I: inscriptions on stone*, Stroud, Alan Sutton.
RIB(II:1) (1990) *The Roman inscriptions of Britain II, fascicule 1: instrumentum domestian*, Gloucester, Alan Sutton.
RIB(II:4) (1992) *The Roman inscriptions of Britain II, fascicule 4: instrumentum domesticum*, Stroud, Sutton Publishing.
Richardson, L. (1929) *Memoirs of the geological survey: England and Wales: The country around Moreton-in-Marsh*, London, His Majesty's Stationary Office.
Richardson, L. (1933) *Memoirs of the geological survey: England and Wales: the country around Cirencester*, London, His Majesty's Stationary Office.
Rippon, S. (1997) *The Severn estuary: landscape, evolution and reclamation*, Leicester, Leicester University Press.
Rivet, A. L. F. and Smith, C. (1979) *The place-names of Roman Britain*, London, Batsford.
RMP(I), R. o. M. a. P. I. (1996) *Recorded monuments protected under section 12 of the national monuments (amendment) act, 1994, County West Meath*, Dublin, National Monuments and Historic Properties Service.
Robinson, P. (2001) Religion in Roman Wiltshire. In, P. Ellis (ed.) *Roman Wiltshire and after*, 147–164, Devizes, Wiltshire Archaeological and Natural History Society.
Rodwell, W. (2001) *Wells Cathedral: excavations and structural studies, 1978–93, part 1: historical and structural sequence*, London, English Heritage Archaeological Report 21.
Ross, A. (1967) *Pagan Celtic Britain*, London, Routledge and Keegan Paul.
Royce, D. (1883) 'Finds' on, or near, the excursion of the society at Stow-on-the-Wold, *Transactions of the Bristol and Gloucestershire Archaeological Society* 7, 69–80.
Roymans, N. (1990) *Tribal societies in Northern Gaul: an anthropological perspective*, Amsterdam, Albert Egges van Giffen Instituut voor Prae- en Protohistories (Cingula 12).
Rudder, S. (1779) *A new history of Gloucestershire (comprising the topography antiquities, curiosities, produce, trade, and manufactures of the that county)*, Cirencester, Samuel Rudder.
Rudge, T. (1803) *The history of the county of Gloucester: brought down to the year 1803, volume 2*, Gloucester, G. H. Harris.
Russell, J. (1991) The Roman villa at Newton Saint Loe, *Bristol and Avon Archaeology* 9, 2–23.

Russell, J. R. and Williams, R. G. J. (1984) Romano-British sites in the city of Bristol – a review and gazetter, *Bristol and Avon Archaeology* 3, 18–26.

Sagona, A. G. and Webb, A. (1994) Toolunbunner in perspective. In, A. G. Sagona, (eds) *Bruising the red earth: ochre mining and ritual in Aboriginal Tasmania*, Melbourne, Melbourne University Press, 133–151.

Saint Clair Baddeley, W. (1913) *Place-names of Gloucestershire*, Gloucester.

Saint Clair Baddeley, W. (1924) *History of Cirencester*, Cirencester, Cirencester Newspaper Co. Ltd.

Saint Clair Baddeley, W. (1925) Custum-Scrubs or Roman Tump, *Transactions of the Bristol and Gloucestershire Archaeological Society* 45, 87–90.

Saint Clair Baddeley, W. (1930) The Romano-British Temple, Chedworth, *Transactions of the Bristol and Gloucestershire Archaeological Society* 52, 255–264.

Saint George Gray, H. (1929) Excavations at Kingsdown Camp, Mells, Somerset, 1928–29, *Proceedings of the Somerset Archaeological and Natural History Society* 75, 100–104.

Saint George Gray, H. (1929) Roman pewter, Meare, *Proceedings of the Somerset Archaeological and Natural History Society* 75, 105–106.

Savory, H. N. (1984) *Glamorgan county history II: early Glamorgan, pre-history and early history*, Cardiff, Glamorgan County History Trust.

Scarth, H. M. (1854) On ancient sepulchral remains discovered in and around Bath, *Proceedings of the Somerset Archaeological and Natural History Society* 5, 49–72.

Scarth, H. M. (1876) Roman Somerset, with special relation to recent discoveries in Bath, *Proceedings of the Somerset Archaeological and Natural History Society* 22, 1–30.

Scarth, H. M. (1879) On the Roman occupation of the West of England, particularly the county of Somerset, *The Archaeological Journal* 36, 321–336.

Scarth, H. M. (1888) Hoard of Roman coins, discovered on the property of W. W. Kettlewell esq., of Harptree Court, East Harptree, on the slope of the Mendip Hills, *Proceedings of the Somerset Archaeological and Natural History Society* 34, 21–28.

Schumer, B. (2004) *Oxfordshire Forests 1246–1609*, Oxfordshire Record Society Series 64.

Sellwood, L. (1984) Tribal boundaries viewed from the perspective of numismatic evidence. In, B. Cunliffe and D. Miles (ed.) *Aspects of the Iron Age in central Southern Britain*, 191–204, Oxford, Oxford University Committee for Archaeology monograph 2.

Sermon, R. (1996) Gloucester archaeological annual report, 1995, *Glevensis* 29, 12–24.

Sheppard, J. A. (1979) *The origins and evolution of field and settlement patterns in the Herefordshire manor of Marden*, London, Department of Geography, Queen Mary's College, University of London Occasional Paper 15.

Sherratt, E. S. (1992) 'Reading the texts': archaeology and the Homeric question. In, C. Emlyn-Jones, L. Hardwick and J. Purkis (eds) *Homer: readings and images*, 145–165, London, Duckworth and Co.

Shoesmith, R. (1980) The Roman buildings at New Weir, Herefordshire, *Transactions of the Woolhope Naturalists' Field Club* 43 (2), 135–154.

Sims-Williams, P. (1990) *Religion and literature in Western England 600–800*, Cambridge, Cambridge University Press.

Smith, A. H. (1964a) *The place-names of Gloucestershire: part 1, the rivers and road names, the East Cotswolds*, Cambridge, Cambridge University Press.

Smith, A. H. (1964b) *The place-names of Gloucestershire: part 2, the North and West Cotswolds*, Cambridge, Cambridge University Press.

Smith, A. H. (1964c) *The place-names of Gloucestershire: part 3, the lower Severn Valley, the Forest of Dean*, Cambridge, Cambridge University Press.

Smith, A. H. (1965a) The Hwicce. In, J. B. Bessinger and R. P. Creed (eds) *Frankiplegius: medieval and linguistic studies of Francis Peabody Magoun Jr.*, 56–65, New York.

Smith, A. H. (1965b) *The place-names of Gloucestershire: part 4, introduction, bibliography, analyses, index, maps*, Cambridge, Cambridge University Press.

Smith, A. H. V. (1996) Provenance of coals from Roman sites in United Kingdom counties bordering River Severn and its estuary and including Wiltshire, *Journal of Archaeological Science* 23, 3–389.

Smith, A. H. V. (1997) Provenance of coals from Roman sites in England and Wales, *Britannia* 28, 7–324.

Stanford, S. C. (1959) Excavations at the Roman outpost at Clifton-on-Teme, *Transactions of the Worcestershire Archaeological Society (New Series)* 36, 19–32.

Stealens, Y. J. E. (1982) The Birdlip cemetery, *Transactions of the Bristol and Gloucestershire Archaeological Society* 100, 19–31.

Stevenson, J. (1965) *A New Eusebius: documents illustrative of the history of the church to AD 337*, London.

Stevenson, J. (1966) *Creeds, councils and controversies: documents illustrative of the history of the Church AD 337–461*, London.

Taussig, M. (1980) *The Devil and commodity fetishism in South America*, Chapel Hill, University of North Carolina Press.

Taylor, C. and Tratman, E. K. (1957) The Priddy Circles: preliminary report, *Proceedings of the University of Bristol Spelæological Society* 8 (1), 7–17.

Thomas, C. (1981) *Christianity in Roman Britain to AD 500*, London, Batsford.

Thorn, F. and Thorn, C. (1982) *Domesday Book: Worcestershire*, Chichester, Phillimore.

Thornton, D. E. (1991) Glastonbury and the Glastening. In, L. Abrams and J. P. Carley (eds) *The archaeology and history of Glastonbury Abbey*, 191–203, Woodbridge, Boydell Press.

Timby, J. (1998) *Excavations at Kingscote and Wycomb, Gloucestershire: a Roman estate centre and small town in the Cotswolds with notes on related settlement*, Cirencester, Cotswold Archaeological Trust.

Todd, M. (1996) Pretia Victoriae? Roman lead and silver mining on the Mendip Hills, *Münstersche Beiträge zur antiken Handelsgeschicte* 15, 1–18.

Todd, M. (2001) Charterhouse on Mendip: interim report on excavations in 1995, *Proceedings of the Somerset Archaeological and Natural History Society* 143, 151–4.

Todd, M. (2003) Iron-Age material from Charterhouse on Mendip, *Proceedings of the Somerset Archaeological and Natural History Society* 145, 53–55.

Tolkien, J. R. R. (1932) The name 'Nodens'. In, R. E. M. Wheeler and T. V. Wheeler (eds) *Report on the excavation of the prehistoric, Roman, and post-Roman site in Lydney Park, Gloucestershire*, 132–137, Oxford, The Society of Antiquaries.

Tomlin, R. S. O. (1996) A five-acre wood in Roman Kent, J. Bird, M. W. C. Hassall and H. Sheldon (eds) *Interpreting Roman London: papers in memory of Hugh Chapman*, Oxford, Oxbow Monograph 58, 209–215.

Thompson Watkin, W. (1888) Recent discoveries of Roman remains in Britain, *Reliquary* 2, 26–29.

Tratman, E. K. (1923) First report on Kings Weston Hill, Bristol, *Proceedings of the University of Bristol Spelæological Society* 2 (1), 76–82.

Tratman, E. K. (1925) Second report on King's Weston Hill, Bristol, *Proceedings of the University of Bristol Spelæological Society* 2 (3), 283–243.

Trotter, F. M. (1942) *Geology of the Forest of Dean: coal and iron-ore fields*, London, His Majesty's Stationary Office.

van Arsdell, R. D. and de Jersey, P. (1994) *The coinage of the Dobunni: Money supply and coin circulation in Dobunnic territory with a gazetteer of findspots*, Oxford, Oxford University Committee for Archaeology.
VCH(Gl5) (1996) *The Victoria history of the counties of England: a history of the county of Gloucester 5, the Forest of Dean*, Oxford, Oxford University Press.
VCH(So1) (1906) *The Victoria history of the county of Somerset 1*, Haymarket, James Street.
VCH(Wo1) (1901) *The Victoria history of the counties of England: a history of Worcestershire 1*, Haymarket, James Street.
von der Lieck, K. (1933) *Xenophon's De vectigalibus*, Würzburg, K. Trittsch.
Wacher, J. (1995) *The towns of Roman Britain (second edition)*, London, Book Club Association.
Walters, B. (1989) A survey of prehistory in Dean circa 12,000 BC to AD 43, *Dean Archaeology* 2, 9–29.
Walters, B. (1992) *The archaeology and history of ancient Dean and the Wye Valley*, Cheltenham, Thornhill Press.
Walters, B. (1999) *The Forest of Dean iron idustry first to fourth centuries AD*, Lydney, Dean Archaeological Group Occasional Publication 4.
Waters, G. (1999) *The story of Churchdown*, King's Stanley, Past Histories.
Watt, S. (2002) Reports: West Midlands archaeology in 2002, *West Midlands Archaeology* 45, 27–165.
Watts, D. J. (1991) *Christians and pagans in Roman Britain*, London, Routledge.
Watts, D. J. (1998) *Religion in late Roman Britain*, London, Routledge.
Watts, L. and Leach, P. (1996) *Henley Wood, temples and cemetery: excavations 1962–69 by the late Ernest Greenfield and others*, York, Council for British Archaeology Research Report 99.
Watts, V. (2004) *The Cambridge dictionary of English place-names*, Cambridge, Cambridge University Press.
Webster, G. (1955) A note on the use of coal in Roman Britain, *The Antiquaries Journal* 35, 199–217.
Webster, G. and Smith, L. (1982) The excavation of a Romano-British rural establishment at Barnsley Park, Gloucestershire, 1961–1979: part II, *Transactions of the Bristol and Gloucestershire Archaeological Society* 100, 65–189.
Webster, J. (1995) Sanctuaries and sacred places. In, M. J. Green (ed.) *The Celtic world*, 445–464, London: Routledge.
Wedlake, W. J. (1982) *The excavation of the shrine of Apollo at Nettleton, Wiltshire, 1956–1971*, London, The Society of Antiquaries of London.
Welch, F. B. A., Crookall, R. and Kellaway, G. A. (1948) *British regional geology: Bristol and Gloucester district (second edition)*, London, His Majesty's Stationary Office.
Welch, F. B. A. and Trotter, F. M. (1961) *Geology of the country around Monmouth and Chepstow*, London, Her Majesty's Stationary Office.
Westwood, J. O. (1849) On the ancient portable hand-bells of the British and Irish churches, *Archaeologia Cambrensis* 4, 167–176.
Wheeler, R. E. M. and Wheeler, T. V. (1932) *Report on the excavation of the prehistoric, Roman, and post-Roman site in Lydney Park, Gloucestershire*, Oxford, The Society of Antiquaries.
Whimster, R. (1981) *Burial practices in Iron Age Britain*, Oxford, BAR British Series 90.
Whitehead, T. H. and Pocock, R. W. (1947) *Memoirs of the geological survey of Great Britain: England and Wales: geology of the country around Dudley and Bridgenorth*, London, His Majesty's Stationary Office.
Williams, B. J. and Whittaker, A. (1974) *Memoirs of the geological survey of Great Britain, England and Wales: geology of the country around Stratford-upon-Avon and Evesham*, London, Her Majesty's Stationary Office.

Wilson, D. (1992) *Anglo-Saxon paganism*, London, Routledge.
Wilson, D. R. (1972) Roman Britain in 1971: 1, sites explored, *Britannia* 3, 299–351.
Winterbottom, M. (1978) *Gildas' The ruin of Britain and other works*, Chichester, Phillimore.
Woodward, A. (1992) *English Heritage book of shrines and sacrifice*, London, Batsford.
Woodward, A. and Leach, P. (1993) *The Uley Shrines: excavations of a ritual complex on West Hill, Uley, Gloucestershire: 1977–9*, London, English Heritage Archaeological Report 17.
Worssam, B. C., Ellison, R. A. and Moorlock, B. S. P. (1989) *British geological survey: geology of the country around Tewkesbury*, London, Her Majesty's Stationary Office.
Yeates, S. J. (2004) The Cotswolds, the Codeswellan, and the goddess Cuda, *Glevensis* 37, 2–8
Yeates, S. J. (2006) *Religion, community and territory: defining religion in the Severn Valley and adjacent hill from the Iron Age to the early medieval period (3 volumes)*, Oxford, BAR British Series 411 (i–ii–iii).
Yeates, S. J. (2006b) River-names, Celtic and Old English: their dual medieval and post-medieval personalities, *Journal of the English Place-name Society* 38, 63–81.
Yeates, S. J. (2007a) Religion and tribe in the Northwest Provinces: a goddess for the Dobunni. In, R. Häussler and A. King (eds) *Continuity and innovation in religion in the Roman West: volume 1 Archaeological and regional studies*, Portsmouth, Rhode Island, *Journal of Roman Studies* supplement 67, 55–69.
Yeates, S. J. (forthcoming 2007b) Still living with the Dobunni. In, S. Semple and H. Lewis (eds) British Archaeological Report (International Series).
Zeepvat, R. J. (1979) Observations in Dyer Street and Market Place, Cirencester, in 1849, 1878 and 1974/5, *Transactions of the Bristol and Gloucestershire Archaeological Society* 97, 65–73.

Index

Abberton, Worcs 43
Ablington Camp, Glos 73, 75
Abona: see Sea Mills
Abundantia 23
Acton Beauchamp, Heres 41
Adam 118
Adderbury, Oxon 155
Ælfred 5
Æthelred 63
Æthilberht 5
Æthilhard 5
Æthilric 5
Æthilweard 5
Aesculapius (god) 94
Africa 90
Agathodaemon 91
Akeman Street 85, 87, 152
Alcester, Warks 26, 43
Alchemists 91
Alcock's Arbour, Warks 26
Alder 108
Aldhouse-Green 9, 15
Aldsworth, Glos 138, 143
Alkington, Glos 41
All Souls/Hallows 125, 131
Almondsbury, Glos 96, 154
Alne 42–43
Altars 49, 74–75, 102, 118–119, 121, 135
Altrip 59, 62
Alvechurch, Worcs 43
Ambury, Oxon 84–85
Ammianus Marcellinus 7
Ampney Brook 36
Andoversford, Glos 148
Andredesweald, Sussex 12

Anglo-Saxon 8, 12, 18, 31, 73, 98, 112, 127, 129–130, 149, 152–154
Anglo-Saxon charters 4–5, 34, 39, 42, 50, 53, 55–56, 71, 77, 96, 110
Anglo-Saxon kingdom 106
Anglo-Saxon kingship 5
Anglo-Saxon legislation 63
Anglo-Saxon parochiae 62, 71
Anted 3
Antonine Itinerary 42
Apollo Cunomaglos: see Cunomaglos
Apple tree 158
Aquis Sulis: see Bath
Aquitaine 118
Arden (Forest of) 10, 23, 25–28, 36, 42–43, 91–92, 111–112
Arden Hill 25, 111
Ardennes 29
Arduenna Silva 28–29
Arduinna (goddess) 26, 28–29
Arianism 147
Ariconium 159
Arle (river) 41
Arle Grove, Glos 71
Arles, France 147
Arrow (river) Warks 42–43, 60
Arrow (river) Heres 48, 154
Arrowsaeta 60
Arrowtop, Worcs 43
Arthur 23, 115, 159
Ash 108
Ashberry, Glos 122
Ashleworth, Glos 22
Ashmolean Museum, Oxon 135
Asthall, Oxon 53, 134, 136

Astley, Warks 42
Aston Cantlow, Warks 43
Atrebates 118
Attis (god) 159
Aubrey 45
Aust, Glos 35
Australia 100
Auxilliary Fortress 104
Avebury, Wilts 56
Avening 41
Avon (Bristol) 9, 20, 30, 42, 44–45, 47, 120
Avon (Warwick) 22, 25, 27, 30, 40, 42
Avon Gorge 20, 22, 62
Axe (river) So 57
Aymestry, Heres 80–82

Bablock Hythe, Oxon 50
Bacchic 121
Badesaeta 60
Badewella 60
Badminton, Glos 44
Badsey, Worcs 27, 44
Bagendon, Glos 74, 126
Baginton, Warks 27, 42, 134
Ballestran: see Little Avon
Bampton, Oxon 122, 155
Banbury, Oxon 55
Banwell, So 98, 156
Barbell 50
Barbourne Brook 39
Barford Wood, Warks 84
Barmoor, Warks 103
Barnsley Park, Glos 118
Barnwood, Glos 114, 125–126
Barrows 125, 131, 136
Barrow Place, Oxon 55
Barton, Cirencester, Glos 113
Bass 35
Bath 7–8, 11, 16, 31, 45–47, 77, 120–122, 126, 135–137, 140–142, 148, 156
Batheaston, So 46
Bathford, So 46
Bathampton, So 78
Bathwick, So 78, 135
Batsford, Glos 54
Battledown, Glos 67
Bays Meadow, Droitwich 38

Beachley, Glos 35
Beam, Oxon 122
Beane (river) 157
Beaver 39
Beaver Island, Worcs 33, 37
Beckbury, Glos 70, 72
Beckford, Worcs 40, 92, 133
Bede 4–5, 143–144, 148–149, 156
Bedminster, So 77, 79
Beesmore Brook 44, 70
Beferic 39
Belgic 18, 118, 157
Beningas 157
Berkeley 20, 22, 34, 41, 133, 153
Berkshire Downs 28
Berroc Silva 28
Berry, Siston 96
Berwick, So 78
Beverstone, Glos 153
Bibury, Glos 73, 75, 152
Bidford-on-Avon, Warks 128
Birch 108
Birdlip Hill, Glos 126, 137–138, 143
Birmingham 9, 22, 25
Bishop's Cleeve 67–68, 70, 130, 151
Bishop's Frome, Heres 149, 154
Bishop's Wood, Glos 23, 95
Bisley, Glos 40, 113, 119, 135, 152
Bitton, Glos 153
Black Banks, Worcs 128
Black Country 26
Black Ditch, Oxon 155
Bladen: see Evenlode
Bladon Heath 18–19, 86
Bladud 31, 46
Blaize Castle, Glos 77–78
Bleak 50
Bleddyn 57
Blenheim Lake, Oxon 55
Blockley, Glos 11, 44, 75, 151, 153
Bloxham, Oxon 12, 99, 155
Blunsdon Hill, Wilts 20
Blunt's Green, Warks 114
Boar 26–27, 54, 135
Bodenham, Heres 24
Bodvoc 3
Bolivian 101

Book of Dennis, the 100
Book of Taliesin, the 160
Bosworth, Leics 42
Bould, Oxon 54
Bourton-on-the-Water, Glos 53–54, 73, 76, 130, 148, 152
Bow Brook 42
Box, Wilts 46, 113
Boyd (river) 48, 96
Bradford-on-Avon, Wilts 11–13, 16, 18, 28, 155
Bradley Brook 36
Bran (god) 158
Brandon Hill, Heres 81
Braudel 2
Braydon Forest 9–10, 20, 28, 49, 56, 100
Braydon (river) 20, 50, 56
Bredon, Worcs 12, 103, 154
Bream 35, 50, 95
Brean Down, So 7, 21, 127–128
Brecknockshire 36
Bregans (god) 146
Breiddin 31
Breinton, Heres 36
Brigantia 59, 146
Briganties 59, 146
Brimpsfield, Glos 41
Bristol 77, 96, 126
Britain 4, 7, 9, 28, 30, 102, 107–108, 117–118, 135, 145, 147, 157, 159
Britannia 59
British (language) 12, 23–24, 26–27, 31, 37, 40–41, 46, 50, 54–55, 59, 62, 132, 143–145, 149, 154, 156
British Church 5
Brittonic 31
Broadstone, Stroat 35
Broadwater Brook 46
Brockworth, Glos 64–65
Bromyard, Heres 9, 22, 24, 154
Bronsil, Heres 103
Bronze Age 33, 37, 44–45, 50, 54, 61, 64, 79–80, 84–85, 92, 100, 102, 104, 108, 111, 115, 124, 129–132, 150–151, 152, 154
Brue (river) 57
Bruidean Mór 104
Bruiden Dá Choca 104

Bubbenhall, Warks 119, 121
Burials 102, 124–131, 137, 143, 152, 154
Burton Dassett, Warks 44, 99, 155
Burwalls, So 79
Bury, Wigmore 81
Bury Hill, Heres 81, 83, 128
Bury Hill, Winterbourne, Glos 96, 101
Buryhill, Aust 35
Bwlch 16
By Brook 46

Cada 105
Cadbury, Congresbury, So 21, 80, 103, 105–106
Cadbury, Tickenham, So 21, 104–105
Caer Loyw: see Gloucester
Caerwent, Mons 36
Caesar 7, 107, 144
Calcote Barn, Glos 135
Calidonia Silva 28
Calne, Wilts 155
Cam (river) Chipping Campden, Glos 75
Cam (river) Dursley, Glos 20, 41
Cam (river) So 46
Camelon, Scotland 118
Camp Field, Heres 81, 83
Campsfield, Oxon 55
Camulos (Mars) 18–19, 28, 62
Cannop (river) 23
Canterbury 5
Capitolium 19, 121, 128
Carboniferous limestone 98
Carnwell, So 46
Carnutum, France 62
Carrant (river) 40
Carved heads 23
Cassington Big Ring, Oxon 84–85, 125–126
Castle Combe, Wilts 46
Castle Ditches, Winson, Glos 73, 75
Cattle 37
Catti 3
Catuvellauni 118
Caucasus Mountains 91
Cawcombe, Glos 51
Celtic (language) 27, 33, 39, 40–43, 46, 48–49, 51, 56–57, 60, 96, 112, 149, 159
Chaceley, Glos 104

Chalice Well, So 57
Changé, France 62
Chariot 132
Charlbury, Oxon 54, 83, 85, 87, 155
Charlemagne 117
Charterhouse, So 78–79, 98–99, 101
Charwelton, Northants 55
Chase End Hill 24
Chase Wood Camp, Heres 80, 83, 104
Chavanage, Glos 129
Cheddar, So 78–80, 156
Chedworth 16, 52, 113, 148
Chelt (river) 40, 66
Cheltenham, Glos 66–68, 151
Chepstow, Mons 36
Cherwell (river) 50, 55–56, 86
Cherwell Farm, Northants 55
Chessels (The), Lower Slaughter 12–17, 27–28, 43, 51, 53–54, 128
Cherington, Glos 113
Chew (river) 20, 48
Chew Stoke, So 114
Chewton Mendip, So 20, 48, 97, 101
Chi-rho 148
Chicken 48
Chippenham, Wilts 27, 45, 100, 155
Chipping Campden, Glos 11
Chipping Norton, Oxon 54
Christian Malford, Wilts 45
Christianity 5, 8, 89, 118, 123, 145, 147–157
Chub 50
Church (The) 5, 63, 81, 148–149
Churchdown, Glos 65–66, 125
Churchill, Worcs 43
Churchill Mill, Oxon 54
Churn (river) 50–51, 74
Cinderford, Glos 114
Cirencester, Glos 3, 11–13, 15–16, 18, 28, 62, 74–75, 108, 113, 121, 126, 128, 135–138, 140, 142, 148, 152
Clapley, Glos 11
Claydon Pike, Glos 52–53
Clayhome Brook 55
Clee Hillsm Salop 25
Cleeve Hill, Glos 44, 66–68, 119
Cleeve Hill, So 80–81
Clent, Worcs 26

Clevedon, So 20
Clifford, Heres 36
Clifton, Deddington 55
Clifton Camp, Glos 79, 160
Clifton-upon-Teme, 154
Clun (river) 40
Clutton, So 98
Clutton-Temple Cloud, S 98
Cnebba 157
Coal 92, 96, 98, 100
Coal Pit Heath 96
Coca (god) 104–105
Cocidius (god) 104
Cockbury, Nottingham Hill, Glos 67, 70, 104–105
Cockbury, Heres 80, 83, 104
Cod (fish) 35
Codesbyrig, Glos 61
Codeswellan (river) 12–14, 17, 53–54
Coin hoards 95, 99, 148
Colchester, Es 62
Cole (river) 51
Colesbourne 51, 159
Coleshill, Warks 25–26, 51
Coln (river) 11, 50, 52–53, 73, 113
Coln Saint Aldwyn, Glos 152
Colwall, Heres 51
Combe Down, So 78
Combend, Glos 13
Comux 3
Condicote, Glos 62
Conglomerate 96
Congresbury, So 80–81, 156
Constantine 147
Constantius II 147
Coombe Hill, Glos 77–78
Cooper's Hill, Glos 64, 162
Copper 91–92, 96
Corbridge, Northumberland, 159
Corinium: see Cirencester
Corio 3
Cornish 33
Cornovii 136
Cornucopia 119
Corse 22
Corse (Forest of) 10, 22, 28, 114, 143
Corston, So 98

Corswell (river) 22
Corve (river) 40
Cotswold Waterpark 18
Cotswolds 3, 8–10, 11–19, 22, 28, 30–31, 38, 43–44, 48–49, 55, 64–65, 76, 99–100, 107, 110, 112–113, 115, 137, 143, 151, 159–160
Coughton, Warks 154
Coughton Brook, Heres 80
Coventina's Well, Northumberland 45
Coventry 25, 149
Cow skulls 133
Coxwall, Heres 82
Cradley, Heres 115
Cranmere 55
Crawfish 57
Crayfish 53
Crew Hill 22
Cricklade, Wilts 155
Crickley Hill, Glos 64, 126, 133–134, 137–138, 143
Crida 157
Crodesaeta 60
Croft Ambrey, Heres 81–82, 103
Cromhall, Glos 96
Cropredy, Oxon 55–56, 155
Croscombe, So 57
Cruachan, Ireland 125
Cruciform building 105
Crudwell (river) 60, 159
Cuda (cognomen) Cisalpine Gaul 15
Cuda (goddess) 12–18, 27–28, 43, 53, 58, 128, 159
Cuda (river) Lusitania 15
Cudon 17
Cult statue or images 47, 81, 110, 114
Cunomaglos (god) 46, 50, 52, 107–116, 145, 160
Cupulation 96
Curl Stream 60
Custom Scrubs, Glos 119, 121
Cutsdean, Glos 12–14, 53
Cuttlefish 35
Cybele (goddess) 159
Cynewald 157
Cynfael 46, 110, 160

Dab 35

Dace 50
Daglingworth, Glos 12–13, 15, 18, 152
Daniel's Brook 40–41, 76–77
Danu (goddess) 16
Dath-í 117
Daylesford, Glos 150
Dean (Forest of) 9–10, 22–23, 92–96, 98, 98–101, 104, 114–115, 138
Dean Brook 40
Dean Farm, Brockworth 39
Deddington, Oxon 55
Delat 57
Deer 50
Deerfold Hill, Heres 81–82
Deerhurst, Glos 33, 151–152
Demetae 157
Dene (river) Warks 44
Dennshill 22
Derks 7, 9, 29, 115
Dervold Hill, Heres 82
Devil 90
Devil's Pool, Oxon 55
Devil's Well, Glos 103
Diana (goddess) 26–27, 113
Di-chronological 1–2
Dickler (river) 18, 53, 128
Dio Cassius 2–3
Diocletian 147
Diodorus Siculus 7
Ditchley, Oxon 55
Dimet 157
Dobunni 2–5, 7–9, 19, 22, 27–28, 30–31, 33, 46–47, 55–56, 58–59, 90, 98, 100, 103–105, 110, 112–113, 116–119, 121–124, 132, 134, 136–137, 139, 141–143, 145–146, 148, 150, 156, 158, 160–161
Dobunnic coinage 3, 18
Dodderhill, Worcs 154–155
Dodington, Glos 48
Doferic 39
Dog 26, 50, 110, 113–114, 116, 153
Dogfish 35
Dogon 90
Dolphin 50
Domesday Book 24
Dorn, Glos 75, 137
Dornford (river) 54

Dory 35
Doulting (river) 57–58
Doverle 39, 41, 133
Doward, Heres 125
Dowdeswell, Glos 66, 69, 159
Dowles (river) 38
Down Farm, Purton, Wilts 20
Doynton, Glos 97, 101
Drinkwater 9
Droitwich 37–38, 122
Druids 107, 144
Drummond 7
Drybrook Quarry, Glos 92
Dudley, Worcs 25
Dudstone Hundred, Glos 122
Dumbleton, Glos 40
Durbridge, Glos 40
Durkheim 6
Durotriges 98
Dursley, Glos 153
Dyfed 147, 157
Dyrham 5

Ealdred 5
Ealdwulf 148
Eanberht 5
Eanfrid 5
Eanhere 5
Eagle 19, 44, 117, 159
Eardisland, Heres 154
East Anglia 148
East Harptree, So 98
Eastern 100
Eastington, Glos 126
Easton Grey, Wilts 12–13, 15, 28
Eccles Brook 149
Eccleswall, Heres 81
Eckington, Worcs 42
Edgar 63
Edge Hill, Glos 22–23
Edge Hill, Warks 11
Edward the Confessor 24
Eels, Elvers 35, 53, 57
Eggleton, Heres 149
Eign (river) Heres 48–49
Eisu 3, 118
Elborough, So 125

Ell (river) 22
Elm 43, 108
Elmley Brook 39
Elmore, Glos 76–77
Elmstone Hardwick, Glos 40
Enabarri 3
England 1, 104, 148
Engels 6
English (language) 3, 5, 10, 12, 23, 24, 26–28, 30–31, 33, 37–38, 40, 42, 53, 60–61, 63, 90, 108, 111, 143–144, 157–158, 160–161
Ennick: see Piddle
Éo Magna 117
Eo Rosa 117
Eoves 27, 158
Epona (goddess) 59, 132
Erging 159
Ermine Street 18
Ersebury 61, 76–77
Esa 60, 118
Esingas 60
Esus 107, 118
Europe 1–3, 7, 28, 95, 100, 123, 132, 157–158
Eve 118
Evenlode (river) 11, 30, 50, 54, 85
Evesham 25, 42–43, 128, 150, 156
Evesham Abbey 26–27, 130, 158
Evesham (Vale of) 9, 25
Exhall, Warks 149
Eye (river) 12, 18, 53, 128
Eynsham, Oxon 83–85, 124, 155
Eynsham Park, Oxon 84–85

Fair Rosamund's Well, Oxon 55
Fallow Deer 23
Faringdon, Berks 20
Farmington-Radstock, So 98
Farnworth: see Chessels
Farthinghoe Brook 55
Feckenham, Worcs 26–27, 43
Feldberg 59
Feldon 9–10, 25, 43
Feuerbach 6
Fifield Hill Farm, Oxon 88
Finberg 71, 74–75
Fish 57

Fladbury, Worcs 154
Flag Fen 30
Flatholm, Glam 35
Flounder 35
Flukes 57
Folk-groups 59, 63, 106, 120, 156–157, 161
Folk-lore 31, 157, 160–161
Folk-names 5, 60, 63, 85, 87–89
Folk-tradition 35, 159
Folk-territories 63
Forge Barrow, Rodney Stoke, So 101
Forest landscapes 9–10
Fortuna 23, 33, 62
Fosse Way 18, 128
Fostering 104–105
Fox 39
Foxhill, Glos 129
Frampton Cotterell, Glos 96
France 103, 159
French 33
Freshford, So 45
Frocester, Glos 153
Frocester Court, Glos 134
Frome (river) Bristol 48
Frome (river) Glos 41
Frome (river) Heres 41, 48
Frome (river) So 41, 46
Frome, So 156

Gaesmere Oak 117
Galerian 147
Gallic 39, 42, 102–103, 118, 144
Ganarew, Heres 36
Garesbourne 20
Garnets 91–92
Gaul 7, 29, 59, 62, 107, 117, 132, 144–145, 159
Gaulish 43
Gaveller 100
Geertz 6
Gellygear, Glam 118
Gender 100
Genealogies 157, 160
Genii Cucullati 15–17, 28
Genio Germaniae Superioris 59
Genio Leucorum 59
Genio Viciniae Castellanae Olbiensium 62

Genius 15, 50–51, 53, 62, 75, 89, 137, 158
Genius Centurie 59, 62
Genius Eboraci 62
Gentleman's Magazine 108, 127
Geoffrey of Monmouth 23, 35
Gereint and Enid, Mabinogion 23
Germania 59
Germanic Mythology 145
Germany 8, 59, 107, 117, 143–145
Ghyst 160
Ghyston Rock: see Saint Vincent's Rock
Gildas 147
Gill Mill, Oxon 53, 135
Giraldus Cambrensis 23
Gladder (river) 38
Glastingas 60
Glastonbury, So 57, 122, 149, 156
Glastonbury Abbey, So 158
Glevum: see Gloucester
Glevensis 60, 63–66
Glimehaeme 60
Gloucester 9, 33–34, 38–41, 62–67, 76, 104, 109, 114, 120, 122, 125–128, 130–131, 135–138, 141–143, 148–150, 159–160
Gloucester (Vale of) 22, 151, 160
Gloucestershire 9, 12, 15, 24, 60–61, 71, 96, 118, 122, 127, 129, 151–154, 160
Glyme (river) 50, 54–55, 60, 86
Glyme Farm, Oxon 55
Glynch (river) 40
Glywys 63, 158–159
Glywysinga 60, 63, 145, 158, 160
Gold 91–92
Gold-mine, Worcs 91
Goldburg 117
Goloring 117
Gournay-sur-Aronde, France 102, 132
Grand Mere, Beach, Bitton 48
Granville Monument, So 127
Great Packington, Warks 25
Great Witcombe, Glos 39, 65
Great Wolford, Warks 155
Greco-Roman temple 118
Greece 132, 134, 157
Green Street, Brockworth 39
Gregory (pope) 148
Greyling 53

Grickstone, Glos 44
Grim (god) 116
Grim's Ditch, Oxon 112, 116
Groundwell, Wilts 20, 56
Grove Park, Warks 84
Gudgeon 50
Guest, Lady Charlotte 158
Guiting Power, Glos 151
Guma 157
Gumeninga hearh, Midds 157
Gurnard 35
Gwent 122, 145
Gyston Cliff: see Saint Vincent's Rock
Gyting (river) 14, 53

Haddock 35
Hagley, Worcs 26
Hailes Brook 37–38, 44, 60, 68, 70–72
Hailes Camp, Glos 68
Hailey Wood, Glos 50
Hake 35
Halibut 35
Hampshire 117
Hampton-in-Arden, Warks 25
Hampton Lucy, Warks 154–155
Hanbury, Worcs 43, 149
Hankerton, Wilts 20
Harborough Banks, Warks 111
Harrow, Midds 157
Hanbury, Worcs 154
Harbury, Warks 155
Hare 110, 116
Harescombe, Glos 40, 76
Harescombe Camp, Glos 76–77
Haresfield, Glos 76
Haresfield Beacon and Camp 76–77
Harptree, So 97, 99, 101
Harrow Farm, Glos 40
Harrow Hill, Glos 23
Harrow Hill, Worcs 27
Hartlebury, Worcs 154
Hasenbury, Glos 73, 75
Hatherley Brook 39
Hauser-an-der-Zaber, Germany 121
Hawford, Worcs 37
Hawkes 7
Hawkesbury, Glos 153

Hayling Island, Hants 117
Hazel 51, 108
Heathcote Hill, Warks 84
Hen 43
Hen (river) 87
Henbury, Glos 77, 130
Henig 9, 15
Henley-in-Arden, Warks 25
Henley Wood, So 7, 21, 127–128
Hennuc (river) 58
Hensingas 60, 87
Hensington, Oxon 86
Hercynia Silva 28
Hereford 9, 23–24, 36, 49, 128, 149–150
Herefordshire 9, 23–24, 39–40, 48, 60, 80, 91, 129, 149, 154
Hermes Trismegistos 91
Herriott's Bridge, Worcs 135
Herons 57
Herring 34–35
Herse: see Daniel's Brook
Hewlett's, Glos 67, 70
High Brotheridge, Glos 64
High Nash, Glos 23
Highfurlong Brook 55
Hilcot Brook 51
Hill-forts 61, 64–70, 78, 80–82, 85–86, 90, 94–106, 114–115, 117, 120, 124–125, 129–131, 133–134, 136, 150–156
Hill of Eaton, Heres 81, 83
Hinchwick, Glos 53
Hoarwithy, Heres 36
Hobditch, Warks 111, 114
Holt, Wilts 45
Holt, Worcs 33
Holt Heath, Worcs 134
Homer 157
Hook Norton, Oxon 99
Horse 105, 118, 132–136
Horse skulls 132–136
Horsebere Brook (river) 38–39, 63–66, 120
Horseland, So 45
Horsley Brook 41
Hotwells, Clifton 45, 160
How Culhwch won Olwen 159
Hucclecote, Glos 64, 124

Human remains 103, 120, 133–134
Human sacrifice 107
Human skulls 103, 133–134
Humber (river) Heres 48
Humber (river) Oxon 55
Hundred of Saint Briavels, Glos 100
Hunt's Mill, Wilts 45
Hunter God: see Cunomaglos
Hwicce 2–6, 8–9, 27, 31, 33, 38, 59, 104, 118, 123, 124, 143–146, 147–149, 160–161
Hyam Farm, Wilts 45
Hyde Brook 40
Hyères, formerly Olbia 62
Hymel: see Bow Brook

Icauna (goddess) 58
Icel 157
Icelingas 157
Icombe Hill, Glos 53
Idbury, Oxon 88, 129
Idover 20
Ilbury, Oxon 100–101
Ilkley, Yorks 37
Illyrian 33
Ilmington, Warks 44
Inam 3
Ine 63
Inkberrow, Worcs 154
Inkford Brook 43
Interpretatio 145
Ireland 104, 117, 125
Irish (language) 24, 37, 91, 149, 158
Irish Mythology 16, 104, 106, 117
Irminshul, Germany 117
Iron 91–92, 96, 98–100
Iron Acton, Glos 96
Iron Age 8, 18–19, 30–31, 35, 37–38, 47, 50–51, 61, 64–68, 71, 77–80, 84, 86, 89–90, 92, 94–95, 98–99, 101, 105, 108, 111–112, 114–117, 119–126, 128–137, 143, 150–151, 153–155, 158, 161
Iron Age coinage 3, 95, 118, 134–135
Iron-Age currency bars 27
Iron Gorge 31
Iron Works, Park End, Glos 95
Ironstone Hill, Oxon 100
Isbourne (river) 11, 42, 44, 118, 159

Ismere 37
Itchen 58
Ivington Camp, Heres 129
Ivy Lodge, Glos 129

Jason and the Argonauts 91
Jupiter 13, 19, 43–44, 55, 117–118, 121, 132, 136
Jurassic 99

Kemble 18, 152
Kemble (Forest of) 10, 13, 18–19, 22, 28, 49, 110
Kempsford 18, 135, 152
Kempsey, Worcs 133, 154
Kenchester 3, 128, 139
Kennet (river) 56–57
Keuper Marl 46
Key (river) 50, 56
Keynsham, So 155
Kidderminster 154
Kilkenny, Glos 71
King's Weston, Glos 77–78, 126
Kingsbury, Wilts 155
Kingscote 13, 16
Kingsdown Camp, So 120
Kingsholm, Glos 104, 127, 130
Kingswood 9–10, 22, 48, 92, 96–98, 100–101
Kington Saint Michael Park, Wilts 45
Kinver, Stafs 26–27
Kinwarton, Warks 43
Knave Hill or Bury 61
Knaves castle, Glos 76
Knee Brook 39, 44, 75
Knollbury, Oxon 85, 87
Kurorte 47
Kynwarton, Warks 154
Kymesbury, Glos 65
Kyre 40
Kyvwich 16

Lam Brook 119
Lampray 34–36
Lamyatt Beacon 7, 21, 127–128
Langford, Oxon 12
Langley Brook 44
Langley Mount, Glos 70, 72

Lansdown Hill, So 46, 127
Lapworth, Warks 25
Latin (language) 39–40, 52, 149
Latton 18
Laughern 39
Le Donon 29
Leach 50
Lead 91, 96, 98
Lead curse tablets 50
Lead pigs 98
Leadon 22, 40
Leam (river) 42–43
Leanington Spar, Warks 43
Lechlade, Glos 49
Leckhampton, Glos 66, 69, 126, 133–134, 137–138
Ledbury, Heres 154
Leek Wootton, Warks 26–27, 155
Lee's Rest, Oxon 54
Leicestershire 42–43
Leint (river) 40
Leintwardine, Heres 80, 82, 154
Lene (river) 24–25
Lenus (god) 52
Leominster, Heres 24–25, 48, 154
Leuci 59
Lickey Hills, Worcs 25–26, 43
Lidbury, Glos 74
Life of Saint Wulstan, The 122
Lime 108
Limekiln Spa, So 46
Limb Brook 84
Lincombe, Worcs 33
Linear boundaries 108, 110, 112, 114–115
Linton nr. Ross, Heres 23, 149
Lionehaeme 60
Little Avon 39, 41–42
Little Compton, Oxon 54
Littledean, Glos 22–23
Littleham Brook 44
Little Rollright, Oxon 54
Llandovery sandstone 103
Lleu the eagle 117
Loach 50, 57
Lockingas 60
Locking Rind 60
Lodon (river) 48

Loikop 90
London 28, 118, 145
Long Ashton, So 96
Long durée 2
Longford, Glos 65, 120–122, 126
Longney, Glos 122
Longwell Green, Glos 96
Lord Chock 101
Lower Sapey, Worcs 130
Lower Slaughter: see Chessels
Lox Yeo 60
Lucan 107, 118
Lugg 9, 24, 41, 48, 58, 154
Lugus (god) 48, 58
Lumpfish 35
Lydiard Millicent 20
Lydney, Glos 154
Lydney Park Temple 7, 23, 36, 94–95, 98, 101, 114
Lyncombe Spa, So 46
Lyneham, Oxon 88, 129
Lynge 35
Lyon 62
Lypiat, Glos 41
Lyre 113
Lysons, D. 7
Lysons, S. 113

Mabinogion 16, 46, 110, 114, 116, 145, 158–160
Mabon 159
Macedonian 118
Mackerel 35
Madmarston, Oxon 103
Maesbury, So 114, 160
Magana 24
Magonsetum 24
Maiden Hill or Bury 61
Maiden Hill, Glos 76, 125
Malmesbury, Wilts 18, 44–45, 149, 155
Malvern (Forest) 10, 22–24, 91, 93, 115, 138, 143
Mansell Lacy, Heres 48
Maponus (god) 159–160
Marden, Heres 24, 149, 154
Marlstone 99

Marne (river) 159
Mars (god) 19, 52, 104, 119, 132, 134–136
Martinmass 63
Martlesham, Suffolk 135
Marx 6
Mathon, Heres 115, 124
Matrona (goddess) 159–160
Maugersbury 61
May Day 125, 131
Mayence, Germany 59
Meare Lake, So 22, 57
Medieval multiple estates 5
Medlartree 51
Mearhead, So 114
Melksham, Wilts 45
Mellitus (bishop) 148, 156
Mells, So 62, 98
Mells Stream 41, 46
Mendip Beacon, So 114
Mendips 9–10, 20–21, 46, 78, 80, 92, 97–101, 114
Meon Hill, Warks 103, 129
Mercia 4–5, 18, 123, 157
Mercury 7, 21, 25, 54, 139–144, 160
Mere Hill, Heres 81–82
Merk (giant) 160
Mesolithic 35, 108
Mesozoic 99
Metalworkers 91
Middlesex 157
Midlands 11
Midsummer Hill, Heres 103
Migration 106
Milan (edict) 147
Military shrines 104
Miller's thumb and Cole 50, 57
Millhampost, Glos 70, 72
Minchenhampton, Glos 153
Minerva 19, 47, 62, 143
Minety, Wilts 18, 20, 56
Minerva 17
Mining and Minerals 90–101
Minnow 50, 57
Minsters 62–63, 67–68, 70–73, 75, 77, 79–81, 83, 88, 147–156
Mitcheldean 22
Mithras 36

Model Farm, Oxon 113
Modron 159
Monastic culture 8
Mons Huucciorum: see Wiggold
Mont, Lower Lydbrook, Glos 92
Montgomeryshire 31, 36
Moorgrave Wood, Glos 96
Mothers 15, 27, 59, 90, 137–146, 156, 158–161
Mouriès, Bouches-du-Rhône, France 132
Much Marcle, Heres 154
Mullet 35
Mussels Well, Glos 125
Mythe, Glos 42

Nâges, Gard 132
Nailbridge, So 98
Nailsea, So 98
Naix, France 59
Naunton, Glos 11, 76
Nash Hill, Wilts 100–101
Nehalennia 34
Neigh Bridge 13, 19
Nemeton: see Sacred grove
Nemetovala 114
Nennius 4, 35–36, 38, 47, 122
Neolithic 92, 100, 108, 119, 124–125, 129, 131
Neptune (god) 51
Nettleton Scrubs, Wilts 46, 110, 137, 142
New Forest 9
New Weir, Heres 36
New Wintles, Oxon 85
Newent, Glos 40, 154
Newton Saint Loe, So 114
Nine hags 159–160
Nodens 7, 23, 94–96, 101
Noleham Brook 44
Norbury, Farmington, Glos 129
Norman 107, 112
Norman Conquest 27
Norman French 28
North Aston Brook 55
North Cerney, Glos 51, 154
Northamptonshire 55, 100
Northamptonshire Uplands 55
Northamptonshire sands 99

Northleach, Glos 152
Nottingham Hill, Glos 67, 70, 102, 104–105, 126, 137–138
Numerian 3
Nunney, So 98, 114
Nustles, Lydney, Glos 94
Nut tree 122
Nymphaeum 36
Nympsfield, Glos 113
Nyoro 90

Oak 107–108, 117
Oceanus (god) 51
Ochre 90, 92, 96, 100
Ock (river) 56
Old Mere, Longford, Glos 39
Old Weir, Heres 30, 36
Oldbury, Warks 111–112, 114–115
Oldbury, Worcs 25
Oldwalls, Glos 73, 75
Ollioules, Gaul 119
Olludius 119
Olveston, Glos 154
Omna 117
Onny (river) Heres 48
Onny (river) Salop 40
Oppidum 112, 137
Orderic Vitalis 23
Orpheus 113–114
Oshere 5
Osred 5
Osric 5
Osthanes 91
Oswald 5
Ousel or blackbird 159
Ovid 91
Owl 159
Oxford 49, 55–56
Oxfordshire 9, 50, 60, 83, 100, 124, 129, 155

Pagan revival 148, 156
Pagans Hill, So 21, 114
Pagi 59
Painswick Brook 41
Painswick Beacon 65, 103–104
Palaeobotany 108
Palaeozoic 92

Paleolithic 100
Pannonia 3
Paris, France 62
Parochial system 8
Patera 119
Pauntley, Glos 40
Payford, Glos 40
Pegglesworth Home Farm, Glos 51
Pelagian heresy 147
Pembridge, Heres 133–135
Penarth, Glam 33
Penda 157
Penkridge, Stafs 25
Pensions 63
Perch 50
Perdiswell, Worcs 37
Peredur 159
Peredur, son of Evrawg 159
Perry Grove, Coleford, Glos 95
Pershore, Worcs 154
Pewsham, Wilts 27
Phrygian cap 110, 113
Pickerel 57
Piddle (river) 42–43
Pigeon 17, 53
Pike 57
Pilchard 35
Pine 24
Pinnock, Glos 54
Piriho (Forest) 18
Plaice 35
Pliny the Elder 91, 107
Plum 120
Plynlymon 31
Polden Hills, So 22
Porpoise 34
Portbury, So 156
Portions 63
Portway, Glos 114
Posidonius 7
Powick, Worcs 30, 33, 122
Powys 57
Prawns 35
Pre-Christian Religion 1, 4–5, 8–9, 144–145, 148, 156, 160
Prestbury Hill, Glos 71
Priddy 97–98, 101

Priddy Circles, So 62, 79–80, 124
Prides 57
Ptolomey 3, 33
Puckham, Glos 71
Pucklechurch, Glos 48, 153
Pypba 157
Pyon Hill, Heres 81–82

Quaver 35
Quedgeley, Glos 76–77
Quobwell, Wilts 45

Radnorshire 36, 39, 48
Raedwald 148, 156
Ragstone 100
Ram 91, 96
Randwick Wood, Glos 76–77, 125
Ray (fish) 35
Ray (river) Oxon 19
Ray (river) Wilts 20, 37, 50, 56
Rea (river) Warks 51
Read 53
Red Book of Hergest, the 158
Red Sandstone 91–92
Reliefs 15–16, 53, 102, 104, 119, 140–141
Religion 6
Religious inscriptions 117
Rendcomb, Glos 113
Rhaetic Shale 46
Rhine (river) 157
Ribemont-sur-Ancre, France 102
Ridgemoore Broo, Heres 48
Rindern 19
Ripple, Worcs 24, 154
Ring-fort 104
Ritual shafts 70
Rivers 30–58
Roach 50, 57
Roel Gate, Glos 70, 72
Roman 5–8, 12, 17–19, 23–24, 26–29, 31, 33, 37, 41–45, 47–56, 58–59, 62, 64, 67, 70–71, 73–77, 79–83, 85, 87–89, 92–96, 98, 101, 104, 106–108, 111–112, 116–118, 120–123, 126–131, 133, 136–137, 143, 145, 147–148, 150–161
Roman coins 33, 35
Roman ethnography 107, 115, 132

Roman Fields, Glos 133
Roman tombstones 135
Romano-Celtic temples 19, 21, 55, 118
Rome 134
Rookery Farm, Green Ore, Wells 98
Rosebury, Bristol 79, 126
Rosmerta (goddess) 140
Ross-on-Wye, Heres 36, 80–81, 104, 149–150
Rowel Brook or Begbrook 55
Roymans 7, 59
Rudhall (river) 22, 80
Ruffe 50
Ruspidge, Glos 23
Ryeham, Glos 41, 133, 135

Saalburg, Germany 59
Sabrina: see Severn
Sacred Groves 107–117, 150
Sacred Topography 9–29 (landscape) 30–58 (rivers) 107–116, 143
Sacred Vessel 4, 137, 143, 145–146, 160
Saint Alban 147
Saint Aldhelm 58
Saint Andrew's Well, So 58
Saint Augustine's Oak 5
Saint Cuthbert's Without, Wells, So 98
Saint Dogmael 157
Saint Ethelbert's Well, Heres 49
Saint Jacob's Well, Bristol 48
Saint Mary de Lode, Gloucester 33–34, 128, 149
Saint Oswald's priory, Gloucester 33, 130
Saint Stephen's Well, Oxon 55
Saint Vincent's Rock, Clifton 45, 160
Saint Werburgh, Glos 130
Saint Winifred's Well, So 46
Salbury, Glos 44, 70
Salenses 59–60, 68, 70–71, 72
Salford Priors, Warks 149, 154
Salia: see Hailes Brook
Salinae: see Droitwich
Salmon 34–36, 38, 40, 50, 56, 159
Salmonsbury, Glos 76, 130, 152
Salperton, Glos 54
Salt Brook, Stoulton 38
Saltmarsh, Heres 41
Saltpool, Stanley Pontlarge 40

Saltwells Spa, Kingswinford 36, 38
Salty Brook 37–38
Salwarpe (river) 37
Samson's Platt, Oxon 86–87
Sapey, Worcs 24, 40, 130
Sawbrook 43
Sawcombe, Winchcombe 38
Saxon burh 70
Saxons (Germany) 117
Scotland 118
Sea Mills, Glos 42, 77–78, 148
Seals 35
Sedgeberrow, Worcs 44
Seine (river) 15
Selwood (Forest) 57
Semnoni 107
Senuna (goddess) 43, 58
Sequanna (goddess) 15
Seven Springs 51
Sevenhampton 51
Severed heads 132
Severn (river) 3, 5, 8–9, 20, 22–23, 25, 30–35, 38–42, 45, 50, 57, 65, 98, 104, 108, 151
Severn Bore 35, 36
Sèvre (river) 33
Sèvres (river) 33
Shad 35, 36
Sheep 96
Sheperdine 34
Sheppey (river) 57–58
Sherbourne, Warks 84
Sherbourne Brook, Glos 54
Sherston, Wilts 44, 155
Shield 19, 104
Shipton-under-Wychwood, Oxon 12, 54, 88, 155
Shipton-upon-Cherwell, Oxon 55
Shorncote Quarry, Glos 124
Shrewsbury 31
Shrimps 35
Shrines 11–12, 16, 19–20, 35–8, 41–42, 44–45, 51–53, 56–57, 90, 98–100, 112
Shropshire (Salop) 31, 39
Shute Shelve, So 135
Silbury, Wilts 56
Silva: see Sacred Topography
Silver 91–92, 98

Sims-Williams 8, 63, 106
Sivy Yarn Field, Sapey 24
Slad Brook 41
Slimbridge 34
Small Down Knoll, So 124, 131
Smerstow Brook 36
Smite (river) 43
Snitterfield, Warks 26
Sodbury, Glos 96, 153
Sole 35
Solinus 47
Solsbury Hill, So 46, 78
Somerset 9, 41, 60–61, 77, 124, 127, 135, 160
Somerset Levels 9–10, 20, 30
Sor (river) 55
Soul-scot 63
South Brewham, So 57
South Cadbury, So 38, 105
South Cerney, Glos 74
Southwark Cathedral 50
Southstone Rock, Worcs 40
Sow 158
Sowe (river) Warks 27, 42–43, 134
Sowe (river): see Whitelake
Spear 19, 33, 104, 129
Spelbury, Oxon 85, 87
Spell Bury or Wall 61
Spelwall, Churchdown 65
Spoils of Annwn, the 160
Sponwælle: see Beesmore
Sprats 35
Spring Hill, Stafs 25
Square Ditch Farm, Glos 71
Staffordshire 25–26
Stag 46, 110–111, 115–116, 159–160
Stanburrow, Glos 76–77
Stancomb Wood, Glos 113
Standish 41, 62, 76–77, 152
Stanton (Forest) 18
Stanton Harcourt, Oxon 50, 155
Stanway, Glos 151
Staple Hill, Warks 128
Staples Hill, So 45
Stapleton, Glos 48
Steepholm, So 35
Stickleback 50
Stockend, Glos 40

Stockley Cross, Staunton-on-Arrow, Heres 48
Stoke Bishop, Glos 96
Stoke Priors 37
Stokeleigh Camp, So 79
Stonbury, Oxon 86
Stour (river) Warks 11, 36, 42, 44
Stour (river) Worcs 26, 36–37
Stow-on-the-Wold, Glos 104, 129–130
Stratford-upon-Avon, Warks 155
Stratton, Glos 13, 15
Stoneleigh, Warks 42
Strabo 7, 107
Sturgeon 34, 36, 50
Sub-Roman 85, 94, 105, 128–131, 135, 149
Sucks Bank, Burton Hills, Heres 48
Sulis Minerva 7, 47, 58, 78, 140–141
Sun 47
Sun-fish 35
Sutton Bog, Northants 55
Sutton Walls, Heres 25, 103, 129
Swan 57
Swanwell, Coventry 27
Swainswick, So 46
Swell, Glos 129
Swilgate (river) 40, 68
Swill (river): see Braydon
Swindon 37
Swine 158
Sword 19
Swordfish 35
Sylbeam, Worcs 122
Sylvanus Urban 108
Symond's Yat, Glos 36
Syreford Mill, Glos 51, 135
Syvwich 16

Tacitus 33, 107
Tackley, Oxon 86
Tadmarston Hill, Oxon 44, 129
Tame (river) 50
Tanworth-in-Arden, Warks 25
Taranis (god) 107
Tasmania 90
Tavistock, Dev 3
Teme (river) 23, 25, 30, 39–40, 50
Temple locations 10–11

Temple Cloud, So 98
Templeborough 3
Temples 7, 10, 19, 21, 23–27, 41, 44, 47, 50, 52, 54, 56, 90, 94–96, 98, 100–102, 124, 128–130, 133, 140, 148, 150, 151, 152, 156
Tenbury Wells 39, 154
Tench 57
Tetbury, Glos 44, 153
Teutates (god) 107
Tewkesbury, Glos 40, 42, 151
Thames 9, 18–19, 30, 49–54
Theodningc (river) 14, 53–54
Theodore 156
Thornbury, Glos 154
Thornpoles 35
Throckmorton, Worcs 43
Tiddington, Warks 42, 128
Timbingas 67
Time period specific study 1
Tin 91, 96
Toadsmore Brook 40
Tor Hill, So 57
Tortu's tree 117
Trafalgar Farm, Glos 12
Tredington Rise 68, 70
Tree shrines 117–123
Trent-Humber 30, 63
Trout 35, 53, 57
Trym (river) Glos 48, 62, 77
Turbot 35
Turch (river) 53–54
Twait 35
Twyver (river) 38, 40, 64–66
Tyches 62, 122
Tyrel (river) 40
Tytherington, Glos 129

Uhtred 5
Uley 7, 113, 119–121, 127, 148
Upper Sapey Common Camp 24
Upwich, Droitwich 38

Venus 36
Verbia 37, 58
Verlucium Silva 28
Vienne, France 38
Vigora (river) 25, 28

Virgil 91
Virgin Mary 150, 156
Viridomix 157
Vosegus (god) 29
Vosegus Silva 29
Vosges 29
Votive material 15, 19, 21–22, 24, 30, 42, 44–45, 51, 91, 94, 99, 102, 153
Votive wells or shafts 17, 50–51, 103
Vulcan (god) 100

Waden Hill, Wilts 57
Walcot, So 78
Waldegrave Old Map of Mendip 101
Wales 104, 118, 147, 158–159
Walford, Leintwardine, Heres 82
Wall, Stafs 26
Wall Hill, Weston, Heres 80
Wallborough, Oxon 85, 87, 113
Walls Hill, Ledbury, Heres 129
Walton, Glos 40
Wansdyke, So 116
Warfare 102–106, 127
Warwick 83–84, 130, 155
Warwickshire 9, 25, 60, 83, 103, 128, 154
Washbourne 40
Wasperton, Warks 128
Webster, J. 9
Weaponry 102–104
Wedmore, So 57
Welford, Warks 44, 154
Wellesbourne, Warks 44
Wellow (river) 20, 46
Wells, So 58, 156
Wells and votive shafts 31
Welsh (language) 7, 12, 18, 22–24, 27, 31, 33–34, 36, 38–39, 43, 49, 54, 57, 149, 157–159
Welsh Mythology 117
Wenlock Edge, 25
Weogorena 25, 59–60
Wessex 5, 8
West 101
West Hill, Glos 119
West Midlands 63
West Saxon 4
Westbury-on-Severn, Glos 154

Westbury-on-Trym, Glos 77–78, 96, 130, 154
Westbury-sub-Mendip, So 124
Western 97, 100
Weston-in-Arden, Warks 25
Weston-super-Mare, So 33
Weston-under-Penyard, Heres 81, 83, 95, 128
Whales 35
Wharf 37, 58
Whistley Hill, Glos 51, 66
White Book of Rhydderch, the 158
White rush 53
Whitehill, Wilts 45
Whitegate Farm, Bleadon, So 133
Whitelake (river) 22, 57
Whitinge 35
Whitminster, Glos 41
Whorlebury, So 35, 98, 101
Whyle (river) 48
Wicca/Wicce 4, 144
Wick, Pucklechurch, Glos 96–97
Wick Saint Lawrence, So 80
Wickham, Oxon 87
Wickham, Worcs 27
Widemarsh, Heres 49
Wiggington, Oxon 148
Wiggold 11
Wigmore, Heres 81–82
Wilcot, Oxon 85
Willersey Hill, Glos 125, 129, 131
William Worcester 45, 57, 160
Wiltshire 9, 20, 37, 60, 83, 160
Winchcombe, Glos 44, 70–72, 113, 151
Winchester 59
Windcliff, Mons 122
Windrush (river) 14, 50, 53–54
Windrush Mere 53–54
Windsor Forest 10
Winford, So 114
Winterbourne 56
Winterswell, Glos 73, 75
Witch: see Wicca/Wicce
Withington, Glos 51, 71, 73–74, 113, 152
Withy Brook 43
Wittantree Farm, Glos 119
Woburne 20

Woden (god) 116, 157
Wolf 54
Wolston, Warks 155
Woodchester, Glos 113
Woodeaton, Oxon 13, 19
Woodstock, Oxon 86–87
Wookey Hole, So 57
Woolhope 22
Woolaston, Glos 68, 70, 154
Wootton, Oxon 54, 83, 86–87
Worcester 4–6, 25, 33, 37, 39, 133, 134, 147, 149, 151, 154
Worcester Cathedral 8, 149
Worcester See 5–6, 147
Worcestershire 9, 12, 23, 25–26, 60, 83, 92, 103, 122, 149, 154
Wormington, Glos 133–134
Wotton, Glos 114, 123
Wotton Bassett, Wilts 20, 45
Wotton-under-Edge, Glos 113
Wotton Wawen, Warks 62
Wroxeter 31, 136
Wudetunnincga 60
Wych Cutting 91
Wychbury, Worcs 103, 133

Wychwood 11–12, 112–113
Wycomb, Glos 13, 16, 52, 71, 73, 135
Wye (river) 22, 30, 35–36, 49, 122
Wyndbrook 40
Wyrd Sisters or Norns 145
Wyre Forest 9–10, 22, 25, 28, 38–39, 91–92, 138
Wytham Hill, Berks 18–20

Xenophon 91

Yardley, Worcs 25
Yarnton, Oxon 55, 84, 125
Yarsop, Heres 48
Yate, Glos 96
Yeo 20
Yew 120
Yewbury, Glos 122
York 62
Yorkshire 3, 37

Zinc 91, 98
Zoyland, So 22, 28
Zugmantel, Germany 59